ABSORPTION

Human Nature and Buddhist Liberation

Buddhism Series

ABSORPTION

HUMAN NATURE AND BUDDHIST LIBERATION

Johannes Bronkhorst

UNIVERSITYMEDIA
2012

Copyright © 2012 Johannes Bronkhorst
Published by UniversityMedia, Wil / Paris
www.universitymedia.org
All rights reserved.

Printed on acid-free and lignin-free paper

Library of Congress Cataloging-in-Publication Data
Bronkhorst, Johannes, 1946–
    Absorption. Human Nature and Buddhist Liberation. / Johannes Bronkhorst.
    p. cm. — (UniversityMedia, Buddhism Series)
    Includes bibliographical references and index
    ISBN 978-3-906000-24-4 (acid-free paper)
    1. Buddhism—Psychology—Meditation.
    2. Psychology—Psychotherapy—Sigmund Freud.
    3. Language—Semantics—Symbolism—Origin.
    4. Mind—Body—Brain—Sexuality.
    5. Religion—Mythology—Mysticism—Ritual.

    I. Title.

ISBN 978-3-906000-24-4

For Joy

whose encouragement has been unflinching

Contents

PREFACE 3

PART I: THE SYMBOLIC MIND

INTRODUCTION 9
  1. Symbolic representation 9
  2. Mysticism 25
  3. Ritual 31
  4. Mythology and Religion 41
  5. Culture 43

APPENDIX 1: Semantic etymologies 48
APPENDIX 2: Symbolic reference and the origin of language 55

PART II: THE PSYCHOLOGY OF THE BUDDHA

INTRODUCTION 73
OUTLINE OF A PSYCHOLOGICAL THEORY
  1. Fundamentals 95
  2. Comparison with neurological findings 109
  3. Psychotherapy and its obstacles 117
  4. A "complete cure" 125
  5. The theory adapted 135
  6. The theory refined 142
  7. Sexuality and sublimation 149
  8. The result of a "complete cure" 157
SUMMARY AND CONCLUDING REFLECTIONS 163
APPENDIX 1: The main texts, with a psychological commentary
  1. The path of liberation as a whole 176
  2. Guiding one's thoughts 183
  3. Avoiding hunger 187
  4. Awareness 189
  5. Mindfulness 190
  6. Fear of being alone 194
  7. Who succeeds? 197
  8. The liberated person 200
APPENDIX 2: Absorption & Pleasure in Mysticism & Meditation 202
APPENDIX 3: Psychology and Free Will 208

Technical Terms and their Sanskrit and Pali Equivalents 216
Abbreviations 216
Bibliography 217
Index 245

> *My most fundamental objective is to urge a change in the perception and evaluation of familiar data.*[1]

Preface

The two studies announced in the subtitle overlap only minimally. They find expression in Part I and Part II of this book respectively. These two parts can be read and evaluated independently. The one point they have in common is the important role they attribute to attention, or rather absorption, in the functioning of the mind.

Apart from this common point, the two parts present two theories — one in Part I, another in Part II — meant to provide answers to a set of questions. Several of these questions (especially those discussed in Part I) have been asked before, and answers have been proposed. It is not the aim of this book to discuss those answers. This would be impractical: those answers belong to widely different fields of enquiry, and are not always relevant to the answers proposed in this book. This book will rather focus on its own intended contribution, which does not wholly fit in any existing field in particular. It offers two new theories, and concentrates on issues that have a direct bearing on those theories. To the best of my knowledge, the two theories do not contradict but rather complement each other.

Matters not directly required for a presentation (and understanding) of the two theories are mostly relegated to the notes, which readers who merely wish to acquaint themselves with the theories are free to ignore. The notes are for those who wish to be informed about sources of information (and

---

[1] Thomas S. Kuhn, *The Structure of Scientific Revolutions* (p. viii-ix).

of ideas), concurring views of others, possible objections, and further issues to be explored. There are references to neurological findings, yet the theories presented do not amount to interpreted neuroscience. Indeed, it is a fundamental claim of this book, argued especially in the Introduction to Part II and in Appendix 3 of Part II, that there is a need for genuine psychological theory beside an understanding of underlying and accompanying neurological processes.

Part I, to put it briefly, deals with the human faculty of speech, and shows that this faculty is inseparable from some other human particulars, most notably religion and culture. It argues that, largely as a result of language acquisition, humans have two levels of cognition, which in normal circumstances are simultaneously active. Absorption is a (or the) means to circumvent some, perhaps all, of the associations that characterize one of these two levels of cognition, the symbolic one (symbolic in a sense to be specified), thus leaving the non-symbolic level of cognition. The result is what is sometimes referred to as a mystical experience, but which is not confined to mysticism. It plays a role in ritual, mythology and other "religious" phenomena, and elsewhere.

Part II takes as point of departure what John Brockman would call a "dangerous idea" (What Is Your Dangerous Idea?), whose consequences it explores (but on whose correctness it does not insist). In doing so, it has to develop a rudimentary psychological theory centered on motivation. Absorption has its place in this theory, too, in that it reveals itself as an important source of pleasure. Since the human mind is at least in part guided by pleasure, which it seeks to repeat, states of absorption leave memory traces that subsequently direct the mind. However, these memory traces do not "recall" the states of absorption, but rather the objects or circumstances that accompanied them. The resulting activity of the mind differs in this way from person to person, and can pursue wildly diverging goals. The theory in Part II also accounts for an important characteristic of absorption: it cannot normally be evoked at will. Without this characteristic, absorption could not play the roles it does in the two theories of Part I and Part II.

The theories here presented do not easily fit into usual academic categories. If pressed, I would propose "human science": the scientific study of the way humans function which, while using material from all relevant domains, refuses to be boxed into any of them.

Inevitably, I am no specialist in all the domains that are being touched upon in this enquiry. Yet I believe that something important is missing in any and all of them. I am aware of the risks of venturing into foreign territory, and cannot but request readers to bear with me and concentrate on the positive that this enquiry may contribute. In spite of helpful comments from anonymous referees, insufficiencies will no doubt remain, perhaps even plain errors. Still, I do hope and believe that it may help to make progress toward a fuller understanding of human nature.

An earlier version of Part I has appeared under the title "Ritual, holophrastic utterances, and the symbolic mind" in the Proceedings of the International Conference "Ritual Dynamics and the Science of Ritual" that was held at Heidelberg University, 29 September to 2 October 2008 (Bronkhorst, 2010). A preliminary PDF version of the whole book was available on the internet from 2009 onward;[2] it has now been removed. The present book contains the definitive text and incorporates substantial improvements on the earlier versions.

---

[2] It has evoked at least one published response: "Re-introducing philosophical soteriology: Bronkhorst on absorption" by Eddy Van Laerhoven (2010).

PART ONE

The Symbolic Mind

Introduction

The evolutionary proximity of human beings to other primates is sufficiently established for studies of "the naked ape" or "the third chimpanzee" to be possible and justified.[1] Nevertheless, many of those working in the human sciences insist that there are fundamental differences between humans and the other primates. Something happened in our evolutionary past which led to the rise of a number of features that we do not share with our evolutionary cousins. The most notable of these are language, culture and religion.[2] What happened that had these momentous consequences? The following pages will propose an answer. Given the nature of the question, it is appropriate to begin with primates different from us.

§1 Symbolic Representation

In research carried out during the seventies at Georgia State University, two chimpanzees—called Sherman and Austin—participated in an experiment meant to investigate whether chimpanzees could be taught to use language, and to what extent they would do so.[3] Since the vocal tract of chimpanzees does not allow them to pronounce the sounds of human language, a different method was employed: The apes were taught to use a special computer keyboard made up of so-called lexigrams.

---

[1] These are the titles of two popular books on human behavior by Desmond Morris (1967) and Jared Diamond (1992) respectively.

[2] Perhaps one should add (certain forms of) madness, which some (Crow, 1991; 1995; 1998; Bentall, 2003: 203) consider inextricably linked to language.

[3] See Savage-Rumbaugh & Rumbaugh, 1978, esp. p. 279 ff.

The more specific aim of the experiment was to find out whether they would be able to use lexigrams in combinations. These combinations might then be looked upon as elementary syntactical relationships. The chimps were trained to chain lexigram pairs in simple verb-noun relationships. For example, the lexigram GIVE followed by the lexigram BANANA would result in the giving of a banana. GIVE followed by ORANGE would be similarly successful, but other combinations would not. The following scheme, where ✚ means "successful", and ✖ means "unsuccessful", illustrates this:

GIVE + BANANA ⇒ ✚
GIVE + ORANGE ⇒ ✚
BANANA + ORANGE ⇒ ✖
ORANGE + GIVE ⇒ ✖
etc.

Initially our chimps would have just two "verb" lexigrams and four food or drink lexigrams to choose from. But the mere learning of a number of lexigram pairs was not sufficient for the chimps to understand the general system (viz., "verb" followed by "noun" leads to the appropriate result). They could learn individual associations between specific pairs and their result, but for a long time they failed to grasp the system of relationships of which these correlations were a part. In the end they did grasp the system, but at the cost of thousands of trials in which they had to find out what combinations of lexigrams led to no result whatsoever. Once they had grasped the system, they had *crossed the symbolic threshold*. They had succeeded in using "words" as symbols in the special sense used here: as signs that do not only refer to "their" objects, but also to each other.

For a correct appreciation of what follows it is essential to understand that the word *symbol* is not used here in its usual sense and that it should on no account be confused with it. I

§1 Symbolic Representation

borrow the word in this specific sense — i.e., signs that do not only refer to "their" objects, but also to each other — from Terrence Deacon, who in turn has borrowed it from the philosopher Charles Sanders Peirce. Symbols of this kind play a role in what we will call *symbolic reference*.

Even the highly condensed presentation of long and elaborate experiments given above shows how much is required to acquire symbolic reference. To cite Deacon (1997: 86):

> What the animals had learned was not only a set of specific associations between lexigrams and objects or events. They had also learned a set of logical relationships *between the lexigrams*, relationships of exclusion and inclusion. More importantly, these lexigram-lexigram relationships formed a complete system in which each allowable or forbidden co-occurrence of lexigrams in the same string (and therefore each allowable or forbidden substitution of one lexigram for another) was defined. They had discovered that the relationship that a lexigram has to an object *is a function of* the relationship it has to other lexigrams, not just a function of the correlated appearance of both lexigram and object. This is the essence of a symbolic relationship.

What Sherman and Austin learned with enormous and prolonged exertion, *we humans* learn in our childhood, apparently with much less effort.[4] Where the two chimpanzees took a long time to learn to pay attention, not just to the desired ob-

---

[4] Only in extremely unfavorable external circumstances, such as those experienced by so-called feral children, may human infants not succeed in acquiring language. On feral children, see Candland, 1993; Newton, 2002; Strivay, 2006. The story of Helen Keller who, though blind and deaf from an early age, succeeded in acquiring language is interesting in this context; see Donald, 2001: 232-251 (note esp. p. 249: "The notion of labeling events and objects *simply doesn't occur* to an isolated mind.")

ject of their activity but also to the signs and to their relationships with each other, we learn to do so almost automatically. Indeed, all normal human children learn the language of their care-takers. Yet the complexities of those languages are much greater than those of the simple sets of "words", two in each set, which Sherman and Austin managed to master. All human children cross the symbolic threshold at an early age, without realizing it. They are able do so because evolution has equipped us for this task, primarily by giving us a much enlarged prefrontal cortex.[5]

Let us stay somewhat longer with our two chimpanzees. Initially, they had learned the combination GIVE + BANANA as a indivisible whole, which gave rise to a pleasant result, viz., that a banana was given to them. After thousands of trials and errors they had mastered the system behind it. They had learned, for example, that the lexigram GIVE could be used with a following ORANGE so as to lead to a different result, viz., that an orange was given to them. Meanwhile they had learned that these two outcomes had something in common, and that this common element was somehow represented by the lexigram GIVE. Similarly, other combinations had taught them that the lexigram BANANA was associated with the element banana in various activities. In other words, Sherman and Austin were in the process of creating *representations* corresponding to elements of objective reality. These representations were the result of the overlap of events: the representation "give" resulted from the overlap of "give banana" and "give orange". Human beings appear to arrive at their representations in a similar, though much more complex manner.

These few reflections show that the learning of language facilitates the formation of representations. These representations correspond initially to the shared parts of different lin-

---

[5] See Deacon, 1997, Part Two: Brain (pp. 145-318).

§1 Symbolic Representation

guistic utterances, i.e., primarily words. However, these same reflections show that this process, once begun, does not necessarily stop here. We can easily imagine a situation where our chimpanzees wish to receive an object for which there is no lexigram on their keyboard, say a piece of chocolate. In that case they might create a symbolic representation, *chocolate*, which they would know how to deal with syntaxically if only there were a lexigram CHOCOLATE, for example in GIVE + CHOCOLATE. In other words, once the learning of language has initiated the capacity of creating symbolic representations, the animal may be in a position to create new symbolic representations for which there are no words. This accounts for the human capacity not only to create new words but also to have symbolic representations for which there are no words.[6]

Consider in this connection another ape, a bonobo called Kanzi. Kanzi, for reasons that will not be discussed at present, acquired language to a degree far superior to Sherman and Austin. Strikingly, his linguistic skills subsequently facilitated other kinds of learning even in domains not directly associated with language. Indeed,

> his understanding encompassed all manner of novel events and even of metaphor. His understanding of language informed his interpretation of real world events and his broadened capacity to interpret and appropriately classify real world events informed his linguistic comprehension in a boot strapping effect. An example of

---

[6] *Symbolic representations* must be distinguished from *concepts* (even though some authors use the word *concept* for what we call *representation*, and *category* for what we call *concept*; so Bickerton, 2009: 192 ff.). An animal of prey may have a concept of the animals that it hunts, in the sense that it will know and recognize them. Without symbolic representation, however, it cannot think about those animals the way those endowed with symbolic representation can.

this was the ease with which Kanzi learned to flake stone tools given a modicum of both visual and verbal instruction. Similar attempts by other apes required long and arduous conditioning and shaping regiments.[7]

Crossing the symbolic threshold, it appears, involves more than being able to learn to use language. It opens up a world of representations which, by the *boot strapping effect* mentioned in this passage, extends well beyond the representations covered by the words of one's language.[8]

It is tempting to connect these reflections with what neurobiologists tell us about human consciousness. Consider the following passages from a recent book by Gerald M. Edelman, a neuroscientist (2004: 105 f.):

> By its very nature, the conscious process embeds representation in a degenerate,[9] context-dependent web: there are many ways in which individual neural circuits, synaptic populations, varying environmental signals, and previous history can lead to the same meaning.
>
> [...]
>
> There is no single circuit activity or code that corresponds to a given conscious "representation". A neuron may contribute to that "representation" at one moment, and in the next have no contribution to make. The same is true of context-dependent interactions with the environment.

---

[7] Savage-Rumbaugh, Fields & Taglialatela, 2000: 916.

[8] It is for this reason hardly surprising that Kanzi is reported to have made, all on his own, four new "words", standing for 'banana', 'juice', 'grapes' and 'yes' (*New Scientist*, 2 January 2003). Everett (2012: 258) shows that Pirahãs can describe colors they have no word for, and concludes: "People *can* think beyond their language."

[9] On p. 43 Edelman explains: "Degeneracy is the ability of structurally different elements of a system to perform the same function or yield the same output."

§1 Symbolic Representation

> A shift of context can change the qualia that are parts of a representation, or even recompose some qualia and still keep that representation.
>
> [...]
>
> [D]epending on input, environment, body state, and other contexts, different core states can underlie a particular representation. The interactions are relational and have the properties of polymorphous sets. These are sets, like Ludwig Wittgenstein's "games", that are defined neither by singly necessary nor by jointly sufficient conditions.

Elsewhere (p. 99), Edelman draws attention to the hippocampus, a neural structure in the brain which is "necessary for episodic memory, the long-time memory of sequential events, the brain's 'narrative'". He comments: "Higher-order consciousness rests in part on episodic memory, and in the absence of such memory coherent semantic activity would not be likely to develop."

It seems probable, then, that the overlap of episodic memories and other mental events plays an important role in the creation of representations in the mind, just as for Sherman and Austin the intersection of the useful units of communication GIVE + BANANA and GIVE + ORANGE led to the representation **give**. Symbolic reference greatly increases the number of representations thus created. It seems that Sherman and Austin had not extracted the representation *give* out of the numerous situations in which they had been given things. Only the exercises with the lexigrams taught them to do so. We may assume that the same happens to human children when learning to speak.

In this way, symbolic reference makes possible an almost limitless multiplication of representations as well as their combination in countless ways. Indeed, worlds of imagination can now be created that take us away from our immediate impulses and experience. The results are multiple. Symbolic representation, to begin with, permits us to think, and speculate, about our own past and future and, what is more, to think about ourselves as characters in numerous scenarios. Hence we can think about ourselves the way we think about others. This is what Deacon refers to in the following passage (1997: 452):

> Consciousness of self in this way implicitly includes consciousness of other selves, and other consciousnesses can only be represented through the virtual reference created by symbols. The self that is the source of one's experience of intentionality, the self that is judged by itself as well as by others for its moral choices, the self that worries about its impending departure from the world, this self is a symbolic self. It is a final irony that it is the virtual, not actual, reference that symbols provide, which gives rise to this experience of self. This most undeniably real experience is a *virtual* reality.[10]

Symbolic representation influences our experience.[11] We will return to this below. It also allows us to be objective with regard to ourselves, which in its turn is behind our tendency to judge ourselves the way we judge others (at least to some extent).[12] This in its turn allows for empathy on a wider scale than might otherwise be possible. *Without* symbolic representation there

---

[10] This self is what Dennett (1991: 418) calls the narrative self; see below.

[11] George Van Driem, private communication: "The idea that language exerts an unfavorable effect on perception itself and blinds us to reality is an old idea already espoused by Bertus Brouwer and Frederik van Eeden."

[12] Symbolic reference, and the acquisition of language that underlies it, are also a necessary prerequisite for the understanding of others' false beliefs; Pyers & Senghas, 2009.

§1 Symbolic Representation

would be *no* detachment from immediate arousal and compulsion, *no* possibility to judge oneself the way we judge others, *no* place for moral choices, *no* developed forms of empathy, *no* ordinary sense of self, and much else.

Symbolic representation does not stop at self-representation. The immediate arousal and compulsion mentioned earlier, too, are objectified and find a place in the "outside world" in the form of values and institutions. The result is as described by Roy A. Rappaport (1999: 8), who uses the word *symbol* approximately in the same way we do:[13]

> The epochal significance of the symbol for the world beyond the species in which it appeared did not become apparent for many millennia — perhaps hundreds of millennia — after it had emerged. But earlier effects of language and even proto-language upon the lifeways of the hominids in its possession must soon have become enormous. [...] [L]anguage permits thought and communication to escape from the solid actualities of here and now to discover other realms, for instance, those of the possible, the plausible, the desirable, [...] [However,] [l]anguage does not merely *permit* such thought but both *requires* it and *makes it inevitable*. Humanity is a species that lives and can only live in terms of meanings it itself must invent. These meanings and understandings not only reflect or approximate an independently existing world but participate in its very construction. The worlds in which humans live are not fully constituted

---

[13] Cp. Rappaport, 1999: 4: "only humans, so far as we know, are possessed of languages composed, first, of lexicons made up of symbols in Peirce's sense of the word [...] or Buchler's [...]: that is, signs related only 'by law', i.e. convention, to that which they signify, and second, of grammars, sets of rules for combining symbols into semantically unbounded discourse."

> by tectonic, meteorological and organic processes. They are not only made of rocks and trees and oceans, but are also constructed out of symbolically conceived and performatively established [...] cosmologies, institutions, rules, and values. With language the world comes to be furnished with qualities like good and evil [...]

Once again, this description concerns the world experienced with the help of symbolic representation. The world experienced without it, if such a thing is possible, lacks these features.

The effects of symbolic representation go even further than this. Objective reality is in part social reality. This is what John R. Searle set out to show in his book *The Construction of Social Reality* (1995).[14] And indeed, it cannot be denied that there is "an objective world of money, property, marriage, governments, elections, football games, cocktail parties and law courts in a world that consists entirely of physical particles in fields of force, and in which some of these particles are organized into systems that are conscious biological beasts, such as ourselves" (p. xi-xii). In other words, "there are portions of the real world, objective facts in the world, that are only facts by human agreement" (p. 1). This social reality, which is real, is yet *language-dependent* (chapter 3). In institutional reality, language is not used merely to *describe* the facts but, in an odd way, is partly *constitutive* of the facts.[15] And being language-dependent, it depends on symbolic representation.

Largely as a result of symbolic representation, human thought is, at least to some extent, narrative in nature.[16] To cite the philosopher Daniel Dennett (1991: 417-18):

---

[14] See further Searle, 2010.

[15] Searle, 1999: 115.

[16] See, e.g., Turner, 1996; Deacon & Cashman, 2009: 496 ff.; Boyd, 2009.

§1 Symbolic Representation

Our human environment contains not just food and shelter, enemies to fight or flee, and conspecifics with whom to mate, but words, words, words. These words are potent elements of our environment that we readily incorporate, ingesting and extruding them, weaving them like spiderwebs into self-protective strings of *narrative*. Indeed, [...] when we let in these words [...] they tend to take over, creating us out of the raw materials they find in our brains.

Our fundamental tactic of self-protection, self-control, and self-definition is not spinning webs or building dams, but telling stories, and more particularly concocting and controlling the story we tell others — and ourselves — about who we are.

One of the characteristics of narrative is its so-called 'chunking' of experience. As a matter of fact, "[i]t is easier to organize knowledge and behavior if the vast realms of experience are subdivided; indeed, the world would quickly become unmanageable if I had to sort through every possible concept and potential course of action at every given moment." (Herman, 2003: 172). To avoid the threatening chaos, the narrative—i.e. symbolic—mind sifts through the data of perception and apportions different parts to different narratives.[17] Depending on the "stories" in which "I" figure, certain objects receive extra attention while others are neglected. This sifting process is, once again, at least in part the result of symbolic representation.

---

[17] Cp. Hirstein, 2005: 239: "The creative process of confabulation, its character and persistence, is emblematic of what it is to be human. ... [I]t places actions and events in a particular human context we find easy to understand. ... It is capable of providing the peace of mind an explanation brings, whether or not that explanation is a good one. ... [W]e find stories ... easy to understand and convenient to use ..."

We may sum up what precedes by citing once more Deacon (1997: 423):

> Because of our symbolic abilities, we humans have access to a novel higher-order representation system that not only recodes experiences and guides the formation of skills and habits, but also provides a means of representing features of a world that no other creature experiences, the world of the abstract. We do not just live our lives in the physical world and our immediate social group, but also in a world of rules of conduct, beliefs about our histories, and hopes and fears about imagined futures.

Here two points have to be emphasized. First, symbolic representation not only affects the way we think or communicate, it also affects our cognition and the way we experience the world. Second, the way we experience the world with the help of symbolic representation — in short, *symbolic experience* — is based on, and cannot exist without, non-symbolic experience. In other words, we have *two levels of cognition*,[18] one of which (the symbolic one) cannot exist without the other, but not viceversa. Let us look at these two points:

1. *Symbolic representation affects the way we experience the world.* As symbolic beings we live in a constructed world which contains many things that the objective world (which is "outside" and independent of us) does not contain, or which it only contains by human agreement. Among these constructed things, as we have seen, we must count our objectified self ("self", "soul"), our objectified urges ("values", "morality"),

---

[18] One might speak of "dual processing", a notion that attracts the attention of researchers, but which does not so far appear to have led to a study of the phenomena which our two levels of cognition will bring up below; see Evans, 2008.

§1 Symbolic Representation

objects to which a function has been attributed (bank-notes where there are only pieces of paper), and much else.

2. *Symbolic experience is rooted in non-symbolic experience and would become seriously dysfunctional without it.* Without non-symbolic experience, we might lose contact with objective reality altogether, being locked, without possibility of escape, into a world of imagination that symbolic representation creates for us.[19] The young child has pure non-symbolic experience, which allows it to subsequently "cross the symbolic threshold" and make the quantum leap into the world of symbolic experience. But even after this leap it needs non-symbolic experience to mold the world it constructs into objective fact.

The conclusion we are led to draw is that we, normal human adults, experience the world in a double manner: a constructed world of symbolic representation is added onto a world of "raw" experience that underlies and accompanies it.

What would non-symbolic experience be like, if it could free itself from symbolic representation? Consider first the following passage from Searle's book (1995: 12):

> From a God's-eye view, from outside the world, all the features of the world would be intrinsic, including intrinsic relational features such as the feature that people in our culture regard such and such objects as screwdrivers. God could not see screwdrivers, cars, bathtubs, etc., because intrinsically speaking there are no such things. Rather, God would see *us treating* certain objects as screwdrivers, cars, bathtubs, etc. But from our standpoint, the standpoint of beings who are not gods but are inside the world

---

[19] According to certain sleep researchers, this is what happens in dreams. See Llinás & Paré, 1991; Jouvet, 1999: 106 f.; Hirstein, 2005: 242; Warren, 2007: 137 f.

that includes us as active agents, we need to distinguish those true statements we make that attribute features to the world that exist quite independently of any attitude or stance we take, and those statements that attribute features that exist only relative to our interests, attitudes, stances, purposes, etc.

We may not be gods, but our experience of the world without symbolic representation would be close to the one attributed to God in this passage: we would see no screwdrivers, cars, bathtubs, etc., but only the objects that people who *do* use symbolic representation treat as screwdrivers, cars, bathtubs, etc. On the basis of our earlier reflections, we may add further features. If we could free ourselves from symbolic representation, we would have no "objective" notion of self, we would inhabit a world without values, and our expectations of the future and many of our memories of the past would not affect our present experience. And finally, we would not filter out many of the features of the world that have been neglected because they do not fit into any of our present narratives.

Once again it will be interesting to cite the observations of a neurologist. Antonio Damasio deals with the question of consciousness in his book *The Feeling of What Happens* (1999). He distinguishes between two kinds of consciousness that he calls *core consciousness* and *extended consciousness*. Core consciousness, he argues, is of a nonverbal nature. Extended consciousness is based on core consciousness and cannot exist without it. The reverse is not true: core consciousness *can* exist without extended consciousness, and this is indeed what happens in certain neurological disorders. Extended consciousness, in the words of Damasio (p. 195-196), "goes beyond the here and now of core consciousness, both backward and forward. The here and now is still there, but it is flanked by the past, as much past as you may need to illuminate the now effectively, and,

§1 Symbolic Representation

just as importantly, it is flanked by the anticipated future. The scope of extended consciousness, at its zenith, may span the entire life of an individual, from the cradle to the future, and it can place the world beside it. On any given day, if only you let it fly, extended consciousness can make you a character in an epic novel, and, if only you use it well, it can open wide the doors of creation". About the experience of core consciousness he says (p. 202):

> In a neurologically normal state, we are never completely deprived of extended consciousness. Yet it is not difficult to imagine what a possessor of *only* core consciousness probably experiences. Just consider what it may be like inside the mind of a one-year-old infant. I suspect objects come to the mind's stage, are attributed to a core self, and exit as quickly as they enter. Each object is known by a simple self and clear on its own, but there is no large-scale relation among objects in space or time and no sensible connection between the object and either past or anticipated experience.

For our present purposes it is important to remember that extended consciousness cannot exist without core consciousness, so that core consciousness is present in some way in every normal conscious human being. To this may be added that extended consciousness, whatever its neurological basis, is largely shaped by symbolic representation. Damasio's extended consciousness may therefore be considered as coinciding for a large part with the consciousness that results from symbolic representation. Damasio's observations confirm in this manner that symbolic experience is based on, and cannot do without, non-symbolic experience.

Edelman, whom we mentioned before, distinguishes between what he calls primary consciousness and higher-order consciousness. Even though he thinks that "it is likely that [such primates as chimpanzees] have a form of higher-order consciousness", he recognizes that the acquisition of language makes a major difference. About this he says (2004: 103):

> Clearly, one of the largest steps toward the acquisition of true language is the realization that an arbitrary token — a gesture or a word — stands for a thing or an event. When a sufficiently large lexicon of such tokens is subsequently accumulated, higher-order consciousness can greatly expand in range. Associations can be made by metaphor, and with ongoing activity, early metaphor can be transformed into more precise categories or intrapersonal and interpersonal experience. The gift of narrative and an expanded sense of temporal succession then follow. While the remembered present is in fact a reflection of true physical time, higher-order consciousness makes it possible to relate a socially constructed self to past recollections and future imaginations. The Heraclitean illusion of a point in the present moving from the past into the future is constructed by these means. This illusion, mixed with the sense of a narrative and metaphorical ability, elevates higher-order consciousness to new heights.

Note that more is needed than just a "sufficiently large lexicon" of arbitrary tokens that stand for things or events. These tokens — as has become clear from the experiments involving Sherman and Austin — should be recognized and employed as *symbols* in the sense used here, i.e. as referring not just to "their" things or events, but also to each other, and as constituting a system of logical relationships with each other.

In view of what precedes we can use the image of a web that symbolic representation weaves between us and the objects of our perception, a web that separates us from the outside world.

This is of course only an image: there is no real web, and there is no real separation from the outside world. In reality, incoming signals are interpreted in the light of the numerous associations which they evoke. In the case of those who master symbolic reference, these associations are richer and more intricate than for those who don't.[20]

§2 Mysticism

In spite of its obvious insufficiencies, I will continue to use the image of a web woven by symbolic representation that situates itself between us and the outside world. Is it possible to push the web aside and experience the world in a more direct manner? Are we condemned to remain separated from the objects of our perception by this artificial construction that has interposed itself between us and the world? Some of the testimonies of people variously referred to as mystics, madmen and meditators suggest that the web sometimes tears, or is torn, whether on purpose or by accident.[21]

---

[20] It is of course conceivable that incoming signals will be interpreted in the light of other associations than the usual ones, in which case we may be entitled to speak of *hallucinations*. Cf. Bentall, 2003: 364 ff.

[21] Cf. Pyysiäinen, 1993: 36 (cp. 2001: 114 f.): "mystical experiences may count as an exception to the linguistic quality of man's being-in-the-world"; Staal, 1990: 139: "mysticism is characterized by the absence of language. It points to a pre-linguistic state which can be induced by ritual, by recitation, by silent meditation on mantras, or by other means". On the link of epileptic seizures with "deeply moving spiritual experiences, including a feeling of divine presence and the sense [of being] in direct communion with God", see Ramachandran & Blakeslee, 1998: 179 f. Deacon & Cashman (2009) propose a somewhat different explanation of mysticism and religion.

Since William James, mystical experience is often characterized as being *ineffable* and as possessing a *noetic quality*.[22] Literal-minded philosophers find the idea that it is ineffable, and therefore beyond the realm of language, puzzling.[23] Less caviling readers may find this a particularly appropriate manner of describing experience that is no longer co-determined by symbolic representation, and therefore by language. Mystical and related experience is also said to give access to a different, higher, reality, or to allow its subject to perceive things as they really are (this is James's noetic quality). Indeed, a universal effect of mystical experience is said to be "an understanding that what was experienced was more real/important than any prior experience."[24] The second of these two claims corresponds to what we would expect to hear from someone who has succeeded in discarding symbolic representation, if only for a short while and perhaps only in part. Such a person may be expected to experience the world differently, and in a more direct and immediate fashion, since ordinary human experience is always separated from its objects by the web of symbolic representation. The claim that mystical experience gives access to a different and higher reality is, though not strictly true, almost correct. Experience through symbolic representation is indirect, mediate. Experience without it, or with less of it, is direct, immediate. Strictly speaking it is the same "objective"

---

[22] Wulff, 2000: 400. For a collection of passages from Western literature on what cannot be said, see Franke, 2007.

[23] See Gellman, 2005: § 3.1; Proudfoot, 1985: 124 f. Nelson (2011: 254) thinks that the mystical is not beyond language in a neurological sense. "It is *before* language, residing in ancient brain structures concerned with our Darwinian survival. My strong hunch is that mystical experiences existed long before language came to our species." Inevitably, Nelson is obliged to conclude that "other animals aside from human beings may have mystical feelings." This is not the position here taken.

[24] Paper, 2004: 4.

§2 Mysticism

reality that is experienced, but it is experienced so differently that the experiencer may have difficulty recognizing it. Indeed, recognition itself involves connecting the present cognition with earlier ones. In non-symbolic experience the link with constructed former and anticipated later experiences is weakened, or absent. The subject is, as a result, easily convinced that he or she is confronted with a different reality, where in actual fact it is the same reality that is experienced differently. Let me add that, if our mystic has to answer the question which of the two realities he or she has experienced is more real, the answer can easily be predicted. The mystical experience is so much more direct and immediate, and so undoubtedly real, that the choice is obvious: the reality presumably experienced in the mystical state is more real than that of ordinary experience.

Other features commonly ascribed to mystical experience are easily explained by the weakening or disappearance of the web of symbolic representation. The ordinary self, for example, will tend to disappear. This does not surprise, given the fact that the ordinary self was a construction of symbolic representation to begin with. The unitary and undifferentiated nature of mystical consciousness emphasized by Stace (1960) and others is another feature that fits in well with the absence of symbolic representation. Recall that the symbolic level of cognition divides the world into representations. Without symbolic representation reality presents itself as undivided, and therefore unitary.

It seems safe to conclude from all this that there are ways to liberate experience, if only temporarily and perhaps partially, from the web woven by symbolic reference.[25] This extraordinary experience will subsequently be interpreted in ways prop-

---

[25] It will be argued below (§ 5) that culture, too, weaves a web of symbolic reference which is added on to, or integrated with, the "linguistic" web.

er to the culture of the person concerned. Such interpretations are, of course, of the greatest significance both to those who have these experiences and those who study them on the basis of witness reports. However, they do not interest us in the context of the present investigation.

We note in passing that this non-symbolic experience (the "mystical" experience) is highly valued and sometimes sought after by many of those who have had it. There is a notable tendency to ascribe deep significance to it. We will have more to say about this below.

Having established that there appear to be ways of discarding the web of symbolic representation, we may give some thought to the question of how this result is obtained. The aim is not to enumerate techniques and methods that are *de facto* used by mystics and others who succeed in having mystical experiences. Rather, we wish to consider what mechanism we would expect, in the light of our reflections so far, to lead to that result.

In order to make progress, we have to abandon the image of a web woven by symbolic reference, and try to understand in a more factual way what happens when a person crosses the symbolic threshold. The case of Sherman and Austin will once again be helpful. Whereas these two chimpanzees had initially learned the connection between the pair of lexigrams GIVE + BANANA and the giving of a banana that followed, they had, after extensive supplementary learning, come to associate the single lexigram GIVE with a variety of situations and elements, among them other lexigrams. These numerous associations — with other lexigrams, with the order of lexigrams to be respected, with situations in which different things were given — allowed them to use this particular lexigram in a simple system of symbolic reference.

§2 Mysticism

Essentially the same applies to human language users. A vast number of associations allows them to use words the way they do. Many, perhaps most, of these associations are not conscious. But they are there, below the surface.[26] Without them, language use would not be possible.

What should one do to remove the web woven by symbolic representation? The obvious answer is: Stop the extra associations that constitute symbolic reference. How does one stop innumerable associations, most of which are not even conscious? Focusing the mind presents itself as a plausible method.

Focusing the mind is a faculty which humans and many animals possess. Situations that are particularly threatening, to take an example, make us forget almost everything else.[27] This faculty is to some extent subject to ordinary conscious control. We then speak of concentration. It can take more extreme forms, in which case the expression *absorption* is to be preferred.[28] Absorption typically accompanies mystical experiences. Absorption, we must assume, reduces the number and perhaps the intensity of associations, including unconscious associations.[29] What remains is an experience in which the

---

[26] Cp. Deacon, 1997: 265-66: "The symbolic reference emerges from a pattern of virtual links between [neurological] tokens, which constitute a sort of parallel realm of associations to those that link those tokens to real sensorimotor experiences and possibilities."

[27] The filtering of irrelevant information is preceded by activity in the prefrontal cortex and basal ganglia, particularly in the globus pallidus; McNab & Klingberg, 2007.

[28] "Absorption is the tendency to alter our perceptions and surroundings while in a state of highly focused attention with complete immersion in a central experience at the expense of contextual orientation" (Maldonado & Spiegel, 1998: 59). On the exclusion of irrelevant information, see Rees et al., 1997.

[29] For references to literature dealing with the neurological correlates of focused attention, in particular the reduced activity of certain brain parts, see notes 150 and 151 below.

associations that are responsible for symbolic representations have been reduced or suppressed: a non-symbolic, mystical experience.[30]

This explanation of mystical experience has an additional advantage. If focusing the mind can reduce the number and/or intensity of associations, there is no reason to insist that in its strongest forms it affects only those associations that participate in symbolic representation. No symbolic representation is required to associate present with past experience: animals that have not crossed the symbolic threshold can yet learn from past experience, and therefore interpret the present in the light of the past.[31] Mystical experiences that are completely timeless and therefore without any associative connection with the past, can be understood as resulting from a state of absorption in which all associations with the past, including those that do not contribute to symbolic representation (if such exist), are

---

[30] Compare these reflections with the following passage from Pyysiäinen's book *Belief and Beyond* (1996): "If we now define the so-called external mystical experience [...] as an experience with sensory input but with no thoughts, it corresponds rather well to [the] description of the receptive mode in which [...] logical thinking and categorization are reduced to a minimum [...] [S]uch experience would mean that syntax and the linguistic aspects of consciousness [...] as well as off-line thinking are turned off. Moreover, also consciousness of one's own conscious nature [...], on which (together with language) the experience of self is based, supposedly disappears. What remains, is [...] on-line thinking, and an awareness of one's sensations. The external world does not disappear from one's consciousness, but is experienced as a here and now continuity with which oneself is coextensive."

[31] See Rose, 2003: 155 ff. There is a debate about the question whether and to what extent different animals (bonobos, orangutans, scrub-jays, squirrel monkeys, rats) can anticipate the future; see *New Scientist* of 1 November 2008 p. 32-35 ("Chrono-creatures: do animals ponder the past and contemplate the future?" by Henry Nicholls) with references to Mulcahy et al., 2006; Naqshbandi et al., 2006; Raby et al., 2007; Correia et al., 2007; Clayton et al., 2008.

interrupted. In other words, focusing the mind can serve as an explanation for mystical experiences that are free from symbolic representation, but also for aspects of such experiences that cannot be fully understood by the mere absence of symbolic representation.

The explanation of mystical experience by means of absorption has a further consequence. There can be degrees of absorption, with as upper limit the total interruption of all associations. This upper limit is not necessarily reached by all those who have mystical or semi-mystical experiences. It follows that there is a sliding scale connecting "ordinary" and "mystical" experience.[32] A slight reduction of the number and intensity of associative mental connections may be part of everyone's daily experience, yet may not strike those who undergo it as particularly remarkable; they may not even take notice.

§3 RITUAL

Ritual is often accompanied by formulas, strings of speech sounds. In India the term used is mantra, and I shall occasionally speak of mantras when referring to these kinds of formu-

---

[32] Damasio (2010: 168-169) makes a similar comparison in connection with his *core consciousness* and *extended consciousness*: "Today I see the changes in consciousness scope as far more mercurial than I first envisioned them; that scope constantly shifts up or down a scale as if it moved on a gliding cursor." Further, "the levels of consciousness fluctuate with the situation" (p. 169), "I have always envisioned many grades between the core and autobiographical endpoints of the scale" (p. 171). Lewis-Williams & Pearce (2005: 56 etc.; also Lewis-Williams, 2010: 140 ff.) speak of a "spectrum of consciousness" and mention intense concentration as one of the factors that intensify its introverted end; "religious experience is, in the first instance, a result of taking the introverted end of the spectrum at face value — within a given cultural context" (p. 55).

las. Frits Staal, in several publications (e.g. 1984; 1985; 2006), has drawn attention to the fact that mantras, *when used as mantras*, do not express meaning, at least not in the ordinary way. He does not deny that many, though not all, mantras have a form that resembles or is identical with linguistic utterances. He emphasizes, however, that mantras, even those that *consist of* language, are not *used as* language. Formulas used in ritual settings are not analyzed.[33] Indeed, often they cannot be analyzed. They may be in a language that is no longer used and that is unknown to those who hear or even pronounce the formulas. This is as true of the Latin of the Catholic mass[34] as it is of the Vedic Sanskrit used in Brahmanical ritual. Sometimes the formulas are in no known language. This applies to many of the mantras used in Tantric forms of Hinduism and Buddhism. A more familiar example may be *abracadabra*. Whether or not this formula has a historical etymology, it is and has been unanalyzable and "meaningless" for most if not all of its users.

Why should ritual formulas be unintelligible, "meaningless"? This question may find its answer in the observation that ritual formulas are, or perhaps have to be, holophrastic. Ordi-

---

[33] Cp. Rappaport, 1999: 151: "It is virtually definitive of ritual speech that it is stereotyped and stylized, composed of specified sequences of words that are often archaic, is repeated under particular, usually well-established circumstances, and great stress is often laid upon its precise enunciation. As Maurice Bloch [...] has emphasized, in contrast to ordinary discourse in which considerable choice is open to speakers at a number of points in any utterance, in ritual formulae the 'features of juncture', those components of speech indicating relations among the referents, are immutable. In M. C. Bateson's [...] terms, ritual utterances are 'fused'. This is to say that meaning is derived from them as unsegmented wholes, or as wholes only segmented into minimal meaningful units of considerable length, usually much greater length than is the case in ordinary speech."

[34] For an ethnographic description of the Latin mass, see Jucker, 2007.

§3 Ritual

nary holistic phrases — i.e., the formulas we use in daily life — do have functions. They may have a literal meaning as well, but this literal meaning plays a reduced role in the formula *when used as formula*. Sometimes the literal meaning may even be misleading. The phrase "how do you do?" is not a question about the way the person addressed *does* something. But even though the constituent words are misleading, the phrase is not without function, as anyone who refuses to use it in appropriate circumstances will soon discover.

Ritual formulas, then, are like ordinary formulas, but more so. Ritual formulas often do not even pretend to have a literal meaning. Indeed, it seems to be a plus for ritual formulas to be unintelligible. Let us therefore forget about their literal meanings. What remains? Recall that ritual formulas, being holistic utterances like formulaic phrases in ordinary language, can still have a function. Ordinary holistic utterances, as recent research has shown, often "seem to be geared towards manipulating the situation in which the speaker finds him- or herself".[35] Nothing prevents us from assuming that ritual formulas do the same. And indeed, it would be easy to provide illustrations of the frequently manipulative intent of the use of ritual formulas. In India, "mantras are understood by the tradition as polyvalent instruments of power";[36] "their function [...] is a direct action, generally a ritual one, or a psychological or mystical one".[37] It seems natural to conclude that ritual formulas do have a function, but unlike ordinary formulas they no longer pretend to have a linguistic meaning as well. Ritual formulas, seen this way, are the perfect holistic utterances. Compared to ritual formulas, formulaic expressions in ordinary life are holistic only in the sense that we do not bother to analyze them.

---

[35] Wray, 2002b: 87.
[36] Alper, 1989a: 6.
[37] Padoux, 1989: 302

Ritual formulas are different: they are unanalyzable. *Like* ordinary formulaic expressions they have a function, often a manipulative one. *Unlike* ordinary formulaic expressions, they perform this function directly, without the intervention of the elements that are designated by the words that occur in ordinary formulas.

Recall now the experiments in which the two chimpanzees Sherman and Austin learned, with great effort, to master symbolic reference. They started with what we might call holistic phrases like GIVE + BANANA. Once they had crossed the symbolic threshold, they could use the constituents of these phrases independently. They could, for example, use the lexigram BANANA in a new context created by themselves. Our ordinary language use is of that type, though infinitely more complex. We can use words in a virtually limitless number of contexts of our own choosing. However, ritual utterances are different. They are holistic. They correspond to the combined lexigrams GIVE + BANANA *before* Sherman and Austin had learned to segment this sequence. This suggests that people who opt for the use of holistic phrases — which is what we all do in specific, "ritual", circumstances — attempt, by so doing, to step back *out* of the realm of symbolic representation *into* the immediacy of non-symbolic experience.[38]

---

[38] The question of the relationship between mantras and music presents itself here, rather than that of the relationship between language and music (see on this, e.g., Mithen, 2005: Part One). In this connection it is of interest that an often and exactly repeated phrase, as the psychologist Diana Deutsch discovered, begins to sound like song. (Verify this by listening to www.tinyurl.com/65tcer, and see further *New Scientist* of 8 November 2008 p. 17 ("Fine line between speech and song revealed").) Deutsch "suspects our brains normally suppress musical cues when we hear speech, so that we focus on interpreting the words. But repetition of the words, which we've already processed, can sometimes override this." If a phrase has already been processed and is not processed anew, it becomes a holistic utterance, like the formulas used in ritual. This

§3 Ritual

To avoid confusion, let me add that not all formulaic expressions are, for that reason, ritual formulas. Quite on the contrary, it seems clear that formulaic expressions are also used in ordinary language, in play, and perhaps elsewhere. The question why certain formulaic expressions are accepted as ritual formulas whereas others are not, is interesting and deserves attention in its own right. It cannot be dealt with in this study.

Let us turn to ritual action. Is it possible to maintain that ritual activity relates to ordinary activity in the same way as ritual utterances relate to linguistic utterances?[39] Recall that ritual utterances are holistic, unlike most utterances used in ordinary language. What is more, normal linguistic utterances exemplify symbolic reference, whereas holistic utterances don't. Is it possible to say the same, or approximately the same, about ritual and ordinary activity? Is it true that ritual activity is holistic in some sense whereas ordinary activity is guided by symbolic representation?

I suggest that this last question can be answered with a double *yes*. Yes, ritual activity is holistic and therefore *not* guided by symbolic representation as understood here, and yes, ordinary activity *is* guided by symbolic representation.

The holistic nature of ritual activity can be established with relative ease.[40] Scholars have often observed that ritual actions

---

suggests not only that repeated phrases are likely to do good service as mantras, but also that certain forms of music fit well into ritual. Note in this connection that "the most prominent and perhaps the only universal context [of music] is that of religion: music is used everywhere to communicate with, glorify and/or serve the divinities identified within any particular culture." (Mithen, 2005: 13)

[39] This was Rappaport's (1999: 151) position: "As far as form is concerned, ritual formulae are to ordinary language as ritual postures and gestures are to ordinary instrumental activity."

[40] Cp. Rappaport, 1999: 253: "*to perform a ritual is not to analyze it.*"

are divorced from their usual goals. Some emphasize that they have no meaning, or that they are not communicative.[41] This does not mean that rituals never have a specific overall purpose; they often do. But "the set of sequences that compose the ritual are not connected to this goal in the same way as sub-actions connect to sub-goals in ordinary behavior".[42] Recall in this context what was said above about the frequently manipulative intent of the use of ritual formulas. Both ritual acts and ritual formulas can be used to reach some end, but

---

Indeed, the import of performance is exactly the converse of that of an analytic operation." The correctness of this observation is not necessarily affected by the fact that many rituals consist of a concatenation of "elements of ritual" (*Ritualelemente*; Michaels, 2007: 242). See Michaels, 2007: 246: "Das Problem aller Morphologie des Rituals ist: Wenn Handlungseinheiten als kleinste Bausteine des Rituals genommen werden, dann entspricht dies nicht den Morphemen einer Sprache, sondern allenfalls den Sätzen [...]". Similarly Lawson & McCauley, 1990: 84 (cited Michaels, 2007: 246): "Returning, then, to the analogy with linguistics, it is the *action* that is the analogue of the *sentence* (which is the fundamental unit of linguistic analysis)." Lévi-Strauss (1971: 603) contrasts the holistic nature of ritual with the analysis that find expression in myths: "Cette tentative éperdue, toujours vouée à l'échec, pour rétablir la continuité d'un vécu démantelé sous l'effet du schématisme que lui a substitué la spéculation mythique constitue l'essence du rituel".

It is of particular interest, and very intriguing (cf. Appendix 1 of Part I, below), that some people resort to semantic etymologizing when trying to explain the elements of ritual: "[A]n important part of the Ndembu explanation of symbols rests upon folk etymologizing. The meaning of a given symbol is often, though by no means invariably, derived by Ndembu from the name assigned to it, the sense of which is traced from some primary word, or etymon, often a verb. Scholars have shown that in other Bandu societies this is often a process of fictitious etymologizing, dependent on similarity of sound rather than upon derivation from a common source. Nevertheless, for the people themselves it constitutes part of the 'explanation' of a ritual symbol" (Turner, 1969: 11).

[41] Staal, 1990; Humphrey & Laidlaw, 1994.

[42] Boyer & Liénard, 2006: 3; similarly Pyysiäinen, 2001: 89.

§3 Ritual

both seek to do so in a holistic manner, forgoing the functions which their constituent actions and words (if there are any) would normally accomplish.[43]

What about ordinary activity? Must we accept that it is guided by symbolic representation? Yes, and the distinction between two levels of cognition introduced above explains why. Our dominant level of cognition is the one determined by symbolic representation.[44] It is the level of cognition that allows us to plan our lives and carry out projects of some complexity. It is this cognitive level that gave our ancestors, and us, an edge over competitors. It is the level of cognition on which our well-being, even our life, depends.

Ritual activities, seen this way, are, like ritual formulas, a *denial* of symbolic representation. Like ritual formulas, they are an attempt to step back *out* of the realm of symbolic representation *into* the immediacy of non-symbolic experience. Neither ritual activities nor ritual formulas are symbolic in the sense used here. Both concern a "different", "higher", reality, a reality not touched by symbolic representation. Rituals and ritual formulas have their role to play, but in the "higher" reality that is concealed by symbolic representation rather than in our ordinary world.

---

[43] Cp. Rappaport, 1999: 390: "It may be suggested [...] that ritual recaptures a state having its ontogenetic origin in the relationship of pre-verbal infants to their mothers. If this is the case the ground of the numinous precedes the development of any awareness of the sacred or the sanctified for, being discursive, that awareness can come only with language."

[44] Cp. Deacon, 1997: 257: "In general terms, human information processing should be biased by an excessive reliance on and guidance by the kinds of manipulation that prefrontal circuits impose upon the information they process. We humans should therefore exhibit a 'cognitive style' that sets us apart from other species — a pattern of organizing perceptions, actions, and learning that is peculiarly 'front-heavy', so to speak."

Does this mean that ritual activities are carried out, and ritual formulas uttered, with the intention of reaching mystical states? Scholars have pointed out that altered states of consciousness do often accompany ritual.[45] It is also known that ritual formulas are used in a number of traditions to evoke altered states of consciousness: the use of mantras in Indian yoga and the so-called *dhikr* in Islam come to mind. Nor is it surprising that these activities or recitations might bring about such results. We have seen that mental absorption can be a means to reach such states, perhaps the only one. Ritual activities and utterances may be conducive to mental absorption. The fact that the difference between ordinary and mystical experience is not abrupt, so that people can have "weak" or "partial" mystical states, supports the claim that altered states of consciousness may accompany many if not all rites.

In spite of this, I hesitate to look upon the search for altered states of consciousness as the only explanation for ritual in all of its manifestations. I rather assume that most if not all human beings, including those who are unfamiliar with altered states of consciousness, are *implicitly aware* of the fact that the world created by symbolic representation is not the only world there is. This assumption gains in credibility if we recall that even "ordinary", i.e. symbolic, experience is not always to the same extent accompanied by associative mental connections: concentration and absorption reduce them, if ever so little. Even the person least susceptible to mystical experience is likely to undergo the resulting fluctuations in the thickness of the web woven by symbolic reference.

---

[45] Cf. Rappaport, 1999: 227: "ritually altered consciousness is widespread if not, indeed, culturally universal." Staal, 1990: 139: "mysticism [...] points to a pre-linguistic state which can be induced by ritual [...]" (cited above). According to Michaels (2006: 261), rituals "often create an auratic sphere or arena of timelessness and immortality". See further Goodman, 1988: 34 f.

§3 Ritual

In a way we are obliged to make this assumption of an implicit awareness. The use of holistic utterances and holistic activities in ritual in widely separate cultures indicates that there must be such an awareness of the process that leads to ordinary, symbolic cognition, viz., through the division of an originally undivided cognition. *Without* the assumption of implicit awareness we might have to postulate that ritual utterances and ritual activities have been discovered by chance, presumably because these utterances and these activities gave rise to altered states of consciousness. This postulate does not, it seems to me, deserve serious consideration. We therefore hold on to the view that implicit awareness of the two levels of cognition common to all normal human beings is behind ritual in its various manifestations.

Why should anyone wish to act—as indeed almost everyone does—in or on the reality thought to be hidden below the surface of our ordinary experience? One reason is no doubt that virtually everyone, not only mystics, is convinced that such a different reality exists and that it is more real than ordinary reality. We have already seen that this conviction is almost correct. All humans are in the possession of an alternative level of cognition giving them more direct access to reality than symbolic representation. All of them "know", in some way, that their ordinary experience of the world is incomplete. There is another, "higher", reality, which has to be manipulated to secure one's well-being. It cannot be manipulated with the help of symbolic reference. As a result, the manipulative tools provided by tradition — rituals and ritual formulas — are and have to be free from symbolic reference: they are, and have to be, holistic.

However, the implicit knowledge that people appear to possess about the nature of ordinary experience and its relation to a "different", "higher", reality goes further than this. Symbolic representation is grounded in non-symbolic experience. Symbolic representation allows for deception and dishonesty, because it can create and communicate imaginary worlds and situations. Escape from symbolic representation through ritual is, in a number of cases, an attempt to re-establish reference by grounding it in the real world. Deacon (1997: 403 f.) gives in this context the example of the Yanomamö Indians from Venezuela, notorious for their almost constant warfare among themselves. Occasionally peace is assured by means of an elaborate ritual known as a "Feast". Deacon describes it as follows (p. 404):[46]

> First, the hosts who wish to make peace prepare a meal. When their guests are due to arrive, dressed as for war and carrying their weapons, the hosts put their weapons away and the men recline on their hammocks waiting for the guests to enter their village. The guests enter, dancing and chanting, and circle around the camp stopping in front of each host. There they ritually threaten them, raising an axe or drawing a bow and arrow. The hosts must remain unmoved, trying to show no fear and no offense at provocative remarks. After this has been repeated for a while (and latent hostilities have not erupted in violence), the roles are reversed. The guests recline in hammocks, their weapons hidden away, while the hosts circle around the camp dancing and ritually threatening their guests. Finally, when it is clear that nothing untoward is likely to happen, they break off and the guests are offered food. Later they may chant together, barter and exchange goods, or even arrange a marriage.

---

[46] Cp. Chagnon, 1968: 97 ff. For a brief presentation and discussion of the recent allegation of mistreatment of the Yanomamö by this anthropologist, see Benson & Stangroom, 2006: 154 ff.

It is ritual which protects hosts and guests from the surprise attacks that are otherwise common among this tribe.

Grounding in the real world and the accompanying escape from symbolic representation with its possibilities of lies and deceit[47] may explain the use of ritual at other occasions, too. A wedding ritual goes beyond the promises that are exchanged. These promises are, by means of ritual, grounded in a reality in which no deception is possible.[48] Similar considerations may be applicable to other rituals, but this topic cannot be further explored here.

§4 Mythology and Religion

Many of the points discussed above are relevant to the realm commonly thought of as religion. Symbolic reference accounts for more than just language. It also creates a barrier separating human beings from a more immediate experience of reality. What is more, human beings are in some way aware of this fact. Some succeed in breaking through this barrier and attain a more direct experience of the world; we have called them mystics. Others search by various means for the hidden reality which they believe must exist. We have considered ritual, but there are no doubt others, among them philosophico-religious speculation. The implicit awareness of a more direct access to

---

[47] This theme is taken very seriously by Rappaport in his study of ritual; see Rappaport, 1999: 11 f. and *passim*.

[48] This observation is at variance with Deacon's view according to which marriage is essentially a symbolic relationship the need for which explains the acquisition of language by early humans: "Symbolic culture was a response to a reproductive problem that only symbols could solve: the imperative of representing a social contract." (1997: 401). Bickerton (2009) provides an interesting alternative proposal as to the initial circumstances that may have set off language in early humans.

the world in which we live often takes the form of a deep conviction that there is a higher reality, different from the ordinary world. What is more, there appears to be an implicit awareness that the world of our ordinary experience has emerged from that higher reality. This notion may find expression in "creation myths", stories that speak of the transition from an initial undivided whole subsequently divided. A primordial formless substance takes form, often under the influence of the spoken word. Rappaport (1999: 162 ff.) gives a number of examples from a variety of cultures. The idea that the highest reality is also an encompassing whole is known to religious thought. The present study will not enter into an analysis of these beliefs. It can, however, be suggested that they contain an element of *truth*. Our world has indeed arisen out of an earlier one that was not yet divided. And this undivided whole is really still there and underlies all our cognition. But the transition from an undivided to a multiple world did not happen at the beginning of cosmic time. It took place in our childhood when we, each of us individually, crossed the symbolic threshold.

The preceding reflections, if correct, show that symbolic reference, and symbolic representation which results from it, have a profound effect on the way we experience the world. Symbolic representation is, in an important sense, that which makes us human, that which distinguishes us even from our nearest cousins in the animal realm. It does not just allow us to learn and use language but instills in us the implicit or explicit conviction that there is a "deeper" or "higher" reality behind the "ordinary" reality experienced in our everyday lives. This in its turn impels us to carry out certain forms of activity ("rituals") and induces us to think certain kinds of thoughts. In view of all this, it is hard to overestimate the importance of symbolic reference. This in its turn raises the question whether symbolic reference makes itself also felt in other domains of human activity. The next section will argue that it does, and that culture may be one such domain.

§5 Culture

We have so far considered symbolic representation in connection with language and, in particular, with vocal utterances. But there is no reason to believe that the faculty that allows us to create symbolic representation is only active in the presence of vocal utterances. This same faculty allows the deaf to use sign language which uses gestures rather than vocal utterances. Sign language has syntax like ordinary language and shares many features with it. It is indeed possible that gestures preceded vocal signs in the historical development of language.[49] However, we may go one step further and consider that the faculty which makes symbolic representation possible is not confined to language in *any* of its forms, whether vocal, gestural, or other (including lexigrams).

As pointed out above, the crucial faculty that enables the human infant to learn language is the capacity to pay attention not just to the objects in its environment but also to features — whether vocal, gestural, or other — that it interprets as signs of those objects. This capacity allows, even obliges, the child to pay attention to further signs that are somehow related to these initial signs, and to the relationships between them. We have seen that the child uses this capacity when learning the language of its caretakers. However, this capacity is not confined to the signs that make up this language. It also covers everything else that the infant associates, for whatever reason, with the objects of its experience and which it therefore in-

---

[49] See Rowan Hooper in *New Scientist* of 5 May 2007, p. 6 f.

terprets as signs.⁵⁰ The very capacity that allows the child to learn its language will also make it pay attention to other, non-linguistic, "signs" and look for the ways in which these signs are interrelated. In the case of language, the ultimately adopted system of relationships between linguistic signs is the structure that governs the language of the child's caretakers. In the case of other, non-linguistic "signs", too, the child is likely to adopt the system of relationships that its caretakers adhere to.

These somewhat abstract reflections suggest that the child, at the appropriate age, is not only busy acquiring its language. Alongside language, it explores the relationships that may exist between other potential signs. As in the case of language, it will in the end settle on the web of relationships accepted by those in its surroundings, or one close to it. It follows that the faculty underlying symbolic representation weaves not just one, but two webs that separate us from the outside world. One is the web woven by language that was discussed at some length. The other is the web woven by the non-linguistic signs that have come to be recognized as such in the culture of the individual concerned.

This web of non-linguistic signs can vary from culture to culture. Examples will therefore be culture-specific. As a widely understood yet simple (and no doubt simplifying) example from the western world, we may consider the Christmas tree.⁵¹

---

[50] Cp. Deacon, 1997: 264: "The contributions of prefrontal areas to learning all involve, in one way or another, the analysis of higher-order associative relationships. More specifically, [...] they are necessary for learning associative relationships where one associative learning process must be subordinated to another."

[51] The first four notes of Beethoven's Fifth Symphony constitute another example. Marvin Minsky said the following about them: "no one could remember Beethoven's Fifth Symphony entire, from a single hearing. But neither could one ever hear again those first four notes as just four notes! Once but a tiny scrap of sound, it is now a Known Thing —

§5 *Culture*

The Christmas tree is not just a sign that designates something (Christmas, the birth of Christ, or something else again). It is also, perhaps even primarily, an element in a wide web of associations, at least for those who have grown up in cultures where Christmas was celebrated. Though people grown up in other cultures may learn what the Christmas tree stands for, they will not yet share this wide associative web. A Christmas tree may not "mean" anything to them. In the case of those for whom it "means" something, we may assume that the Christmas tree is treated in a way not dissimilar to the way in which symbols (i.e., Peircean symbols, primarily the words of language) are treated. Like words, the Christmas tree is used to construct a system, a web of associations. (Unlike words, it may here be added, the Christmas tree and other cultural "symbols" are not likely to give rise to the precise representations that the use of words obliges their users to create.)

It may be justified to say that this web, or rather the accumulation of webs of which the Christmas-tree-web may be one, *is* the culture into which the child grows up.[52] As in the case of language, the web of culture may affect cognition. Interestingly, there is some evidence to suggest that cultures do indeed affect cognition differentially, that is to say, members of different cultures cognize the world differently.[53]

---

a locus in the web of all the other things we know, whose meanings and significances depend on each other." (cited in Sacks, 2007: 211)

[52] For a recent discussion of culture, see Plotkin, 2007a.

[53] See Plotkin, 2007: 236 ff., with references to various publications (Lillard, 1998; Nisbett et al., 2001; 2003; 2005; Siok et al., 2004; Atran, 1998; Medin & Atran, 2004; Greenfield et al., 2003; Cole, 2006; for a review of some recent research critical of this conclusion, see "East meets West" by Ed Yong in *New Scientist* of 7 March 2009, pp. 32-35); further Lloyd, 2007. This suggestion is parallel to the hypothesis according to which individual languages are responsible for the way their users understand the world and act in it, the so-called Sapir-Whorf

The web of culture, like the web of language, can be torn, presumably by the same method, viz., when the person concerned enters into a state of absorption. This suggests that the world experienced by so-called mystics is not only free from all that language had superimposed on it, but also from numerous other superimpositions that may be globally referred to as cultural superimpositions.

It follows from what precedes that the very capacity enabling us to learn and use language and underlying certain behaviors and experiences commonly referred to as religious, may also be responsible for human culture.[54] This capacity identifies certain objects and sensory inputs as signs of others and looks for the system of their mutual relationships. A subset of these signs along with their mutual relationships constitute language. Others constitute networks of connections, systematized and rationalized in ways that may differ from one culture to the next (just as languages vary). These networks of connections may incorporate background assumptions about the nature of the world around us. They may also, as in the case of the Christmas tree, have a primarily emotional character and give "meaning" to our world. As in the case of language, these networks of associative connections are likely to be deeply an-

---

hypothesis; see, e.g., Gleitman & Papafragou, 2005; further Boroditsky, 2001; Deutscher, 2010; Everett, 2012: 255 ff. Indeed, some maintain that the two theories cannot be separated: "a language is shaped by its culture, and a culture is given expression in its language, to such an extent that it is impossible to say where one ends and the other begins, i.e. what belongs to language and what to culture" (Grace, 1987: 10).

[54] It goes without saying that the term "religion" as commonly used also covers certain behaviors and experiences that are "cultural" in the sense here employed. In terms of the theory here presented, what is ordinarily understood as religion combines elements that require different explanations: some are "cultural" features, others fall in the category of "attempts to step back out of the realm of symbolic representation".

chored in each person. And, as in the case of a first language, considerable effort may be required for alternative networks to find a place beside the original ones.

Appendix 1: Semantic Etymologies[55]

Symbolic reference is essential for language learning. It allows us to "extract" words from larger utterances, just as Sherman and Austin had "extracted" GIVE from GIVE + BANANA. However, there is no obvious reason why this analytical process should stop at words. We might expect that human beings are inclined to push the analysis further, so that symbolic reference then goes beyond the level at which it is useful in daily life, and "overshoots the mark". This is what happens in the phenomenon to be considered in this Appendix.

Recall that human beings, more than chimpanzees, have the capacity to analyze acoustic and other inputs so as to discover symbols that may be hidden in them. Sherman and Austin had a hard time segmenting the unit GIVE out of the combinations GIVE + BANANA and GIVE + ORANGE. Human children segment countless words out of a linguistic input that contains no clear indications as to where one word ends and the next one begins, even less where one morpheme ends and the next one begins. Yet these same children succeed in attributing meanings to the results of their segmentations. The question is: do children, and adult speakers for that matter, stop at the commonly recognized words of language or do they advance beyond words, perhaps even beyond the morphemes that make up words?

This question is of some importance. If one thinks that words correspond to pre-existing representations, language users will then divide the linguistic input they receive into words that fit those pre-existing representations and no further, because there are no representations further down the line.[56] In

---

[55] Many of the examples given in this Appendix have been taken from Bronkhorst, 2001.
[56] See Pinker, 2007: 89 f. for a discussion of different points of view

Appendix 1: Semantic Etymologies

this book we take a different position: many representations are created, often (but not always) on the basis of the words of language. This position leads to the reasonable expectation that the segmentation that humans apply to their linguistic input is not halted once they arrive at some purportedly natural representations. Rather, we would expect that human segmenting extends also beyond the words of language into the realm of parts of words and perhaps even individual sounds.[57] This is indeed what we find. Human segmenting of this kind finds expression in the phenomenon that I will call semantic etymologizing. This phenomenon is wide-spread.

A *semantic etymology* is to be distinguished from a *historical etymology*. A historical etymology presents the origin or early history of a word; it tells us, for example, that a word in a modern language is derived from another word belonging to an earlier language, or to an earlier stage of the same language. The English word *militant*, for example, is derived from Latin *militans* through the intermediary of French *militant*. And the Hindi pronoun *maim* ('I') is derived from Sanskrit *mayā* ('by me') through Prakrit *mae* (Oberlies, 1998: 17). Semantic etymologies do something different. They connect one word with one or more others that are believed to elucidate its meaning. According to the Vedic *Satapatha Brāhmana* (6.1.3.10) the god

---

regarding representations (there called "concepts") in language and thought. Note further that also Bickerton (2009) takes the position that representations (which he, too, calls "concepts") result from language, rather than vice-versa. He also records a change of mind (p. 226): "I eventually came to agree with Terrence Deacon that it was symbolism rather than syntax that marked the boundary between humans and nonhumans."

[57] The question of individual speech sounds is tricky, for the notion that speech can be analyzed into a sequence of phonemes, and their perception, has been argued to be inseparable from alphabetical writing; Warren, 1999: 169 f.

Rudra, for example, has that name because he cried (*rud-*) in a story about him. Semantic etymologies tell us nothing about the history of a word, but something about its meaning.

Semantic etymologies have largely gone out of fashion these days. Most sensible people have serious doubts about the possibility of finding the meaning of one word by comparing it with other, more or less similar words. We tolerate such semantic etymologizing from children who indulge in it quite freely, as Jean Piaget (1925) and others after him have shown. We are less tolerant with respect to adults who do so; the person who interprets the word *contentment* as "being content with men" or with *tea* (*content-men-t*), is perhaps rightly diagnosed as schizophrenic by modern investigators.[58]

And yet semantic etymologies are wide-spread in all pre-modern cultures. Here are some examples:

In the Sumerian myth of Enki and Ninhursag the former is cured when Ninhursag causes deities to be born corresponding to Enki's sick members: "The correspondence between the sick member and the healing deity rests on the [...] etymologizing of the ancient scribes; the Sumerian word for the sick organ contains at least one syllable in common with the name of the deity. Thus e.g. one of the organs that pained Enki was the 'mouth', the Sumerian word for which is *ka*, and the deity created to alleviate this pain is called Nin*ka*si; similarly, the goddess born to alleviate the pain of the rib, the Sumerian word for which *ti*, is named Nin*ti*, etc." (Kramer, 1969: 37 n. 13).

An ancient Egyptian text carved inside two pyramids dating from the 24th century BCE "is full of plays on words" such as: "O Atum-Khepret, [...] thou didst arise (*weben*) as the *ben*-bird of the *ben*-stone in the *Ben*-House in Heliopolis." (Wilson, 1969: 3). Sauneron (1957: 123 f.) adds further ex-

---

[58] So Werner & Kaplan (1963: 259), citing a patient of Maria Lorenz (1961: 604).

Appendix 1: Semantic Etymologies

amples and points out that 'plays on words' were considered to give an 'explanation' of the world.[59]

In the Hebrew Bible etymologies are common, especially in connection with names: Adam is linked with *adama* 'earth' (Gen. 2.7); woman, *isha*, is derived from man, *ish* (Gen. 2.23); Cain from *qaniti* 'I have gotten' (Gen. 4.1); etc. (Böhl, 1991: 163 f.).

Kirk (1974: 57 f.) emphasizes the use of etymologies in Greek myths and states (p. 58): "The poets of the Homeric tradition were already intrigued by the resemblance of the name 'Odysseus' to the verb *odussomai* 'I am angry'. [...] Pytho, the old name for Delphi, is derived [in the *Hymn to Apollo*, probably late seventh century BCE] from the serpent destroyed there by Apollo and allowed to rot, *puthein*. [...] Heraclitus the Presocratic philosopher found it significant that one word for a bow resembled the word for 'life' (*biós* and *bíos*), and Aeschylus related the name of Helen to the idea that she 'took the ships' (*hele-naus*), that of Apollo to *apollunai*, 'destroy', and that of Zeus to *zên*, 'live'." Similar efforts at etymologizing characterize later Greek antiquity.[60]

An example from medieval Europe is provided by the secret spiritual organization of the Fedeli d'Amore, whose representatives were active in France, Italy, and Belgium from the 12th century onward. They used a hidden language in order to keep their mystery of love secret. Love for them is a soteriological means, and accordingly the word *amor* 'love' is interpreted as *a-mor* 'without death':

---

[59] See further Morenz, 1957; Sander-Hansen, 1946, esp. p. 19f.

[60] For a study of the etymologies in Homer, see Rank, 1951; also Kraus, 1987: 31 f. For an (incomplete) list of etymologies in Plutarch, see Strobach, 1997: 186 f.

A senefie en sa partie
Sans, et *mor* senefie *mort*;
Or l'assemblons, s'aurons *sans mort*.[61]

Caesarius of Heisterbach (ca. 1170–ca. 1240) gives an explanation of the word *mors* 'death' in his *Dialogue on Miracles*:[62]

> Though the transgression of the first created, death entered into the world. Hence death (*mors*) received its name from 'biting' (*morsus*). As soon as man bit (*momordit*) the apple of the forbidden tree, he incurred death and subjected himself as well as his whole posterity to its necessity. Death is also said to have come from 'bitterness' (*amaritudine*), because, as it is said, no pain in this life is more bitter than the separation of body and soul.

Elsewhere he explains the word *puer* 'boy': "*Puer* ('boy') signifies *purus* ('pure')".[63]

An example from ethnographic records is the following: Among the inhabitants of the Trobriand islands the word *vatuvi* occurs in a magical formula.[64] This word has no grammatical form; it is neither noun nor verb. Malinowski (1935: II: 249, cf. p. 260-61) observed: "the real etymological identity of this word will define it as connected with *vitawo*, or the prefix *vitu-*, and the word *vituvatu*, 'to institute', 'to set up', 'to direct', 'to show'. [It has] also [...] fortuitous, but magically significant associations with *vatu*, 'coral boulder', 'coral reef', and the more or less real word *va-tuvi*, 'to foment', 'to make heal.'"[65]

---

[61] See Eliade, 1986: 112. (*A* signifies, for its part, without, and *mor* signifies death; combining them we have *without death*).

[62] Cited in Zaleski, 1988: 50.

[63] Cited in Zaleski, 1988: 52.

[64] Malinowski (1935: I: 96, II: 257) describes it as the most important formula in all Omarakana garden magic.

[65] Regarding the last association, *va-tuvi*, Malinowski observes (p. 260-

Appendix 1: Semantic Etymologies

All these semantic etymologies illustrate one and the same phenomenon: the search for expressive units beyond the level recognized in the speech community concerned. They remind us that the capacity for symbolic reference was not created *for* language learning (even though its usefulness in language learning no doubt explains the selective advantage it offered).

The Chinese language, with its monosyllabic words, lends itself less easily to an analysis beyond the level recognized in the speech community. However, its many homonyms invite its users to connect unrelated things that have the same name. Indeed, "Han commentators applied a form of correlative thought in their philological studies, frequently explaining the meaning of obscure characters by sound analogy on the assumption that a phonetic correspondence indicated a semantic relation".[66] "Sometimes highly complex circular *shou* emblems [symbols of long life or immortality] had incorporated into their design a swastika (pronounced *wan*), to express by a pun the concept of *wan shou*, meaning 'ten thousand years of long life'." Similarly: "The endless knot [was] interpreted [...] as symbolizing Buddha's intestines (*ch'ang*). [...] [S]ince its name, *ch'ang*, made a pun on the word for long, the whole figure [...] symbolized [to the later Chinese] a long life [...],"[67] etc. An example closer to our time is found in the weekly journal *Newsweek* of July 6, 1987, p. 18: "Hong Kong's new British governor, Sir David Wilson, bowed to local tradition by changing his Cantonese name, Ngai Tak-ngai, shortly before assuming office last April. Its characters were homophones for the phrase 'so hypocritical it's dangerous'; his new moni-

---

61): "As a matter of fact, one or two natives [...] gave me this explanation of the word when commenting upon the spell." It is not clear whether any native made the association with *vatu* explicit.

[66] Henderson, 1984: 19-20.
[67] Cammann, 1962: 98, 99-100.

ker, Wai Yik-shun, means 'guardianship' and 'trust', conjuring up more soothing images to colony residents [...]". These examples do not illustrate the search for expressive units beyond the level commonly recognized, but something different. They illustrate the search for a shared semantic interpretation of minimal units, even where the speech community assigns different interpretations to them. This search is, of course, similar to the search that allowed Sherman and Austin to arrive at one representation for GIVE, starting from GIVE + BANANA and GIVE + ORANGE.

Appendix 2: Symbolic Reference and the Origin of Language

The origin of language is increasingly debated. To get an impression of some current opinions, we turn to a recent issue of the journal *Lingua* (vol. 117 no. 3, 2007, pp. 503-604) dedicated to language evolution. One of the contributors, Derek Bickerton, points out that this is "an interdisciplinary game, played by biologists, neurologists, anthropologists, archaeologists, computer scientists, philosophers, and more — as well as [...] by linguists" (2007: 510). On the following page he emphasizes the distinction between *language* evolution and changes in *languages*. Whereas the former is part of the biological evolution of humans, the latter belongs to the realm of cultural change.

An essential concept in the study of language evolution is *protolanguage*. Says Bickerton (2007: 515): "The notion that the earliest stages of language evolution involved a largely if not entirely structureless protolanguage [...] is now so widely accepted that the term seems to have passed into the general vocabulary of language evolutionists." This protolanguage is, as indicated, largely if not entirely structureless. What were its constituents? According to Bickerton "there does not, as yet, exist any compelling reason for rejecting the original concept of a protolanguage as containing a categorially complete, if severely limited vocabulary of items roughly equivalent to modern words, but lacking a sophisticated phonology and any consistent structure" (2007: 517).

Not everyone accepts this position. A competitor is the theory according to which protolanguage was holophrastic. Bickerton describes it as follows (2007: 516-517):

[T]he most radical proposal with regard to the constituents of protolanguage is that these were holophrastic rather than synthetic. This proposal has been most thoroughly developed by [Alison] Wray [...]. Wray's proposals support genre continuism, since [...] animal calls are roughly equivalent to holophrases, rather than words. Wray claims that protolanguage simply increased the number of such units to a point where they began to impose an excessive memory load, at which point the holophrases were decomposed on the basis of phonetic similarities. Here we can do no better than quote Wray's own example: "So if, besides *tebima* meaning *give that to her*, *kumapi* meant *share this with her*, then it might be concluded that *ma* had the meaning *female person + beneficiary*." ([Wray,] 2000: 297)

Bickerton does not agree with this proposal, as is clear from his comments (2007: 517):[68]

---

[68] In a more recent publication (2009), Bickerton still rejects the notion of a holistic protolanguage (pp. 65 f.) but presents a picture of the simultaneous appearance of words and representations that is not all that different; see e.g. p. 219: "Gradually the sound is getting divorced from the situation that gave rise to it. Put something into enough different contexts and its particular details become blurred; it gets closer to becoming an arbitrary symbol. At the same time, a representation is formed in the brain ..." Even more recently (2010) his change of mind seems to be complete: "Initial displacement signals might well have been holistic; a signal, rather than meaning simply 'elephant' like a modern word, might have been interpreted as something equivalent to 'There's dead elephant out there and we can eat it if we all move quickly' (there is no need to suppose that the underlying semantics of such a modern-language message would have been represented — a mental picture of a dead elephant plus the thought of all that meat would have been enough). While such a usage of 'elephant' might qualify technically as displacement (insofar as it conveyed information that might be already several hours old about a sight perhaps several miles distant), its meaning, unlike that of words, would be tied to one kind of situ-

Appendix 2: Symbolic Reference and the Origin of Language

This leaves out of account the possibility that, although the syllable *ma* might occur as Wray suggests, it would also occur in a number of holophrases lacking any references to either females or beneficiaries. Not only is this extremely likely, but the only possible alternative is, if anything, even more damaging to Wray's case. For if *ma* occurred always and only where female beneficiaries were involved, the holophrastic protolanguage would be a hollow charade, a mere disguise for a medium already fully synthetic. But if *ma* also occurred where a female + beneficiary was impossible — contexts perhaps as numerous as, or more numerous than, those that can bear such a reading — why would the hearer assume that it referred to a female beneficiary in just those cases where such a reading was possible, and how would that hearer account for the other cases?

For further arguments against the holophrastic model, Bickerton refers to one of his own earlier publications (Bickerton, 2003) and to the contribution of Maggie Tallerman in the same issue of *Lingua* (Tallerman, 2007).

Alison Wray, the main target of Bickerton's criticism, also contributed an article co-signed by George W. Grace to this issue of *Lingua*. These two authors describe their understand-

---

ation involving elephants. However, once this degree of displacement was available (that is, once the 'elephant' signal was freed from its dependence on a physically-present, sensorily-accessible elephant), the road was opened to further developments: use of the same signal on seeing elephant footprints or dung, or imitations of elephants in children's play, for example. Use of a constantly widening range of contexts would move the signal closer to becoming a true symbol — closer to the kind of meaning exemplified by the modern word 'elephant.'" (p. 171) See further note 56, above.

ing of the first language users in the following words (Wray & Grace, 2007: 570-571):[69]

> [W]e must understand that what made the very first language users different from their parents was that they possessed the capacity to identify patterns inside their existing message units and extract (apparently) recurrent material for recombination. [...] The first 'segmenters' need not have stood out all that much from those around them, for theirs would have been a marginal activity relative to the general use of holistic forms with agreed functions. Those who *could* segment out sections from holistic utterances for recombination could do so [...], while the others carried on using what they already knew. The analysis, operating in direct response to interactional need, could thus be naturally very slow, and indeed would need to be, both because the analyticity of the modern speaker would be little challenged by the holistic usages of his pre-modern companions, and because, in the short term, his novel expressions, while meaningful to him, would be impenetrable to the rest, unless they learned them whole. But little by little, under the influence of even one analytic operator and his/her descendants over a number of generations, an initially immutable protolanguage could progressively transform into something more flexible, until a command of the flexibility became advantageous to survival and/or reproduction.

This passage is slightly puzzling in that it calls those with the capacity to segment existing units "the first language users".

---

[69] The idea of a holistic protolanguage is not new. As Van Driem (2004) points out, Hugo Schuchardt argued already in 1919 that the first utterance arose from the splitting of a holistic primeval utterance ("Sprachursprung" I & II, *Sitzungsberichte der Preussischen Akademie der Wissenschaften* 52, 716-720 & 863-869).

Appendix 2: Symbolic Reference and the Origin of Language

One would rather have expected that these segmenters be called "the first word users": through their segmenting they would have arrived where Bickerton's protolanguage users were all along, viz., in the possession of "a categorially complete, if severely limited vocabulary of items roughly equivalent to modern words, but lacking [...] any consistent structure" (see above). This is no doubt what Bickerton had in mind when he wrote (2003: 87): "All the substantive problems in language evolution — how symbolism got started and fixed, how, when, and why structure emerged, where and to what extent any of this got instantiated in neural tissue — remain to be solved, *whether one accepts a holistic account or* not" (my emphasis). Bickerton concludes from this that "it is more parsimonious to assume that language began as it was to go on — that discrete symbols, whether oral or manual, were there from the beginning" (ibid.).[70] I am not sure whether parsimony settles this issue, even if we were to follow Bickerton in other respects. It is at least conceivable that language evolution passed through various phases, starting from a holophrastic phase, which was then (partly) succeeded by a synthetic phase.[71] Alternatively,

---

[70] Interestingly, Wray (2000: 287) invokes Occam's razor to argue for the continuity between the holistic communication used by primates and the holistic language we use today.

[71] This is Mithen's position (2005: 260): "This 'words before grammar' is the type of language evolution that Bickerton proposed — so we can see that his views are not necessarily wrong, but are simply chronologically misplaced and require a pre-existing history of holistic proto-language to be feasible." Wray (2002a) speaks of "the holistic system that I propose pre-existed and provided the context for the emergence of the analytic system" (p. 116) and of "the holistic protolanguage that I propose coexisted with — and preceded — the simple analytic system from which our modern grammatical capability developed" (p. 118); see also the following: "there is a place for a simple analytic protolanguage of the kind that Bickerton proposes, but not as the sole medium of communication" (p. 118). Arbib (2003: 183; cp. 2005: 108, 118 f.) intro-

one might think that the very process whereby segmenting became possible was also responsible for at least some structure. We will return to this issue below.

Let us assume, for argument's sake, that there was once an exclusively holophrastic protolanguage. The first segmenters differed from their parents on account of a new capacity, the capacity to segment holophrastic phrases. This new capacity may have had a biological basis. This, at any rate, is what Wray and Grace assume. Only in this way "even one analytic operator and his/her descendants over a number of generations" can exert the influence referred to in the above passage: if this capacity were cultural, there would be no need to wait a number of generations, and the novel expressions of the first language users would not necessarily be "impenetrable to the rest". We will see below that this is not the only possible point of view.[72] For the time being we will, however, follow Wray and Grace in assuming that the new capacity must be thought of as based on a genetic mutation, and therefore as part of biological evolution.

---

duces the notion of a *prelanguage* which, he suggests, was composed of 'unitary utterances' and which preceded the discovery of *words*: "On this view, words in the modern sense co-evolved with syntax through *fractionation*, a process of discovery and diffusion quite distinct from the formation of a genetic module for grammar." Consider, finally, Searle, 2010: 77: "We are not assuming that reference and predication, the speech acts corresponding to noun phrases and verb phrases, are in any way simple independent elements, but rather that once we have the total speech act we can abstract these as component elements. Following Frege, we think of the noun phrases and verb phrases as derived from the total sentence and not of the total sentence as arrived at by combining noun phrases and verb phrases."

[72] Citing Dennett (2003: 184-85), but replacing *religion* by *language* one might say: "If there are any genes for [language], this is, in fact, one of the least interesting and least informative of the Darwinian possibilities."

Appendix 2: Symbolic Reference and the Origin of Language

The above passage from Wray and Grace's article also presupposes that all members of the group, including those who do not yet possess the capacity to identify segments, are capable of learning new utterances. Only in this way can they "learn whole" expressions that are impenetrable to them. These expressions are not therefore genetically transmitted. This presupposition is not spelled out in Wray and Grace's article, but seems to be important in view of the fact that it takes for granted an important difference between human protolanguage and primate calls, which *are* genetically transmitted.

The specification that the protolanguage out of which modern language eventually arose was different from primate calls, and that it consisted of learned utterances that could be distinguished from each other, answers a number of the objections voiced by Tallerman in her contribution to the *Lingua* issue, notably those that deal with the presumed proximity of the protolanguage to animal calls[73] and with its presumed phonological insufficiency.[74] We cannot deal with them in detail. Some of her other criticisms are summed up and responded to by Mithen (2005: 254) in the following terms:

---

[73] Elsewhere in her article Tallerman accepts that "protolanguages (like languages) are culturally transmitted" (2007: 599).

[74] See in this connection Wray, 2002a: 115: "I have suggested that the holistic cries and gestures of our pre-human ancestors were transformed, *over a long period of time*, into a *phonetically expressed* set of holistic message strings [...]" (emphasis mine, JB). Also Arbib, 2003: 196: "[T]he lowering of the larynx in humans or pre-human hominids might have served a similar purpose (as in the red deer, viz., deepening the animal's roar, JB) — without denying that further selection could have exploited the resultant increase in degrees of freedom to increase the flexibility of speech production. [...] [T]*his selective advantage would hold even for a species that employed holophrastic utterances devoid of syntax.*" (emphasis mine, JB)

Although linguists unsympathetic to Wray's approach, such as Derek Bickerton and Maggie Tallerman, have questioned the feasibility of segmentation, their criticisms have been unsubstantial. Tallerman claims, for instance, that the likelihood of any chance associations arising is remote, but computer simulations have shown that they could easily have happened [...] while Wray herself has explained how the process of segmentation may have been supported by 'near matches'. Tallerman also claims that holistic utterances are unlikely to have contained multiple phonetic strings with the potential for segmentation because they would have been too short. But one need do no more than consider the lengthy holistic phrases of monkeys, apes, birds, and so forth, to appreciate that those of our human ancestors may have been of considerable length,[75] having evolved over millennia and proliferated in number to provide ever greater semantic specificity. Similarly, an argument that Wray's theory of segmentation has to assume the prior existence of discrete segments, which then invalidates her conception of holistic utterances, also has no foundation. Holistic utterances may have been multi-syllabic but they were — by definition — holistic, with none of the individual or

---

[75] Consider in this connection the following: "In a paper with Nobuyuki Kawai, [Tetsuro] Matsuzawa showed that Ai, a young chimpanzee, could remember a sequence of at least five numbers, more than a preschool child; and at a recent symposium in Chicago on 'The Mind of the Chimpanzee', he showed how Ai, with further training, had developed powers of working memory beyond that of most human adults. He suggested that 'our common ancestors might have had immediate memory, but in the course of evolution, they lost this and acquired languagelike skills.'" (Sacks, 2007: 159 n. 8; see further Kawai & Matsuzawa, 2000, and Cohen, 2007)

Appendix 2: Symbolic Reference and the Origin of Language

groups of syllables mapping onto a discrete aspect of the utterance's complex meaning.

It is not the aim of this Appendix to enter into an exhaustive discussion of all the arguments for and against the holophrastic model (whether in the form of the assumption that all human protolanguage was holophrastic, or rather that a holophrastic protolanguage gave rise to an analytic protolanguage which in its turn gave rise to language). What counts at this point is that this model is not dead; far from it, it is alive and kicking. This allows us to consider some of its consequences. Wray and Grace observe (2007: 561): "For reasons that may be partly biological, the older the individual becomes, the more likely he or she is to dissect language more than is strictly necessary for effective general communication." Since the capacity of dissecting language does not respond to a specific need, the result may be surprising (Wray & Grace, 2007: 561-562):

> Any biological influences on the balance between formulaicity and compositionality may be limited to the peripheral capacity to open up a form *before* there is a specific need to do so, thus maintaining a creative edge to one's engagement with language. Since such a capacity would simply need to exist, rather than achieve any specific goal (such as a complete analysis of the language into atomic particles and rules), we might anticipate finding that its effects are haphazard and idiosyncratic — and indeed we do.
>
> One individual might suddenly wonder what it is that is 'done' in *how do you do?*, while another notices that *barking* seems to contain the morphemes *bar* and *king*. Such inappropriate analyses will capture attention whereas others, that turn out to be rational in terms of the shared perceptions of compositional structure in the language, are simply absorbed.

The "peripheral capacity" referred to in this passage is central to the holophrastic model (in either of its two forms). The model predicts this capacity, and would indeed be empty without it. The existence of this capacity in modern humans, on the other hand, does not suffice to prove the correctness of the holophrastic model. The fact that one sometimes wonders what is 'done' in *how do you do?* does not, by itself, prove that human language arose out of a protolanguage (or protoprotolanguage) which was holistic. However, if it could be demonstrated that the capacity to open up forms before there is a specific need to do so is more than a capacity—that it is a proclivity manifestimg itself in various ways across human cultures and stages of development—then this would constitute an argument in support of the holophrastic model. Such a proclivity would be harder to account for in the synthetic model, for here words are extracted to correspond to pre-existing concepts. The widely attested use of semantic etymologies (discussed in Appendix 1 of Part I, above) provides such a demonstration.

Let us, to begin with, restate some of the objections that have been voiced against the holophrastic model. Bickerton, in a passage already cited, found fault with Wray's hypothetical example in which, besides *tebima* meaning *give that to her*, *kumapi* meaning *share this with her*, early language users might conclude that *ma* had the meaning *female person + beneficiary*. Bickerton's criticism took the following form. He pointed out that the syllable *ma* might also occur in holophrases that lack references to either females or beneficiaries. Indeed, if *ma* only and exclusively occurred where female beneficiaries were involved, the holophrastic protolanguage would be a hollow charade, a mere disguise for a medium already synthetic. If, on the other hand, *ma* occurred both in contexts where reference

Appendix 2: Symbolic Reference and the Origin of Language

to a female beneficiary is impossible and in contexts where this is possible, how would the hearer know where and when it does indeed refer to a female beneficiary, and how would that hearer account for the other cases? Tallerman (2007: 597) discusses the same hypothetical example and comments:

> A major problem in this regard is that logically, similar substrings must often occur in two (or more) utterances which do *not* share any common elements of meaning at least as many times as they occur in two utterances which *do* share semantic elements. For instance, suppose that a string *mabali* also contains the *ma* sequence, but means 'put that rock down!'. What ensures that *ma* gets associated with 'her'?

Bickerton and Tallerman are probably not aware of the fact that reflections similar to theirs occur already in one of Plato's Dialogues, the *Cratylus*. This Dialogue presents Socrates in discussion with Cratylus, an etymologist. Socrates subjects the procedure of (semantic) etymologizing to a thorough analysis. This procedure is not dissimilar, in Socrates' analysis, to the extraction of *ma* in the above hypothetical examples. Socrates would call *ma* a "primary name"; he further maintains that primary names are by their very nature like the things they denote (p. 169). In the course of his analysis he comes to assign certain meanings to some letters of the Greek alphabet: the letter *rho* is expressive of speed, motion, and hardness; the letter *lambda* conveys smoothness, softness, and other qualities. However, this leads to difficulties in words like *sklêrótês* which, though containing the letter *lambda*, means "hardness" (p. 173). Like Bickerton and Tallerman, Socrates considers these difficulties insurmountable: "I myself prefer the theory that names are, so far as possible, like the things named; but really this attractive force of likeness is [...] a poor thing, and we are compelled to employ in addition this commonplace expedient, convention, to establish the correctness of names" (p. 175).

Socrates was not, of course, discussing the transition from protolanguage to language. He was concerned with semantic etymologies. Just as Bickerton and Tallerman try to undermine the hypothesis of a holistic protolanguage, Socrates' arguments should have discouraged semantic etymologizing. They did no such thing. Consider the reflections by Isidore of Seville, the sixth century author of a monumental work called, precisely, *Etymologies*. About etymologies he says, among other things:[76]

> Etymologies of words are furnished either from their rationale (*causa*), as 'kings' (*rex*, gen. *regis*) from [...] 'acting correctly' (*recte agendum*); or from their origin, as 'man' (*homo*) because he is from 'earth' (*humus*), or from the contrary, as 'mud' (*lutum*) from 'washing' (*lavare*, ppl. *lutus*), since mud is not clean, and 'grove' (*lucus*), because, darkened by its shade, it is scarcely 'lit' (*lucere*).

Isidore should perhaps have followed Socrates' example and pondered upon the question whether there is some meaning that can be ascribed to the sound sequence *hom/hum* and that recurs in all formations of which this sequence is part. He might have offered similar reflections with regard to *lu* and *luc*. He did not. Difficult cases and counterexamples clearly did not discourage him.

Examples of etymologies like these can be cited from widely different cultures and literatures; further examples are provided by children and psychiatric patients. This has been shown in Appendix 1 of Part I. Strictly speaking they do not extract meaningful segments, at least not explicitly. It is however clear that they are based on the similarity or identity of parts of the words compared. In many cases there is no linguistic justifica-

---

[76] Barney et al., 2006: 55 (*Etymologies* I.xxix).

Appendix 2: Symbolic Reference and the Origin of Language

tion whatsoever for these semantic etymologies. This is stated in so many words in a text from ancient India that deals with etymologizing, Yaska's *Nirukta*. Ancient India had also a sophisticated tradition of grammar, which obliged scholars to distinguish between the two activities. Yaska's position in this matter is clear: etymologizing is the complement of grammar, it treads where grammar cannot go.[77]

Consider now Sverker Johansson's (2005: 234) criticism of the idea of a holistic protolanguage:[78]

> It is not obvious to me [...] why the segmentation process envisaged by Wray [...] would be expected to work. A similar process is certainly present in modern-day language acquisition — children first acquire some stock phrases as unanalyzed wholes, and later figure out their internal structure — but that only works because these stock phrases *have* an internal structure, given by the grammar of the adults from whom the child acquires them.

Johansson assumes (as do Bickerton and Tallerman) that the segmentation process can only work where the material already contains, in a consistent and organized manner, the segments that are being extracted. Socrates would agree, for he refers repeatedly to the name-givers who gave names to things in a long distant past. But not all semantic etymologies are based on this belief. Most semantic etymologizing takes place quite independently of it. Semantic etymologizing "works", i.e. it is practiced, in spite of the fact the words and phrases they deal with do *not* have any relevant internal structure. We must conclude that there is a widely attested proclivity to extract segments and assign meanings to them even in cases where the material is inconsistent and resists such segmentation. This

---

[77] Bronkhorst, 1984.
[78] Cited by Tallerman (2007: 594).

proclivity coincides in all essentials with the capacity to segment postulated by the upholders of the theory of a holophrastic protolanguage. It is not limited to situations in which the prior existence of discrete segments has to be assumed. This, then, does away with some of the most serious criticism of the idea of a holophrastic protolanguage.

Having come this far, let us consider in some detail what the transition from holistic protolanguage users to segmenters implies. It has been suggested that a genetic mutation may be responsible, but this remains vague. Indeed, it amounts to little more than giving a name ("genetic mutation") to a process which one does not understand. And yet, the process concerned may not escape understanding, and what is more, it is open to question whether a genetic mutation has to be postulated to explain it.

The event which turns holophrasts into segmenters may be nothing else than crossing the symbolic threshold. Our hominid ancestors have crossed this threshold (phylogenetically) many thousands of years ago, and all human beings who learn to use language do the same (ontogenetically) during their early years.

Symbolic reference even seems able to explain at least some of the syntactic rules of language. Deacon (2003a: 90, with a reference to 1997) argues, to begin with, "that the structure of [Universal Grammar] would not yield to a biological evolutionary solution, nor would it have a neurological explanation".[79] According to him, many structural features of language may derive from semiotic constraints, inherent in the

---

[79] See also Van Driem, 2001: 66 ff. ("The splitting of the symbol and the birth of syntax"). Note that Deacon, in a more recent publication (2012: 69 ff.), argues that Universal Grammar must be considered a "homuncular theory".

Appendix 2: Symbolic Reference and the Origin of Language

requirements for producing symbolic reference. Indeed, "some major universals of grammar may come for free, so to speak, required by the nature of symbolic communication itself" (2003: 138). Deacon is of the view that "it may turn out that many core features of [Universal Grammar] — recursive operations, the minimally diadic structure of sentences, and many subjacency, ordering, and dependency constraints of grammar — trace their origin to [...] indexical [...] requirements [which] apply to all symbolic linguistic relationships" (2003: 133). As a result, "theoretical efforts now directed toward showing how innate [Universal Grammar] could have evolved and how it might be instantiated in brains could well turn out to be mere intellectual exercises" (2003: 139).

It would seem, then, that the crossing of the symbolic threshold had a double effect on the forms of communication of our remote ancestors. Symbolic reference enabled them to segment the holophrastic utterances (or other forms of communication, e.g. gestures) they had hitherto employed. On top of that, symbolic reference imposed certain constraints on the combined use of the resulting segments.[80]

---

[80] For an interesting and plausible account of the way in which minimal early language has given rise to modern languages, see Deutscher, 2005.

PART II

The Psychology of the Buddha

Introduction

This study is an experiment, or rather, it takes you on a voyage of discovery. It begins with a map that shows the way to a treasure. It follows the map faithfully, and exhibits the treasure that it finds.

This study is not about a real map, nor is it about a physical treasure. It starts with the working hypothesis that certain central claims of the early Buddhist texts are true and tries to determine what implications this has for psychological theory. The working hypothesis is the map; its implications for psychological theory are the treasure. You, the reader, are invited to judge the process by its outcome. You are not asked to judge the working hypothesis. In the comparison with the treasure hunter, you are not asked to pronounce on the reliability of the map. You are merely asked to judge the value of the treasure. You may think that this treasure is valuable, and yet be convinced that the map used to find it was unreliable, or indeed was no map at all. You are asked to suspend your disbelief, follow the reasoning and evaluate the outcome.

There are, to be sure, some *a priori* arguments in support of our working hypothesis. The relevant claims in the early Buddhist texts (which we will consider in detail below) concern psychological states and processes that are unusual from a commonsensical point of view. They are not, however, in conflict with any established rules of natural science or psychology. Moreover, historians have to take the evidence of their sources seriously, even about psychological states and processes, until and unless they have reasons to do otherwise.[81] They often do

---

[81] By not observing this rule, even a field like Buddhist studies may run the risk of "degenerating into a 'de-bunking enterprise', based more on

have such reasons. Sources may be in conflict with each other, or report on facts that are in conflict with what established science tells us about the world. Sometimes we have grounds for thinking that texts lie on purpose.[82] No compelling reasons of this kind present themselves in this case. The claims made in the early Buddhist texts may not agree with the way we think about ourselves and other human beings, but that may merely mean that we have to revise our thoughts about ourselves. This is the reason why I propose to accept the veracity of these claims as a working hypothesis, and to explore whether they can add to our understanding of the human psyche.[83]

One might object that historians are not the kind of people to provide data, or ideas, fit to be used in the sciences, including psychology. This is not always necessarily correct. To show that historical data can sometimes provide data that help a scientific discipline to make progress, consider the follow-

---

ideology than evidence"; Csikszentmihalyi, 1996: 17, with a reference to Hannah Arendt.

The history of India offers many examples of the general requirement that historians have to take seriously the evidence of their sources until and unless they have reasons to do otherwise. Particularly important among these are the testimonies of foreign visitors — such as the Hellenistic ambassador Megasthenes around 300 BCE, a number of Chinese Buddhist monks during the first millennium, and the Persian Moslem Al-Biruni around the year 1000. Isolated observations of these visitors — i.e., observations that are neither confirmed nor contradicted by other evidence — are taken very seriously by historians, and rightly so. For a discussion of the determining influence of the accounts of the Chinese pilgrims Faxian and Xuanzang on nineteenth century Indian archaeology, see Leoshko, 2003: 30 ff.

[82] Beckman, 2005.

[83] Cp. Turner, 1996: 114: "In the hard sciences, which attract so much emulation and envy, unusual events are not dismissed as peripheral. On the contrary, unusual events often command the most attention, on the principle that they are the most likely to reveal general processes."

ing. The records of so-called *historical supernovae*, i.e., supernovae whose first appearance has been recorded in historical documents, have been described as "among the most valuable legacies which the ancient world has bequeathed to modern science". They made a significant impact on modern astrophysics.[84] The claims of the early Buddhist texts are admittedly very different from the recordings of supernovae by early observers. Nevertheless, both are entitled to respect from scientists, and both may conceivably contribute to modern science, each in their own way.

Others may object that no conclusions can be drawn from a single case, such as from what presumably happened to the historical Buddha and perhaps some of his early followers. Those who feel this way are invited to recall the complaint voiced by the neuroscientist V. S. Ramachandran: "Imagine that I cart a pig into your living room and tell you that it can talk. You might say, 'Oh, really? Show me'. I then wave my wand and the pig starts talking. You might respond, 'My God! That's amazing!' You are not likely to say, 'Ah, but that's just one pig. Show me a few more and then I might believe you.' Yet this is precisely the attitude of many people in my field."[85]

Others again may fear that the working hypothesis proposed is no more than a covert way to introduce a hidden religious agenda into a scientific debate. They may think that one might as well adopt as "working hypothesis" the Christian

---

[84] Clark and Stephenson, 1977; this book offers a general presentation of historical supernovae, as well as observations about the interpretation of celestial data in China. The most famous of these historical supernovae is the one that was to give rise to the Crab Nebula well known to astronomers; it was observed in 1054 CE by Chinese astronomers. For a translation of the Chinese and Japanese sources related to the Crab Nebula, see Clark and Stephenson, 1977: 140 ff., and Duyvendak, 1942.

[85] Ramachandran & Blakeslee, 1998: xiii.

belief that "Jesus is the son of God". This fear, though understandable, would be misplaced. The working hypothesis here proposed has nothing to do with religious beliefs, and involves no metaphysical assumptions of any kind. If a comparison with early Christianity has to be made at all (which does not seem to me a particularly good idea), then rather with some such statement as "Jesus was a historical person who ended his life being crucified". Research may or may not be able to confirm or falsify this statement, which is yet of the kind that could interest also non-religious researchers.

Returning now to the Buddhist sources, it is true that studies that try to reconstruct facts about the life of the historical Buddha are confronted with innumerable difficulties and rarely, if ever, produce reliable results.[86] Legendary accounts of episodes in the Buddha's life have come into existence for numerous reasons. Popular imagination, in particular, dwelt upon the person of the Buddha, and played an important role in the creation of many of the stories told about him. From among these, it is virtually impossible to separate the wheat from the chaff.

The present study is not interested in the details of the historical Buddha's life. Rather, it concentrates on the central claims of his teaching.[87] Here we are on safer ground, for a tradition of monastic recitation was set up precisely for the purpose of preserving this teaching. Unlike the stories of the Buddha legend, which are largely absent from the oldest texts, the main teachings are repeated over and over again in these texts.

---

[86] For attempts, see, e.g., Bareau, 1963; 1970-71; Nakamura, 2000-2005. Even the tradition as to the final days, death and incineration of the Buddha may be no more than pious fiction; see Bronkhorst, 2011: 206-224.

[87] For a presentation and analysis of the teaching of the historical Buddha, see Bronkhorst, 2009.

Introduction

This is also not a study of the Buddhist religion. It is rather a study based on certain claims which the Buddhist community has preserved in its oldest texts. These claims concern, primarily if not exclusively, the person who referred to himself as the Buddha, "the awakened one", and whom subsequent generations came to accept as the founder (or most recent fully enlightened teacher) of Buddhism. These claims should not be confused with claims regarding psychological attainments that may be found among members of the Buddhist community. In this study we are not interested in the Buddhist community and its attainments, but only in the old texts which it has preserved. These texts go back to a time before the community existed in anything resembling its present form.

There are good reasons to think that it took a considerable time before monks and nuns settled down in monasteries. The Buddha and his early disciples did not live in monasteries: they were mendicants who begged for their food and had no permanent place of residence.[88] The method which the Buddha had followed in order to achieve his goal, and which he subsequently taught to his followers, had to be practiced in isolated places in the jungle and not in monasteries.[89] Indeed, for a hundred years or so following the disappearance of the Buddha, monasteries and the accompanying communal style of living may still not have existed. When the emperor Asoka wanted to bestow a gift in memory of the Buddha's birth, he was not able to donate it to the community of monks and nuns, as would become customary in a later age. Instead he freed the village in which the Buddha was born from all taxes, and had this recorded in one of his famous inscriptions.[90] In other words, he presented

---

[88] An old rule enjoins monks to eat scraps of food, wear rags, and lodge under trees; Hinüber, 2006: 16.

[89] Appendix 1 of Part II §1(8), §6, below.

[90] Bloch, 1950: 157. Cp. Schopen, 2006: 316.

a gift to the inhabitants of this village rather than to the community of monks and nuns. Undoubtedly the reason for this was that the Buddhist community could still not receive gifts at that time. This changed after Asoka, but the development of monastic Buddhism in subsequent centuries tends to obscure the fact that the Buddha and his earliest followers pursued their path in isolation from the world.

The claims dealt with in this study belong to texts that have been handed down by the Buddhist monastic community. The ideas, practices and beliefs of members of this community are not necessarily useful for a correct understanding of the original claims. From the point of view of this study, its main virtue is to have preserved these texts with great care.[91]

Which are these claims? There are several of them. We will study them in detail as we proceed. The most important one in the present context is that a certain practice specified in the texts can lead to both the end of desire and the end of suffering.[92] The claim concerning the end of suffering occurs frequently. We find it in its most condensed form in the so-called Four Noble Truths. These concern (i) suffering, (ii) the origin of suffering, (iii) the cessation of suffering, (iv) the way leading to the cessation of suffering. In other words, the Buddha is supposed to have claimed that ordinary life is suffering; to have identified the causes responsible for this; to have, in his own case, removed those causes; and to have taught the way that has to be followed (and that he claimed to have followed) in order to bring about that result.

---

[91] Wynne, 2004.

[92] This practice is also claimed to lead to the end of rebirth. Since this claim is based on a belief that is hard to reconcile with modern science, it does not constitute a challenge to science. Cf. Flanagan, 2011: 72 ff.

Introduction

Some qualifications are called for. The early Buddhist tradition has preserved an account of the Buddha's last days which records the fatigue and discomfort due to disease and old age that he was experiencing.[93] The early Buddhist tradition, and the Buddha himself, apparently saw no contradiction between this account and the destruction of suffering which he had presumably accomplished.[94] Indications like these allow us to conclude that the destruction of suffering taught here must be understood primarily as the destruction of psychological suffering. The extent to which this affects bodily suffering will be discussed later.[95]

No such qualifications are required with regard to desire. Desire, which is frequently referred to as thirst°,[96] is regularly mentioned as the root cause of suffering. Desire must therefore be eradicated. The traditional explanation of the second Noble Truth is: "This is the Noble Truth of the origin of suffering: the thirst for repeated existence which, associated with delight and greed, delights in this and that, namely the thirst for the objects of sense desire, the thirst for existence, and the thirst for non-existence." It comes as no surprise that the claim of the third Noble Truth is that suffering can be made to cease by getting rid of the thirst that underlies it.

Our working hypothesis, as explained above, is that these claims are true: desire and psychological suffering can be

---

[93] Appendix 1 of Part II §8, below.

[94] Subsequent Buddhism made lists of the afflictions of the Buddha, and attempted to explain them, a topic dealt with by John Strong in a paper ("Explaining the Buddha's afflictions: karmic strands, good means, or just aches and pains") presented at the XVIth Congress of the International Association of Buddhist Studies, Taiwan 2011.

[95] Part II §8 and Appendix 1 of Part II §8, below.

[96] Words followed by "°" are included among the Technical terms and their Sanskrit and Pali equivalents on p. 216.

brought to an end. Desire and suffering are familiar to all of us. This may make us distrustful with regard to the claim that a person could exist without them. Distrust, however, is no disproof, so let us proceed.

How *can* we proceed? The early Buddhist claims confront us with the following questions: What are human beings like if, in appropriate circumstances, they can attain a conscious and enduring state of being without suffering and without desire? What psychological theory would account for such a state?[97] And what further theoretical assumptions are necessary in order that the process described in the ancient texts[98] should lead to this state?

In order to answer these questions, we need to reflect on the *kind* of psychological theory we require. It seems clear from

---

[97] The choice of existing global psychological theories is extremely limited, and may not have progressed much beyond the state referred to by William James in a letter to his brother Henry: "It is indeed strange to hear people talk triumphantly of 'the New Psychology' and write 'Histories of Psychology' when into the real elements and forces which the word covers not the first glimpse of clear insight exists. A string of raw facts, a little gossip and wrangle about opinions; a little classification and generalization on the mere descriptive level ... but not a single law in the sense in which physics shows us laws, not a single proposition from which any consequence can be casually deduced." (cited in Slater, 2004: 251).

Scholars of Buddhism who confront these and similar questions tend to believe that they call for a philosophical rather than a psychological answer; one example among many is David Burton's book *Buddhism, Knowledge and Liberation: A Philosophical Study* (2004). I think these scholars are mistaken. Burton observes (p. 170): "Whether human nature is such that the complete eradication of craving and hence suffering is attainable by one's own efforts is a debatable point." He is right, but the debate concerned would be a psychological debate, not a philosophical one.

[98] For this process, see primarily Appendix 1 of Part II §1, below.

Introduction

the beginning that neither neuroscience nor evolutionary psychology can provide full answers.[99] Let us consider neuroscience first.

Neuroscience might conceivably discover what processes or states of the human brain correspond to a conscious state that is free from suffering and free from desire. It might even discover which neurological interventions would bring about that state. Even if such information existed, it would be of only limited use for understanding the early Buddhist texts. These texts present an enduring and conscious state free from suffering and free from desire as the final outcome of a process described in experiential terms. In order to understand these texts, we need an answer formulated in terms of a theory which has a place for experiential elements; the theory has to show how these are functionally interrelated.[100] Only such a theory might conceiv-

---

[99] This means that we must disagree with Watson (2000: 760) where he states with regard to psychology: "Darwin provides the only hope at the moment, together with the latest advances being made in neuroscience."

[100] William James' emphasis on the "elementary ingredients of the mind" (1890: I: 28: "A science of the mind must reduce [...] complex manifestations [...] to their elements. [...] A science of the relations of mind and brain must show how the elementary ingredients of the former correspond to the elementary functions of the latter.") omits the need to understand the functional interrelationship between the "elementary ingredients of the mind". Similarly, Rose's (2003: 5 f.) "Rosetta stone" that may help to translate between the two languages of mind and brain, if it can exist at all, requires not just a "language of the brain" that supposedly may be provided by neuroscience, but also a "language of the mind", with a "syntax" of its own, i.e. a theoretical structure that brings to light the interrelationship between mental entities. As long as this Rosetta stone contains mere isolated words in the part written in the language of the mind, no such thing as a translation is ever likely to be possible. It is certain that "[the] Rosetta Stone metaphor of translation remains a long way from realisation" (Rose, 2005: 21). In the Afterword added in the reprint, Rose abandons this metaphor ("Older and

ably answer our questions. Neuroscience will certainly have to be taken into consideration. Both the process described in the ancient texts and the personal state that presumably results from it must, if they are at all possible, have counterparts in processes in and states of the human brain. However, mere knowledge of the neuro-physiological correlates of the process and its result will not provide us with the understanding we are looking for.[101] Even a detailed understanding of what happened in the Buddha's brain — if we could obtain it — would not help us understand why and how it occurred.[102] Nor would

---

hopefully wiser, I now see that the Rosetta Stone, much as I love it, is an inadequate analogy" (2005: 308), and "I ... consign my Rosetta Stone to the dustbin of discarded metaphors" (p. 310)).

[101] Komisaruk, Beyer-Flores & Whipple (2006: 265) draw attention to the danger of creating "just so" stories on the basis of mere research findings regarding brain activity. For a discussion of neuroscience's "explanatory gap", see Horgan, 1999: 15 ff. Flanagan (2011: 88) observes: "One reason to hope that the explanatory gap can be closed [by means of a theory that bridges it] is that if it is not, we are left (unless science comes up with radically new laws) with no way to explain mental causation and thus to keep consciousness from, in fact, being epiphenomenal."

[102] Recall that, to borrow a phrase from Boden (2006: II: 1110), "a theory of the brain needs a theory of what it is that the brain is doing", and that "the original conceptual problem of defining what the brain actually *does* psychologically speaking, what its *psychological* functions are, remains as elusive as ever" (Richards, 2002: 119). Similarly, "it is one thing to look at the brain and see where neurons 'light up', it is quite another to have a sophisticated sense of what one is looking for, and looking at" (Lear, 2005: 6). And again: "When it comes to studying mental function, biologists are badly in need of guidance." (Kandel, 2005: 38; Kandel then adds that, in his opinion, psychiatry and cognitive psychology can make a particularly valuable contribution to brain science "as guide and tutor"). Neuropsychologist Seth Horowitz of Brown University, as cited in *Scientific American* (Biello, 2007), states: "You list a bunch of places in the brain as if naming something lets you understand it". "Vincent Paquette ... goes further, likening neuroimaging to phrenology, the practice in which Victorian-era

it explain how he was able to plan the process which led to the intended result, viz., the end of desire and the end of suffering.

Evolutionary psychology can at best be only of marginal use in our investigation. There can be no doubt that in the study of the human mind it is essential to keep an eye on what is, or might be, humanity's genetic heritage. It is evident that the elimination of desire, including sexual desire, brings no evolutionary advantage. Natural selection cannot, therefore, be invoked as a factor that has worked in favor of the development of the faculty to do so, at least not in a simplistic and direct manner.[103] The question remains how humanity's evolutionary past has led to a situation in which, *ex hypothesi*, desire *can* be eliminated. This is a question that can only be meaningfully addressed once we know exactly what happens, in terms of mental functioning, in such a situation.

Having argued that no satisfactory answers to the specific questions raised in this study can be expected either from neuroscience or evolutionary psychology, let me now address the

---

scientists tried — and ultimately failed — to intuit clues about brain function and character traits from irregularities in the shape of the skull" (ibid.). Pribram's (1998: 12) following critical remarks sum it all up: "Today's establishment, in the role of eliminative materialists such Francis Crick, the Churchlands (Paul and Patricia), and Steven Stitch, want to get rid of what they call 'folk psychology'. They claim that if you know all about neurons you don't need to have a science of consciousness; once we know what each neuron does, we have it all. They are, of course, making a 'category error', but Crick passes that objection off as just philosophical nonsense. No turn of the century Viennese was that *unsophisticated*. Nor do we need to be now." According to Edelman (2006: 89), "no adequate reduction of human sciences to the brain's so-called epigenetic rules is realizable". See further Looren de Jong & Schouten, 2005; Looren de Jong, 2006; Van Eck, Looren de Jong & Schouten, 2006; and Appendix 3 of Part II.

[103] This does not, of course, exclude the possibility that celibacy may in certain circumstances be an adaptive strategy; see e.g. Deady et al., 2006.

question what kind of theory offers the best hope for making psychological sense of the claims of the early Buddhist texts. I think the answer is obvious. We need a theory in which experiential terms — and most particularly desire — figure as functional elements. Only such a theory may do justice to our working hypothesis, viz., the reliability of certain claims in the early Buddhist texts.

Let it be clear that I do not claim that experiences such as desire are in principle irreducible to more elementary processes in the brain (or brain and body). In the present context it is not necessary to pronounce on this issue. All that counts is that the theory which allows us to discuss the claim that desire can be eradicated should have a place for desire. There may or may not be deeper — perhaps neurophysiological — levels of explanation, but this is without immediate importance for our project. Moreover, the decision to conduct our discussion on a level where desire and other experiences figure as functional elements brings an unexpected advantage: it allows us to circumvent the much-debated issue of free will.[104]

Few psychological theories that I am aware of have a place for experiential terms. The most serious attempt, in spite of all its flaws, is still Freud's psychoanalytic theory (including what he came to call metapsychology). We will therefore have to take this theory as point of departure, whether we like it or not. We are of course free to depart from it wherever this appears useful or necessary. Freudian psychoanalysis, like the theory we are looking for, was meant to be a coherent theory in which experiential terms play an essential role. In Freudian theory, as

---

[104] See Appendix 3 of Part II. This procedure will also allow us to circumvent the problems — discussed by Roger Penrose, esp. 1994, Part I — connected with the reduction of certain mental functions to computational mechanisms (supposing such a reduction is even theoretically possible).

Introduction

in our ideal theory, experiential elements are embedded in a larger theoretical context in which other elements that are not directly related to experiences also have their place. Repression and the various drives, or instincts, which Freud postulated are examples of elements that do not directly correspond to experiences but which do play essential roles in his theory. Freudian theory as it stands would lend itself to a confrontation with the claims of the early Buddhist texts, most notably because desire plays a central role both here and in those texts. In particular Freud's sexual instinct might be profitably confronted with the claims of our texts according to which all desire, including sexual desire, can be extinguished.

We will see below that Freudian psychoanalysis, as it stands, is not our ideal theory. It will be useful to consider some of the criticisms that have been directed against it. Freudian theory has been accused of being unfalsifiable. Our Buddhist sources show that this criticism is not justified: Freudian theory *can* be falsified. Indeed, it *is* falsified if we accept the testimony of these sources. A theory that postulates the biological, and therefore inborn nature of the sexual instinct as we know it, is in conflict with the claim that sexual desire (along with all other forms of desire) can be eliminated.[105] Freudian theory could however be improved upon, for example, by an appropriate reformulation of the sexual instinct. This could then give rise to a theory which no longer stands refuted.

This first, and as yet extremely superficial confrontation of Freudian theory with the testimony of the early Buddhist texts

---

[105] Don't forget that we are speaking of the elimination of sexual desire, not about sexual restraint or sexual abstinence. Freud later in life elaborated and expanded his ideas about the sexual instinct so as to arrive, for example, at "erotic instincts [that] strive to bring about a synthesis of living things into greater unities" (*New Introductory Lectures on Psychoanalysis*, 1933; SE XXII p. 108). Yet he never abandoned the conviction that sexuality is rooted in biology.

shows promise. This testimony takes us directly to the remotest and least accessible parts of the theory. Freud always spoke about the instincts — including the sexual instinct — in a most circumspect manner.[106] This is understandable, because information about these instincts had to be extracted, or rather excavated, from underneath a jungle of more accessible data. The promise of the early Buddhist texts is that there may be a direct way to the roots of this jungle which avoids the luxuriant overgrowth. More than forty years ago Kurt Eissler, the New York psychoanalyst who founded and directed the Sigmund Freud Archives, stated that "the psychoanalytic situation has already given forth everything it contains. It is depleted with regard to research possibilities."[107] If so, alternative ways to get at the "roots" of Freudian theory merit serious attention.

The sexual instinct as conceived of by Freud is not only in conflict with the testimony of the early Buddhist texts, but also with a vital element in psychoanalytic theory and practice itself, viz., *sublimation*. Sublimation is supposed to be a deviation, a redirection, of sexual energy to higher aims. If, however, sexual energy is indeed rooted in biology, it cannot be redirected: sexual energy should not find satisfaction in different

---

[106] Freud's ideas about the instincts are for this reason open to serious criticism. Cf. Panhuysen, 1998: 41: "There are [...] some serious objections to Freud's approach. In the first place there is the concrete shape of his drive theory. His drives are too little elaborated (and are capable of being elaborated too much): Not only are Eros and Thanatos mythical beings, but also all drives remain vague shadows, principally because the transition from somatic upwelling to drive represented in a psychic way remains too indeterminate."

[107] Kurt Eissler (1969: 469) as cited in Kandel, 2005: 66. Others close to the psychoanalytic movement have been critical. An example is Wilhelm Reich, who wrote in 1954: "I left behind me an age which had finally got hold of a little corner of the Freudian thought system, but had completely thrown overboard Freud's courage to stand alone [...]" (Reich, 1967: 5).

aims than those which are naturally its own. Sublimation is therefore problematic in Freudian theory as it stands.[108] Once again, a reformulation of this and other aspects of the theory could result in a better, more viable theory.

As well as being criticized for being unfalsifiable, Freudian theory is also criticized for being "positivist" and "empiricist". This, it is claimed, is inappropriate for a psychological theory: human sciences supposedly do not fit such a model. This criticism (for being "positivist" and "empiricist") is the opposite of the earlier one (for being unfalsifiable). Indeed, it objects to the very notion that Freudian theory might be, or might want to be, falsifiable.[109] The very notion of a "mechanistic" theory of the mind is reprehensible to those who uphold this view. Cognitive scientists, nevertheless, have no difficulty comparing the mind with a machine — although not quite in the way Freud did.[110]

The position taken here is that falsifiability of a theory is a virtue rather than a vice. An unfalsifiable theory is hardly better than no theory at all, for it is untestable. Such a theory is in danger of becoming merely a manner of speaking about phenomena, or perhaps only a way to feel one's way into them. A

---

[108] See, e.g., Vergote, 1997.

[109] E.g. Frosh, 2006: 40: "[T]he kind of approach to scientific testing advocated in the positivist, empiricist tradition is inappropriate to the human sciences. This is, first, because it cannot account for 'reflexivity' [...]. Secondly, the empiricist approach is geared to highly controlled situations that are not representative of the actualities of human circumstances."

[110] Note the title *Mind as Machine. A history of cognitive science* of a recent publication; its author (Boden, 2006: 9) presents, "broadly speaking", the study of *mind as machine* as a definition of cognitive science. Note further that "[o]ne of Freud's earliest British supporters [T. N. Mitchell, JB] saw him as 'dominated by the [...] prevailing urge to find mechanistic explanations for everything in the cosmos'" (Cioffi, 1998: 85).

satisfactory psychological theory should be more than this. It should allow us to discuss psychological events or experiences in terms that "stick their neck out". Such a theory could, if necessary, be replaced by a better one for other than subjective reasons.

Two noteworthy thinkers — Thomas Nagel and Eric R. Kandel — have contrasting views about this issue. Let us consider these.

In a review that appeared in the *New York Review of Books*, the philosopher Nagel argues that theories like the one we are looking for cannot be expected to go beyond a generalized "feeling into". He writes:[111]

> As Wollheim [the author of the book reviewed, JB] observes, commonsense explanations are a form of understanding "from within"; even when they provide insights into the mind of another, they depend, in part, on self-understanding, since they interpret the other person as another self. To understand someone else's thought, feelings, or behavior requires that we make sense — even if only irrational sense — of his point of view, by using our own point of view as an imaginative resource. Imagination enables us to make internal sense of beliefs, emotions, and aims that we do not share — to see how they hang together so as to render the other's conduct intelligible. But Freud's extension of this form of insight to unconscious thoughts, motives, and fantasies, and into the minds of infants, threatens to deprive ordinary psychological concepts, like belief, wish, and desire, of their familiar empirical support in the common experience and understanding of everyday life. [...]

---

[111] *New York Review of Books* of May 12 1994. I cite from the reprint in Gomez, 2005: 138-150. The quoted passages occur on pages 139, 140 and 142.

Freud extended the range of such explanation to unheard-of lengths, to cover not only memory lapses and slips, but jokes, dreams, neurotic symptoms, and the substructure of erotic life and family ties — with forays into morality, politics, art, and religion. [...]

Yet the entire system remained psychological in the sense Wollheim has specified. It sought to provide an understanding of human beings "from within", so that we could put ourselves in their shoes and make sense of their symptoms and responses by attributing to them beliefs, desires, feelings, and perceptions — with the difference that these were aspects of their point of view of which they were not consciously aware.

Not surprisingly, Nagel comes to the conclusion that unconscious mental processes — i.e. processes that are described in the terminology of ordinary experience, but which are yet not part of it — must be evaluated by the same standard as ordinary experience, and not "by the methods appropriate in particle physics, cancer research, or the study of reflexes". According to him, "we may not be able to run controlled experiments, but we can still try to make internal sense" of them.

Nobel laureate Kandel holds a different opinion. He states (2005: 66):[112] "although psychoanalysis has historically been scientific in its aims, it has rarely been scientific in its methods; it has failed over the years to submit its assumptions to testable experimentation. Indeed, psychoanalysis has tradition-

---

[112] See also Kandel, 2006: ch. 27 ("Biology and the renaissance of psychoanalytic thought"). Further Kandel, 2005: 127: "I ... think that the emergence of an empirical neuropsychology of cognition based on cellular neurobiology can produce a renascence of scientific psychoanalysis. This form of psychoanalysis may be founded on theoretical hypotheses that are more modest than those applied previously but that are more testable because they will be closer to experimental inquiry."

ally been far better at generating ideas than at testing them. As a result of this failure, it has not been able to progress as have other areas of psychology and medicine."[113] Kandel (p. 68) opts in this way for the *scientific* view of psychoanalysis and rejects the *hermeneutic* one, which Nagel represents. In Kandel's opinion, the hermeneutic view of psychoanalysis "reflects a position that has hindered psychoanalysis from continuing to grow intellectually".

In this debate we take sides with Kandel against Nagel.[114] Indeed, Nagel's remarks might be applied to any theory that uses terms related to ordinary experience and then extends their use beyond their habitual field of application. We do not wish our theory to play (merely) the role that Nagel would ascribe to it. We are *not* looking for a theory in order to understand the processes and results described in the early Buddhist texts "from within", i.e. "to try to make internal sense" of them.

---

[113] Similarly Kandel, 2005: 54: "With the perspective of time, we can readily see what has hindered the full intellectual development of psychoanalysis during the last century. To begin with, psychoanalysis has lacked any semblance of a scientific foundation. Even more, it has lacked a scientific tradition, a questioning tradition based not only on imaginative insights but on creative and critical experiments designed to explore, support, or, as is often the case, falsify those insights."

[114] Steven Rose, though not mentioning psychoanalysis, argues in favor of some form of "mind-language" in the following passage (2005: 220): "Some years ago at a symposium on reductionism in the biological sciences I clashed with the distinguished philosopher Thomas Nagel on this matter of levels of explanation. Arguing for the primacy of reductionist explanations, Nagel suggested that whilst higher level accounts, such as mentalistic ones, could *describe* a phenomenon, only the 'lower level' reductionist could *explain* it. I disagree. In many cases, lower-level accounts are descriptive whilst the higher-level ones are explanatory. ... For sure, explaining the brain is helping us describe and understand our minds, but it is not going to succeed in eliminating mind-language by relocating it into some limbo dismissable by the cognitive illuminati as mere 'folk psychology'." Cf. note 102, above.

This is exactly the procedure that we fear might lead us astray by drawing these processes and results back into the realm of *our* experience, where we may be dealing with processes and results that are not part of it.[115] We need a theory that is both formulated in the terms of ordinary experience and broad enough to cover areas that are not part of it and go, in a sense, beyond our common imagination.[116]

Kandel suggests that "one way that psychoanalysis might re-energize itself ... is by developing a closer relationship with biology in general and with cognitive neuroscience in particular" (2005: 64). He continues: "From a conceptual point of view, cognitive neuroscience could provide a new foundation for the future growth of psychoanalysis, a foundation that

---

[115] This attitude of "trying to make internal sense" of the texts explains no doubt the remarkable fact that academic scholarship has so far failed to even notice or comment upon the extraordinary nature of the claims contained in the early Buddhist texts.

[116] It should *not* cover the type of unconscious mental state that is "very commonly discussed in the cognitive science literature [...] where the agent not only cannot bring the mental state to consciousness in fact, but could not bring it to consciousness even in principle, because it is not the sort of thing that can form the content of a conscious intentional state." Searle (2004: 167-168) illustrates this type with the following example: "in cognitive science it is commonly said that a child learns a language by 'unconsciously' applying many computational rules of universal grammar, or that the child is able to perceive visually by performing 'unconscious' computational operations over the input that comes into the child's retina." About this type of unconscious mental state, which he calls *deep unconscious mental state*, Searle rightly says (p. 171): "There are no such cases. There is no such thing as a deep unconscious mental state." See further Searle, 2007: 113: "there are all sorts of subpersonal processes going on in the brain, in the lateral geniculate nucleus, for example, which can be described *as if* they were cases of thinking about information, but of course there is literally no information there. There are just neuron firings, which result in information of a conscious kind at the end of the process but themselves have no semantic content."

is perhaps more satisfactory than metapsychology." Kandel's suggestion is no doubt valuable and promising, yet one regrets that he considers discarding metapsychology altogether, rather than improving it in a manner that it will lend itself to a confrontation "with biology in general and with cognitive neuroscience in particular." It is the latter aim that inspires the following pages.

It is difficult to create a theory that shares elements with Freudian psychoanalysis but avoids its weaknesses because, as it stands, Freudian theory is not one single theory. Freud's ideas developed over his lifetime, and he revised his theory regularly, sometimes radically.[117] A number of his fundamental notions are anthropomorphic and must be avoided in a theory that aims at being scientific. It is not possible at present to deal with all the criticisms that have been raised against the theory, some of which are valid.[118] It is however clear that the theory as it stands cannot be used in the investigation we wish to conduct. What we need is a new theory that will derive inspiration from Freudian psychoanalytic theory where it appears to be useful, but which is otherwise free to deviate from it.

---

[117] This leads Borch-Jacobsen and Shamdasani (2012: 303) to characterize psychoanalysis as being "an empty theory in which one can cram whatever one likes". They explain: "To take an example, Freud's unilateral insistence on the pre-eminence of sexuality was objected to from all sides. No matter, he then developed his theory of narcissism and the analysis of the ego, silently borrowing from some of his critics, Adler and Jung. The traumatic neuroses of the First World War appeared to have conclusively demonstrated that one could suffer from hysterical symptoms for non-sexual reasons. Freud then came up with the theories of the repetition compulsion and the death drive from the ever ready unconscious."

[118] See, e.g., Cioffi, 1998; Crews, 1998; Dufresne, 2003; 2007; Meyer, 2005. Most of these criticisms do not concern the theoretical elements that will be drawn upon in the following pages.

This new theory can be less elaborate than psychoanalysis. Many important elements can be omitted, because they play no useful role in the present investigation. For example, the new theory does not have to deal with transference, a key concept in psychoanalytic theory and practice. Transference plays no role in a process which is brought about by a single individual unaccompanied by a therapist. The Buddha, according to the early Buddhist texts, reached his goal on his own, far away from society and the company of other human beings. Dreams, too, play no role in the path described in the Buddhist texts. There is no need to deal with their place in the new theory, in spite of the fact that for Freud they constituted the royal road to the unconscious. Other key concepts in Freudian theory, such as the Oedipus complex, do not need to be considered. The early Buddhist texts do not mention the specific personal difficulties which individuals are to overcome on their way to the goal. For our investigation the hypothesis *that* that goal can be reached is more important than the specific difficulties encountered. The aim of this study, moreover, is not to show that the path depicted in the Buddhist texts represents some form of psychoanalytic *therapy*, but rather that, though perhaps unique as a path, it can be described and perhaps understood in terms of a theory that has points in common with Freudian *theory*. All that is required is the skeleton of a theory (which may one day be elaborated into a "full" theory). However, without a properly constructed skeleton no body can stand up. This applies to bodies of theory as much as to bodies of flesh and blood. Much of the Freudian superstructure, its "flesh and blood", will therefore remain outside our immediate area of concern. What remains corresponds more or less closely to Freud's *metapsychology*.

The same observations can be expressed through the comparison of the human mind with wild growth in a tropical jungle which I used above. Psychotherapists have, by necessity, approached this luxuriant growth from above, trying to disentangle the multitudes of forms that present themselves to the eye. Their ideas about what hides in the soil, beneath this rich cover, have had to remain tentative because no direct access to it was possible. The approach which we are exploring offers direct access to the roots, but tells us relatively little about the overgrowth. This study will therefore confine itself to the investigation of those "roots", without denying that a complete theory should take into consideration the whole "plant", both the parts that are hidden in the soil and those that protrude from it.

In the following pages a new theory will be constructed along these lines. Though new, it does not deny its obvious indebtedness to Freudian theory. Footnotes will from time to time (though not systematically or exhaustively) cite passages from Freud's collected works which express ideas that are similar to the ones presented here. These footnotes are *not* meant to suggest that the theory presented is in these respects identical with Freudian theory. Nor are they to be read as justifications of the positions put forward.

OUTLINE OF A PSYCHOLOGICAL THEORY

§1 Fundamentals

The observation that human behavior is influenced by earlier experiences must be our point of departure. A pleasurable experience, in particular, will leave a trace in the human mind which can be activated ("remembered") by a renewed encounter with the object or event that was originally associated with it, or with objects or events that are sufficiently similar to these.[119] The activated memory trace may evoke the bodily state (e.g., an activity) which had accompanied the pleasurable experience on the previous occasion.

We can think of the mind (or an important part of the mind) as a large collection of memory traces, each more or less deeply entrenched. Many of these will bring about specific bodily states when activated. A memory trace together with the bodily arousal that belongs to it incorporate a partial map of the world, however primitive.[120] This combination can be

---

[119] Not all memories preserved in memory traces are *episodic* or *explicit*, or more generally *declarative* memories; many are *procedural* or *implicit* memories. See below. Rose (2003: 378) observes that "[p]rocedural memories, unlike declarative, do not seem to become forgotten in the same way, suggesting that they are both learned and re-membered by a very different mechanism from declarative one." He then suggests the following explanation: "Perhaps this is because memories that involve procedural rather than declarative modes — such as riding a bicycle — are not confined simply to the brain but involve whole sets of other bodily memories, encoded in muscles and sinews?"

[120] This is not the opinion of Antonio Damasio (2010: 130 ff.), who distinguishes between dispositions (the brain's "true and tried device") and maps and their images ("a new invention"); the two are said to work in synergy. Others, however, maintain that already at the most elemen-

seen as an embodiment of the "belief" that the object or event

tary level we have to think of physicomental maps rather than of mere sequences of stimulus-response. Cp. Rose, 2003: 177-178: "despite its popularity with psychological theorists, modellers and neurobiological experimenters, association cannot be the only way in which memory occurs ... For instance, on Skinner's theory, rats ought to learn to run a maze correctly by learning each correct turn (first left, second right and so on) individually and sequentially as a chain of stimuli and responses. But it was quite straightforward to show, by rearranging the maze or altering the cues within it, that the animals are not so inefficient; instead they seem after a few trials to be able to form *some sort of a global image of the maze, a map if you like*, in their brains, so that wherever they are placed in it they can deduce where the goal may be and adopt the most efficient route towards it without being excessively confused by the rearrangement of the maze. Animals use strategies when they learn; they can create concepts. To understand such mechanisms it is not adequate to reduce them to linear sequences of stimulus-response, positive and negative reinforcement." (my emphasis, JB). Also p. 269: "Cognitive behaviour is not reducible to simple sequences of contingencies of reinforcement but instead reflects goal-seeking activities, hypothesis making and many other features which had hitherto been dismissed from consideration within the Anglo-American tradition in psychology." Rose, 2005: 22: "[A] free-living cell ... needs to be able to respond appropriately to ... changes. One way of conceiving of this capacity to vary a program is as an action plan, an 'internal representation' of the desired goal — at its minimum, that of survival at least until replication is achieved." Intelligence in cells is also defended in Ford, 2009. See further Kandel, 2005: 118: "investigations which fail to consider internal representations of mental events are inadequate to account for behavior, not only in humans but — perhaps more surprisingly — also in simple experimental animals." The question how such cognitive maps and goal-seeking are to be explained on the level of the memory traces is beyond the scope of this publication; see however Freeman, 1999: 120-121: "the ingredients received by brains from their sensory cortices with which to make meanings are produced by the cortices. They are not direct transcriptions or impressions from the environment inside or outside the body. All that brains can know has been synthesized within themselves, in the form of hypotheses about the world and the outcomes of their own tests of the hypotheses, success or failure, and the manner of failure." The fear of introducing homunculi here cannot

§1 Outline of a Psychological Theory: Fundamentals

concerned, if reacted to with that specific bodily state, will lead to a pleasurable experience. In the simplest case this "belief" is based on one single experience, and may very well be wrong: a repeated confrontation with the same or a closely similar object or event, followed by the same bodily arousal, may *not* bring about a pleasurable experience on this subsequent occasion. In many cases new experiences can correct wrong "beliefs". They can do so because a number of memory traces can mutually INTEGRATE and form a TRACE UNIT or SECONDARY TRACE. A trace unit will incorporate a better map, i.e. a better reality assessment, and will evoke the bodily arousal which its better reality assessment "believes" will give rise to pleasurable expe-

---

be fully removed in the manner suggested by Dennett (2005: 137, also 161): "As long as your *homunculi* are more stupid and ignorant than the intelligent agent they compose, the nesting of homunculi within homunculi can be finite, bottoming out, eventually, with agents so unimpressive that they can be replaced by machines". Deacon (2012: 83-84) comments: "everything depends on mental processes being a cumulative effect of the interactions of tiny mindless robots. Though the homunculus problem is in this way subdivided and distributed, it is not clear that the reduction of complex intentionality to many tiny intentions has done any more than give the impression that it can be simplified and simplified until it just disappears. But it is not clear where this vanishing point will occur. Though intuitively one can imagine simpler and simpler agents with stupider and stupider intentional capacities, at what point does it stop being intentional and just become mechanism?" And again (p. 139): "No fractionation ... into modules of even smaller scope and proportion allows the apparent arrow of causality to reverse." Deacon dedicates much of the remainder of his book trying to show how this arrow of causality can actually reverse.

About remembering, Rose states (p. 381): "Truth to tell, ... we still haven't the slightest idea of just how re-membering occurs, how a simple clue can evoke the sequential memory of an entire scene." Note finally that at the human level memory traces tend to be integrated in such a manner that some kind of essence is attributed to the objects of memory; see Bloom, 2010.

riences.[121] Integrated traces may even change in the process of integration — i.e., they may no longer remember the "same" memory.

By way of example we may think of the hunger of a baby that is appeased when it is suckled at the mother's breast. The initial memory trace of this pleasurable event may contain little understanding of the way in which that event came about, and how it could be brought about again when the need arises. Combined with other memory traces, a trace unit may arise that incorporates a better map of the situation, including knowledge of the kind of activity that might bring about a repetition of that experience. Continued experience may make this map ever more sophisticated. The baby may start to realize, for example, that an effective method to repeat the experience passes through ways of attracting the attention of the mother. This understanding is not attached to one single memory trace but to a number of them that have mutually integrated, thus forming a trace unit.

The process described can be visualized in more detail in the following manner. The primary traces that together make up a trace unit will (if they have not changed in the process; see above) still bring about the states of bodily arousal that they brought about before their integration. At that time this bodily arousal took the direction dictated by its primary trace. After integration, the direction of bodily arousal will no longer be determined by the reality assessment of its original trace but by that of the trace unit as a whole. In this way, the baby's search for appeasement of its hunger will pass through various phases from, say, undirected crying to focused attempts to attract the attention of the mother.

---

[121] The mechanism by which integration takes place and can give rise to a better reality assessment is in need of elucidation (without the help of anthropomorphic homunculi), which cannot be provided here.

§1 Outline of a Psychological Theory: Fundamentals

It will be useful to reformulate the above in terms of (bodily) urges and their satisfaction. An urge is linked to a memory trace which determines its direction. It does so because the memory trace incorporates the "belief" that satisfaction will be obtained in that specific way. After integration of the memory trace into a trace unit, the urge will still be there (it will be put in a state of excitation when the memory trace is activated). However, its direction will no longer be determined by "its" memory trace but by the trace unit as a whole. Part of the excitation associated with the original memory trace, however, will remain free floating and contribute to a general degree of bodily tension in an individual.

The example of hunger shows that at least certain urges can push for satisfaction without the preliminary activation of associated memory traces. (One may feel hunger without being confronted with or thinking of food.) In such cases the excitation of the urge may activate the memory trace rather than vice-versa. We will call such urges independent. We must keep in mind that there may be other urges which do not "announce" themselves on their own. These can only be known, and excited, through the activation of their memory traces. Such urges are dependent, for they depend for their manifestation on the activation of their memory traces or on chance occurrences of satisfaction. More will be said about this below.

As a first approximation we posit an underlying principle of homeostatic equilibrium in all of these cases. The organism "searches" for this state. Excited urges disturb this equilibrium, their satisfaction reestablishes it. Events that reestablish homeostasis are experienced as pleasurable, those that disturb it as unpleasurable.

The principle of homeostatic equilibrium will have to be expanded in order to account for certain pleasurable experiences that will be dealt with later. The expression "homeostatic equilibrium" wrongly suggests that there is a stable state that can be reestablished and that corresponds to a constant level of bodily tension. In reality this level can vary, so that it will be better to speak of *heterostasis* rather than homeostasis.[122] This topic, too, will be further elaborated below.

If all the memory traces of an individual were to be integrated in the way described above, the result would be one single all-embracing trace unit whose reality assessment would be founded upon all the experiences that person had ever had. An individual's urges would aim at satisfaction in the most "realistic" manner possible for him or her.

We will see below that the mind does not consist of one single all-embracing trace unit. It is however true that the majority of memory traces do integrate so as to form one large trace unit. We will call this particular trace unit, the largest of them all, the main unit. The main unit incorporates the reality assessment of the person as a whole. It directs, and often redirects, the majority of that person's urges.[123]

The following can be stated about the inner functioning of the main unit. Since it unites innumerable memory traces, almost any situation encountered will activate a number of these. Many different courses of action would lead to satisfaction of some of the associated urges, yet all of these courses of action cannot be undertaken simultaneously. It is at this point that attention has a role to play. Attention allows the main unit to "choose" between different courses of action.

---

[122] Cp. Panksepp, 1998: 164.

[123] This does not necessarily deny that the main unit may be divided into partly overlapping subunits, responsible for a multiplicity of personalities in one and the same person; see Carter, 2008. For a critical presentation and discussion of multiple personality, see Hacking, 1995; further Nathan, 2011; Reinders et al., 2012.

§1 Outline of a Psychological Theory: Fundamentals

Scientists have pointed out that attention is vital to the life and survival of many animals, not only humans. "An animal that is hungry or being threatened has to select an object or an action from many possible ones. It is obvious that the ability to choose quickly one action pattern to be carried out to the exclusion of others confers considerable selective advantage. Possessing such an ability makes it possible to achieve a goal that would otherwise be interfered with by the attempt to undertake two incompatible actions simultaneously. Survival may depend critically on this ability."[124] The question that interests us at present is: What *is* attention in terms of our theory? What happens when attention "chooses" between different courses of action? The answer to these questions must take the following reflections into consideration.

In the theory so far presented, memory traces belong to the mind, urges (being bodily states) belong to the body. Mind and body interact closely, yet they must be clearly distinguished. In trying to specify the nature of attention, this distinction is important.

Attention may determine that in a given situation one particular trace (or a small number of traces) will be activated (and the corresponding urge put in a state of excitation) at the expense of others: attention can imply selective activation. The other traces that might be activated in the situation are sidelined, if only temporarily. However, attention is not only the selective activation of memory traces. Attention can also be directed at certain aspects of the sensory input. Perhaps this is indeed its primary function. Animals that observe their prey and music lovers who listen to their favorite composer direct their attention to the relevant aspects of their sensory input. This happens once again at the expense of other potential objects. Through the selected aspects of the sensory input, certain

---

[124] Edelman, 1992: 141-142.

memory traces will also be activated, but this is secondary in these cases, not primary as above.

Whether attention is primarily directed at aspects of sensory input or at selected memory traces — either way, this happens at the expense of other aspects of the sensory input and of other memory traces. It will therefore be useful to think of attention as a limited power supply: the more attention is directed at certain parts of the sensory input or at certain memory traces, the less will be available for others.[125] Depending on the amount of attention that is directed at a specific memory trace, this memory trace will be activated to a greater or lesser degree. A more strongly activated memory trace will excite the accompanying urge to a higher degree than one that is less strongly activated. Here, as before, the memory trace is mental, the urge physical.

The exclusion of non-selected memory traces is relative in most cases: Typically a selected memory trace will be activated to a higher degree than non-selected ones. As a result, the urge associated with a selected memory trace will be put into a higher degree of excitation than the ones associated with non-selected memory traces. The greater strength of the chosen urge may in certain cases be called upon to counteract those other urges. It follows that the higher the level of attention, the more easily the main unit will be able to carry out its chosen course of action.

If we now return to the functioning of the main unit, the following picture emerges. Selective activation of memory

---

[125] Cp. Eysenck, 1982: 28: "attention is regarded as a limited power supply. The basic idea is that attention represents a general purpose limited capacity that can be flexibly allocated in many different ways in response to task demands." Spiegel & Spiegel, 2004: 19: "Any intensification of focal attention necessitates the elimination of distracting or irrelevant stimuli. ... We not only pay attention to our given task but also ward off distractions."

§1 Outline of a Psychological Theory: Fundamentals

traces (by means of the faculty called *attention*) will excite different urges to different degrees. This differential excitation of urges gives the selected urges (i.e., urges that are associated with selected memory traces) the extra (bodily) *tension* that can be used to counterbalance other excited urges (should these exist).[126]

It must be emphasized that the activity of the main unit is not exclusively reactive. Memory traces are not only activated by the confrontation with outer objects or events through sensory input, but also by memories (whether real or otherwise) and fantasies. The main unit, in its attempts to anticipate future conceivable events, can construe an almost limitless number of these latter. It is helped in this by its capacity of symbolic representation, which we discussed in Part I (I §1). Attention, when directed at any of these memories or fantasies, will activate the traces in a similar manner to that of unmediated confrontation with the external object or event concerned, though as a rule to a lesser degree.

---

[126] It is not impossible, though perhaps hard to prove, that the opposition between main unit and other trace units finds expression in the different characters that can figure in dreams. Cp. Deacon, 2012: 478: "[T]he unity of consciousness may be more mercurial than commonly imagined. Different loci of teleodynamic activity at the same level may develop in parallel and come into competition as they differentiate and propagate to recruit additional neurological resources. Thus the differentiation of self may also involve a Darwinian component ... The often quite sophisticated alter egos that we find ourselves interacting with in dreams, and who can often act in unexpected ways, suggests that in this state of consciousness, there may be no winner-take-all exigency. In dreams, all action is virtual and thus need never be finally differentiated; but when awake and enjoined to behave by real-world circumstances, action depends on a winner-take-all logic to produce a single integrated action. So the unity of waking conscious experience may in this respect be a special case of a more pluralistic self-differentiation process."

Sometimes, traces are definitely rather than provisionally discarded by the main unit. This kind of trace is linked to urges whose manifestation is so completely opposed to all other goals of the main unit, and so strong, that it has to be countered. This takes place through a forceful mobilization of free tension. Attention plays a key role in this. As long as it is directed at the dangerous trace, it will raise the level of excitation of the threatening urge.[127] To avoid this, attention must be withdrawn from that trace. In order to do so, and in order to recruit the free tension required to oppose the threatening urge, attention has to be directed to other traces or external objects. (These other traces or external objects may become associatively connected with the threatening urge, in which case the displacement can become a symptom.)[128] The result is avoidance, or denial, of everything that might activate the dangerous trace.[129]

This whole process, including the increase in bodily tension and the diversion of attention, takes place with great urgency. As a result the full content of the dangerous trace remains "unknown". This is a way of saying that this trace will not be integrated into the main unit. By not being integrated, the content of this trace will remain unchanged. Since an urge takes its

---

[127] Attention may not be the exclusive property of the main unit. It is perhaps a feature of the organism as a whole, attaching itself to activated memory traces, whether or not "approved of" by the main unit, or to sensory inputs that activate memory traces. See note 132, below.

[128] Cp. Freud in *Inhibitions, Symptoms and Anxiety* (1926; SE XX p. 91): "A symptom is a sign of, and a substitute for, an instinctual satisfaction which has remained in abeyance; it is a consequence of the process of repression." Ibid. p. 103: "It is this displacement, then, which has a claim to be called a symptom."

[129] In Freudian terms, this description accounts for both *primal repression* and the *repression proper* of associated ideas (for details, see Freud, "Repression" [1915]; SE XIV pp. 141-158).

§1 Outline of a Psychological Theory: Fundamentals

direction from the trace to which it is attached, the urge will keep its threatening nature, even if the trace to which it is attached aims it where no satisfaction can be obtained. The misdirected urge will remain misdirected, for it does not "know" better. It cannot "know" better, for it cannot profit from other experiences. In order to profit from other experiences, its trace would have to be integrated into the main unit from which it is excluded.

This fate is not only reserved for primary memory traces. It also concerns trace units of various sizes whose reality assessments, i.e. "beliefs" in the possibility of obtaining satisfaction for the accompanying urges, are so much in conflict with the procedures for satisfaction adopted in the main unit that they threaten it. One might think that even dangerous memory traces will, in due time, lose their threat and end up being integrated in the main unit. However, this does not usually happen. The reason is that the main unit has "taken note" of the danger from which it has so narrowly escaped. The confrontation with the threatening urge and accompanying memory content, which has only been averted *in extremis*, has left a sign-post in the form of a memory trace that contributes to the reality assessment of the main unit. The negative experience associated with this memory trace and its accompanying urge will henceforth be avoided, just as negative experiences in the outer world are avoided.

Why should confrontations with "unacceptable" traces and urges be a source of unpleasure? We have seen that the organism as a whole "strives" after a state of homeostasis (more precisely, heterostasis). Urges are states of excitation that seek discharge. The discharge of an urge (its satisfaction) gives rise to an experience of pleasure. The appeasement of hunger is an example. The confrontation with "unacceptable" traces and urges does the opposite: it gives rise to high levels of bodily tension, for a strongly excited urge has to be countered by tension brought about by means of diverted attention. Given that discharge is pleasurable, the charged situation that accompanies this confrontation, which does not lead to discharge, is experienced as unpleasurable.[130]

At this point the notion of consciousness has to be introduced. Attention and consciousness often go together, even though this is not always the case.[131] Mental contents at which attention is directed are usually conscious; many other mental contents are not. Certain non-conscious mental contents may become conscious once attention is directed towards them. It follows from the exposition above that there are also mental

---

[130] Note that the satisfaction of the "unacceptable" urge is not *itself* the source of unpleasure in these cases. Its source is rather the reaction of the organism as a whole, mobilized to prevent this satisfaction from taking place. Cp. Freud, *Inhibitions, Symptoms and Anxiety* (1926; SE XX p. 92-93): "Repression is an equivalent of [an] attempt at flight. The ego withdraws its (preconscious) cathexis from the instinctual representative that is to be repressed and uses that cathexis for the purpose of releasing unpleasure (anxiety). The problem of how anxiety arises in connection with repression may be no simple one; but we may legitimately hold firmly to the idea that the ego is the actual seat of anxiety and give up our earlier view that the cathectic energy of the repressed impulse is automatically turned into anxiety. If I expressed myself earlier in the latter sense, I was giving a phenomenological description and not a metapsychological account of what was occurring." Ibid. p. 108-09: "It [is] anxiety which produce[s] repression and not, as I formerly believed, repression which produce[s] anxiety."

[131] Moors & De Houwer, 2007: 39 f.; Koch & Tsuchiya, 2007. An exception may further have to be made for certain forms of brain damage; cf. Kentridge et al., 1999. Note also that "the activation of a memory trace is not at all synonymous with conscious remembering" (Turnbull and Solms, 2003: 60). Donald (2001) is critical towards attempts to explain human mental activity without realizing the central role consciousness plays in it.

§1 Outline of a Psychological Theory: Fundamentals

contents to which attention cannot or will not be directed.[132] Attention is withdrawn from these because their accompanying urges represent (or represented) a danger to the main unit. In this way, mental contents fall into two main categories: those that are or can become conscious without the help of a special stratagem, and those that resist becoming conscious. The difference between these two is not confined to the presence or absence of consciousness. The contents that are (potentially) conscious are part of a system: the main unit, whose reality assessment is determined by the majority of the person's experiences. The reality assessments of contents that have no access to consciousness have been stunted in their development and are based on a relatively limited number of experiences.[133]

The theory presented so far shares various features with the psychological ideas of Sigmund Freud. It contains elements

---

[132] The attention talked about here is, of course, the attention of the main unit. One could imagine that the faculty of attention is also available to repressed trace units, but this possibility cannot be explored here.

[133] Our theory does not exclude the possibility of a main unit that is divided into several mutually opposing parts. This might account, for example, for the conscious decision in certain people to hold on to patterns of behavior that they know go against their interest and well-being. Such internal divisions of the main unit should be expected to be accompanied by permanent (relatively) high levels of bodily tension.

We will not discuss posttraumatic *dissociation*. Repression as understood in our theory should be distinguished from it, even though repression may well be a special instance of dissociation. Dissociation is the selective "forgetting" that may result from trauma. Repression, too, is traumatic, but not because of the content of the repressed urge itself, but because of the reaction of the organism; see note 130, above. On dissociation, see Bremner & Marmar, 1998 (various contributions); Gerschuny & Thayer, 1999. Recent developments in the theory of dissociation are discussed in Spitzer et al., 2006. On Freud's initial confusion between repression and dissociation, see Nemiah, 1998.

that correspond more or less closely to the Freudian *conscious* and *unconscious* (later, Ego and Id) and something that corresponds to Freud's *repression*.[134] Our theory, however, omits numerous areas included in Freudian psychology and is therefore much more limited in its scope. Moreover, even where the two overlap, they are not identical. A major difference is that Freud had very little to say about *attention*, which plays virtually no role in his thought.[135] In our account of repression (or what corresponds to it), attention plays a crucial role, so that our account of repression, too, is different from the Freudian one. These differences illustrate that our theory is not meant to be a faithful copy of Freud's theory, or of some of its parts. It should not therefore be judged by its degree of compliance with psychoanalytic doctrine. Rather, it should be looked upon as an independent attempt to create sufficient theoretical structure to support the discussion that follows. Note further that our theory, at least in the presentation given so far, neglects the undeniable fact that the mind does not start off as a *tabula rasa*. We will come back to this.

---

[134] It is possible to state — with V. S. Ramachandran (1994: 324) as cited in Solms, 2006 — that "the repression phenomena [...] form the cornerstone of classical psychoanalytical theory"; cp. Freud, "On the history of the psycho-analytic movement" (1914; SE XIV p. 16): "The theory of repression is the corner-stone on which the whole structure of psycho-analysis rests."

[135] See, however, Freud's remark in *The Interpretation of Dreams* (1900; SE V p. 615): "The system Pcs. [...] has at its disposal for distribution a mobile cathectic energy, a part of which is familiar to us in the form of attention." Freud's use of *cathexis* is sometimes close to our *attention*. The "system Pcs." corresponds, by and large, to our "main unit".

§2 Comparison with Neurological Findings

It will be interesting to see to what extent our theory agrees with what is known about the functioning of the human brain. In this field enormous progress has been made in recent years. The psychological interpretation of its findings, however, is confronted with many difficulties. We are most interested in findings and interpretations that seem compatible with our theory. These exist. There is a tendency among certain researchers to interpret the findings of neuroscience in terms of Freudian theory.[136] But researchers who do not look to Freud for inspiration, too, come up with findings and interpretations that are of interest.

Consider recent ideas about the neurological analogue of consciousness. Watt and Pincus (2004: 81) refer to a number of publications and summarize current thought on this matter in the following words: "many theories support the assumption that consciousness reflects globally integrative processes derivative of neurodynamical interactions between multiple contributing brain systems, particularly communication between the critical triad of thalamus, brainstem, and cortex."

As an example we consider the ideas of Gerald M. Edelman[137] and Giulio Tononi. These authors discuss the theme of integration and consciousness from a neurobiological point of view in their *A Universe of Consciousness* (the European edition is called *Consciousness*; 2000). They point out that neuronal circuits only give rise to consciousness if they are integrated with each other through a process they call *reentry* ("a process

---

[136] For a discussion, see Solms, 2004.

[137] Horgan's characterization of Edelman as a "high-profile Freudophile" (1999: 39) is not based, to my knowledge, on any *parti pris* on Edelman's part in favor of Freudian theory. See Edelman, 2006: 108 f. for his response to psychoanalytic theory.

of signaling back and forth along reciprocal connections", p. 44). Consider the first two of their three conclusions (p. 36):

> First, conscious experience appears to be associated with neural activity that is distributed simultaneously across neuronal groups in many different regions of the brain. Consciousness is therefore not the prerogative of any one brain area; instead, its neural substrates are widely dispersed throughout the so-called thalamocortical system and associated regions. Second, to support conscious experience, a large number of groups of neurons must interact rapidly and reciprocally through the process called reentry. If these reentrant interactions are blocked, entire sectors of consciousness disappear, and consciousness itself may shrink or split.

These conclusions, especially the second one, suggest that mental maps that are embodied in neuronal groups integrate with other maps if the neuronal groups concerned interact through reentry; and they give rise to consciousness if large numbers of such groups are involved. On the other hand, they stay isolated and remain unconscious if the reentrant interactions are blocked. The integrated neuronal groups constitute a *dynamic core*, defined as "a cluster of neuronal groups that are strongly interacting among themselves and that have distinct functional borders with the rest of the brain at the time scale of fractions of a second" (p. 144).[138] This dynamic core corresponds to our *main unit*, in that it is responsible for conscious

---

[138] It would seem that the *dynamic core* is similar to what other researchers call *global neuronal workspace* (Dehaene & Naccache, 2001; Dehaene et al., 2006; Dehaene, 2011; see further Dennett, 2005: 131 f.). This, too, is characterized by "long-distance connections" and forms "a reverberating neuronal assembly with distant perceptual areas". Dennett (2005: 136 f., 160 f.) speaks of "fame in the brain" or "cerebral celebrity."

§2 Comparison with Neurological Findings

experience. Edelman and Tononi take care to point out that the term *dynamic core* does not refer to a unique, invariant set of areas of the brain (whether prefrontal, extrastriate, or striate cortex). The core, moreover, may change in composition over time.[139]

Edelman and Tononi further observe that "there is reason to believe that a substantial portion of neural activity, even in the cerebral cortex, does *not* correlate with what a person is aware of" (p. 140). It is here that we may hope to find the isolated trace units of our theory. Edelman and Tononi do indeed go so far as to introduce the notion of *splinter cores* that exist beside and independently of the dynamic core;[140] they do not, however, formulate explanatory hypotheses about these. They merely ask a number of questions. The following two are of particular interest in the present context (p. 190):

> Is it possible that such active but functionally insulated thalamocortical circuits may underlie certain aspects of the psychological unconscious — aspects that, as Sigmund Freud pointed out, share many of the hallmarks of the "mental" — except that they do not make it into consciousness? Can such circuits be created by mechanisms of repression?

Having raised these and other questions, our two authors limit themselves to observing that "clearly, much work needs to be done to clarify these issues".[141] The questions are however in-

---

[139] This may be looked upon as an example of the "dynamic localization" in the brain of mental functions and processes, advocated by Kaplan-Solms & Solms (2002: 26 ff.), following Luria (and ultimately Freud).

[140] Edelman (2006: 112) emits the hypothesis that certain people — such as those who suffer from the symptoms resulting from disruption of the corpus callosum — may have *two* dynamic cores.

[141] Cp. Edelman, 2004: 95: "I have not dealt with the Freudian un-

triguing, and we may be comforted in thinking that the psychological theory presented so far is not contradicted by the ideas of Edelman and Tononi. The idea of multiple *splinter*

---

conscious and the notion of repression, which remains to some extent a vexed subject." According to Edelman, 2006: 155-56, "nonconscious brain systems [...] have structures and dynamics that interact with and influence the dynamic core. In this respect, Freud's views of unconscious sources of behavior were premonitory." Naccache (2006) is of the view that Freudian repression and neuroscience are incompatible, as are the Freudian and neuroscientific notions of the unconscious: "le coeur même de la psychanalyse freudienne de l'inconscient, c'est-à-dire le concept de refoulement, et certaines propriétés des représentations mentales inconscientes postulées par Freud sont en absolue contradiction avec ce que nous connaissons aujourd'hui du fonctionnement mental et de sa physiologie" (p. 361). However, it is far from obvious that the unconscious functions explored in his book can or should be identified with the unconscious that figures in Freudian theory. Buser (2005) is less absolute; indeed, one of his ambitions is to "explorer, confronter, et tenter d'associer les deux domaines inconscients" (p. 7), i.e., the "cognitive" unconscious and the "thymic" or affective unconscious. His conclusion (p. 191): "nonobstant toutes les inévitables réserves, les incontournables sorties de route de la théorisation psychanalytique, on ne peut nier tout en bloc et ignorer ce pan de l'analyse du psychisme, avec ses trois volets que sont l'inconscient, le préconscient et le conscient, alors que l'on réserverait par ailleurs maintenant le droit de vie au couple inconscient-conscient du domaine cognitif et que l'on reconnaîtrait à ce dernier seul la valeur d'un système scientifiquement prouvé." Magistretti & Ansermet (2010: 9) speak of "les confusions actuelles dans les neurosciences à propos de l'inconscient, et notamment autour de la distinction entre l'inconscient cognitif et l'inconscient freudien." See further Ansermet & Magistretti, 2010a. Ansermet & Magistretti (2004) associate the (Freudian) unconscious with the amygdala: "il n'est pas impossible [...] que les traces inscrites dans l'amygdale soient le substrat, ou l'un des substrats, des scénarios fantasmatiques et des états somatiques associés qui constituent ce que nous avons appelé la réalité interne inconsciente" (p. 198). Elsewhere (2010: 172) they contrast l'"inconscient au sens freudien" with "ce que l'on appelle l'inconscient cognitif."

§2 Comparison with Neurological Findings

cores, if it were to be confirmed, is of course closer to our *trace units* than to the Freudian *system of the unconscious*.[142]

Solms and Turnbull (2002) draw attention to what they call the seeking system in the brain, whose source cells are located in the ventral tegmental area.[143] This system "does not appear to know what it is seeking" (p. 118-119). Its mode of operation "is therefore incomprehensible without reference to the *memory* systems with which it is intimately connected." The clear distinction in our theory between memory traces and associated urges seems in this way to find a confirmation in the physical structure of the brain.

This distinction is further confirmed by some important ideas presented by Antonio Damasio in a number of publications.[144] Recall that the brain is not isolated from the body; it is in constant interaction with it. Experiences, which as a rule affect the brain first, subsequently evoke reactions in the body. These reactions can be of various kinds: muscular, hormonal, and so on. Following Damasio, I will reserve the term *emotion* to designate certain bodily states; emotions are to be distinguished from *feelings*, which are the perceptions of those bod-

---

[142] The "system Ucs" (*The Interpretation of Dreams*, 1900; SE V p. 541). Note, however, that "the ego is an organization and the id is not" (*Inhibitions, Symptoms and Anxiety*, 1926; SE XX p. 97), and (ibid.) "As a rule the instinctual impulse which is to be repressed remains isolated." Similarly Lear, 2005: 53: "it is a mistake to think of [the unconscious] as a second mind with beliefs, intentions and desires all of its own".

[143] Cp. Panksepp, 1998: 144 ff.

[144] These ideas are a weakened version of ideas first published by William James in 1884, and independently by Carl Georg Lange in 1885. See James, 1890: II: 449 ff.; further LeDoux, 1996: 291 ff.; Rolls, 1999: 70 ff.; 2005: 26 ff.; Klein, 2002/2006: 16 ff.; Ansermet & Magistretti, 2010: 39 ff. Lehrer (2007: 1 ff.) draws attention to the influence in this respect of Walt Whitman on James (p. 18: "This psychological theory, first described in the 1884 article 'What is an emotion?' is Whitman, pure and simple"), and of Ralph Waldo Emerson on both of them.

ily states.[145] For Damasio, "emotions are actions or movements, many of them public, visible to others as they occur in the face, in the voice, in specific behaviors. To be sure, some components of the emotion process are not visible to the naked eye but can be made 'visible' with current scientific probes such as hormonal assays and electrophysiological wave patterns. Feelings, on the other hand, are always hidden, like all mental images necessarily are, unseen to anyone other than their rightful owner, the most private property of the organism in whose brain they occur."[146] About feelings it can be said that "the essential content of feelings is the mapping of a particular body state; the substrate of feelings is the set of neural patterns that map the body state and from which a mental image of the body state can emerge. A feeling in essence is an idea — an idea of the body and, even more particularly, an idea of a certain aspect of the body, its interior, in certain circumstances. A feeling of emotion is an idea of the body when it is perturbed by the emoting process."[147] These ideas allow and even oblige us to distinguish strictly between memory traces and the emotional charges that accompany them.[148] The former correspond to neural patterns in the brain, the latter to body states (which are subsequently "perceived" by other neural patterns). This distinction is strictly observed in our theory.

Experiments show that long-term memory, if activated, can be "unbound" and "reconsolidated", i.e., updated and

---

[145] It goes without saying that this terminology is to some extent arbitrary, and that other ways of using these terms are possible; see, e.g., Scherer, 2005.

[146] Damasio, 2003: 28; see further Damasio, 2010: 108-129 ("Emotions and feelings").

[147] Damasio, 2003: 88.

[148] It also obliges us, of course, to distinguish between feelings and pleasure, defined above.

§2 Comparison with Neurological Findings

changed.[149] These findings can be read as a confirmation of the observation that the integration of memory traces *may* involve the modification of their reality assessments.

The effects of focused attention on brain functioning are clear from studies of its "default mode". It appears that certain brain areas are active when the person is at rest, but quieten down when the subject starts concentrating. Indeed, "the posterior cingulate cortex and adjacent precuneus can be posited as a tonically active region of the brain ... It would appear to be a default activity of the brain ... Only when successful task performance demands focused attention should such a broad information gathering activity be curtailed."[150] Indeed, meditating Zen Buddhists are found to deliberately switch off their default network.[151] This appears to be the neural correlate of the selective activation of memory traces at the expense of others which we had postulated as a characteristic feature of attention.

I conclude with some passages from an article about "Recent advances in understanding attention" which will be of use in the further elaboration of our theory (Taylor, 2003a):

> [V]arious experiments have shown that moving the focus of attention is achieved by a different brain network from that involved in processing the input being attended to. The regions exercising control of attention movement are

---

[149] Nader, 2003; Doyère et al., 2007; Ansermet & Magistretti, 2010: 147 ff.; Garner et al., 2012. The extent to which this phenomenon may be obstructed by the "indelibility of emotional memory" (LeDoux 1996: 250 ff.) is not known to me. Recent experiments suggest that memories can be dissociated from their emotional charge; this effect was brought about by administering propranolol (Brunet et al., 2008).

[150] Raichle et al., 2001: 681. See further *New Scientist* of 8 November 2008, pp. 28-31 ("Private life of the brain" by Douglas Fox).

[151] Pagnoni et al., 2008.

in parietal and prefrontal sites, while attended sites are in primary and secondary unimodal cortices in the various senses (and also in motor cortex for response). [...]

Attention control has been found to arise by two mechanisms, one by bottom-up signals from the occurrence of unexpected and strong inputs (such as a brief flash of light), the other by top-down control from some required goal (such as by the face of a friend being searched for in a crowd). It has been thought that bottom-up signals normally achieved attention capture; it is now appreciated that top-down control is usually in charge. Involuntary attention capture by distracting inputs occurs only if they have a property that a person is using to find a target. Thus there is a single control network deciding between the importance of desired (top-down) and unexpected (bottom-up) sites for attention.

These lines suggest that attention is essentially independent of the input and may therefore exist without being directed at any specific object. By emphasizing the "top-down" mechanism, they further suggest that attention can be used "at will", and is not an automatic reaction to certain inputs in every situation. We will make grateful use of these suggestions later on.[152]

---

[152] The possibility of "pure", i.e. essentially contentless, consciousness and attention without object has been argued for in various ways by a number of researchers. See, e.g., Forman, 1990; 1999; Taylor, 2002; 2003b; Lutz, Dunne & Davidson, 2007: 538; also Lachaux, 2011: 101. The article "Mysticism" in the online *Stanford Encyclopedia of Philosophy* (http://plato.stanford.edu/entries/mysticism/; latest revision Feb 9, 2010) provides a number of arguments for and against PCE (Pure Consciousness Events) (§ 5-6). Forman's own contribution to the volume edited by him, which concentrates on Meister Eckhart, emphasizes the rapture, and therefore the pleasurable nature, of the state of "pure consciousness" presumably experienced by this mystic. More on this in Appendix 2 of Part II, below.

It appears, then, that at least certain aspects of our psychological theory are compatible with recent findings in brain functioning. These findings do not prove that our theory is correct. It requires further elaboration in order to be testable. We also need to expand the theory to be able to use it in our present investigation. It would be unrealistic to assume that we can be guided in this by neuroscience alone. This does not imply that our theory and neuroscience now have to part ways. Quite on the contrary. We may hope that the elaborated theory will make predictions that can be tested by neuroscience, or at least raise issues that may suggest experimental inquiry. We will return to this topic at the end of this study.

§3 Psychotherapy and its Obstacles

Repressed trace units can interfere with the activity and wellbeing of the organism in the following way: Various forces affect the behavior of the organism simultaneously. The integrated reality assessment of the main unit guides its principal activity. The main unit has a certain quantity of bodily *tension* at its disposition. Outside the main unit, a number of isolated urges will seek expression guided by the undeveloped reality assessments of their trace units. These isolated urges may interfere with the proposed course of action of the main unit. In order to carry out the activities determined by *its* reality assessment, the main unit will have to counteract these urges. For this task, it uses the available tension. In most cases it may succeed, but occasionally an isolated urge will find expression, usually in a round-about manner.[153] The avoidance of repressed

---

[153] The resulting "slips" are the ones that occupied Freud in *The Psychopathology of Everyday Life* (1901; SE VI), and elsewhere.

memory traces and their accompanying urges will also affect behavior; the resulting behavior is not directly due to the repressed urge but to the memory, recorded in the main unit, of an earlier catastrophe that was barely avoided. The constant interplay of the activity of the main unit and the interference (direct or indirect) by repressed memory traces will, in many cases, lead to some kind of equilibrium. This equilibrium corresponds to what we call *character*.[154] In certain cases the interference by repressed urges is experienced as a source of discomfort. When the discomfort is severe, psychotherapeutic "cures" may be sought.

Psychotherapy, in some of its forms, tries to reduce the interference by methods that aim at integrating isolated units into the main unit. At first sight this looks like an almost impossible task. How can it be achieved?

Recall that repressed memory traces do not themselves affect the behavior of a person. Interference results from the emotional charges they "carry" in the form of associated urges. In order to integrate a repressed memory trace, it has to be activated ("remembered"). This is not possible without exciting the associated urge. This means that a therapy that aims at the integration of repressed memory traces has to gain access to their emotional charges.[155] However, an excited urge that is associated with a repressed memory trace will provoke a reaction from the main unit. To prevent expression of the repressed urge, the main unit will divert attention and in this way mo-

---

[154] More about this below.

[155] This has been accepted by psychoanalysis from its beginning; see Breuer and Freud, "Preliminary communication" (1893; SE II p. 6): "[...] we found, to our great surprise at first, that each individual hysterical symptom immediately and permanently disappeared when we had succeeded in bringing clearly to light the memory of the event by which it was provoked *and in arousing its accompanying affect* [...]" (my emphasis, JB)

§3 Psychotherapy and its Obstacles

bilize the tension it needs to counter that urge. Attention is diverted from the repressed memory trace, and the repression is likely to stay in place. Thus the therapeutic effort is unlikely to succeed. In spite of this, psychoanalysis and related forms of therapy claim certain successes. How can this be explained? What is missing in our depiction of the therapeutic process that might account for this?

What stands in the way of therapeutic success is both the strength of the repressed urge and the level of tension raised by the main unit to counter it. If both are strong, the therapeutic result is likely to be nil. However, in ideal therapeutic situations both are reduced. This can be seen as follows.

The main unit derives most of its (bodily) tension from its activated traces. These traces are activated by experiences (confrontation with objects or situations corresponding to the traces concerned) or by what we may call anticipating the future. An ideal therapeutic environment (the "couch" and other elements in Freudian therapy)[156] is a safe place that provides few stimuli that might activate memory traces. The absence of immediate danger combined with other factors allow the mind to lower its level of preparedness for possible future events. An important contributing factor to this "absence of immediate danger" is the tolerant and non-judgmental attitude of the therapist, the only person with whom the thera-

---

[156] Freud was aware of the importance of the therapeutic environment; see "On beginning the treatment" (1913; SE XII p. 133-34). Whether he succeeded in creating a safe place is another question; Weissweiler (2008: 264) speaks of a "Tradition der Couch und der schweren Eichenmöbel, der verstaubten Perserteppiche und mit Nippeskram überladenen Vitrinen" and of "Möbel ... die Angst machen". Physical and emotional relaxation and calmness are also essential in hypnotic techniques that can facilitate the process of recovery of traumatic memories while still allowing patients to feel in control; Maldonado & Spiegel, 1998: 78 f.

peutic experiences are shared. As a result, the standby level of (bodily) tension will be low. The degree of activation of the recovered traces will be low, too, because these traces are not activated by a renewed experience of the object or event that hold the promise of satisfaction. Quite on the contrary. In the therapeutic situation the traces are recovered in a round-about way (through slips, free associations, and so forth); they are not confronted head-on with the objects or events which constitute the more usual occasion for their activation. It is this relatively low-intensity situation which, in the best of circumstances, allows the integration of repressed traces into the main unit: The degree of excitation of the "dangerous" urges is so low that no threatening activity can result from them. The corresponding traces can therefore be made the object of awareness and hence integrated into the main unit.

Circumstances are not always ideal. The frequency of relapses (or simply failed therapies) indicates that our theory is in need of further refinement. One complication is that the contents of certain repressed memory traces can be known "intellectually", i.e., without putting the associated urge in a state of excitation.[157] Strictly speaking this description is not

---

[157] Freud repeatedly warned against the presentation of repressed fantasies to a patient not yet ready for it; see ibid. (1913; SE XII p. 140): "It is not difficult for a skilled analyst to read the patient's secret wishes plainly between the lines of his complaints and the story of his illness; but what a measure of self-complacency and thoughtlessness must be possessed by anyone who can, on the shortest acquaintance, inform a stranger who is entirely ignorant of all the tenets of analysis that he is attached to his mother by incestuous ties, that he harbours wishes for the death of his wife whom he appears to love, that he conceals an intention of betraying his superior, and so on! I have heard that there are analysts who plume themselves upon these kinds of lightning diagnoses and 'express' treatments, but I must warn everyone against following such examples. Behaviour of this sort will completely discredit oneself and the treatment in the patient's eyes and will arouse the most violent

§3 *Psychotherapy and its Obstacles*

correct. We know that the main unit has an almost limitless capacity for producing fantasies. It can also produce a fantasy that is identical with, or similar to, the images embodied in repressed traces. The main unit may resist producing such a fantasy to some extent, because this takes it dangerously close to repressed material (and may therefore activate it); yet with the help of some prodding by the therapist or by some other means it *can* produce it.[158] Patient and therapist may in this case believe that they have recovered a repressed image where in reality they have created a new one, one which is not and has never been repressed and carries no emotional charge. Such a "recovered" image will not and cannot have a therapeutic effect.

Recovering new fantasies rather than real memories is the opposite of a successful therapy. In both cases a repressed im-

---

opposition in him, whether one's guess has been true or not; indeed, the truer the guess the more violent will be the resistance. As a rule the therapeutic effect will be nil; but the deterring of the patient from analysis will be final." In 1906, he told Jung that the transference "provides the impulsion for comprehending and translating the unconscious; where it refuses to act, the patient does not take this trouble, or does not listen when we present the translation we have found." (Gay, 1988: 301)

[158] Cp. Freud, "The Unconscious" (1915; SE XIV pp. 175-176): "If we communicate to a patient some idea which he has at one time repressed but which we have discovered in him, our telling him makes at first no change in his mental condition. Above all, it does not remove the repression nor undo its effects, as might perhaps be expected from the fact that the previously unconscious idea has now become conscious. On the contrary, all that we shall achieve at first will be a fresh rejection of the repressed idea. But *now the patient has in actual fact the same idea in two forms in different places in his mental apparatus*; first, he has the conscious memory of the auditory trace of the idea, conveyed in what we told him; and secondly, he also has — as we know for certain — the unconscious memory of his experience as it was in its earlier form. Actually there is no lifting of the repression until the conscious idea, after the resistances have been overcome, has entered into connection with the unconscious memory-trace."

age has been "recovered": in the case of a successful therapy by making repressed material available to the main unit; in the case of fantasies by reconstructing (*ex hypothesi* correctly) the contents of the repressed traces. In this last case the repressed traces will remain as repressed as they were, and the associated urges will not become integrated into the general-purpose tension of the main unit.

There may be possibilities intermediate between these two extremes. The newly constructed fantasy may absorb some elements of the repressed memory trace and in this way take on a part of the associated emotional charge. Here the therapeutic cure will be only partial, a result which may appropriately describe the outcome of many psychotherapies.

There is a possible variant of the "intermediate" result of a psychotherapeutic cure. The memory that is believed to have been recovered, but which has in reality been newly created, may not correspond in its main points to the repressed material and yet incorporate some of its elements. In consequence it carries part of its emotional charge. We may assume that this variant is most often found in cases where the new fantasy has been created under the influence of theoretical *a priori* convictions of the therapist.

The situations so far considered start from the assumption that repressed memories can be recovered, at least in theory. This may be in need of clarification. As Solms and Turnbull point out, "On present knowledge, it seems reasonable to assume that *episodic* early infantile memories can never be recovered in any veridical sense. Our earliest experiences can only be *reconstructed*, through inferences derived from implicit (unconscious) semantic and procedural evidence. The same applies, to a lesser extent, to traumatic memories."[159] Even later

---

[159] Solms and Turnbull, 2002: 169. See also Turnbull and Solms, 2003. Note however Doidge, 2007: 381 (with references to Rovee-Collier,

§3 Psychotherapy and its Obstacles

in life, episodic memory appears to be the result of reconstruction: "We remember bits and pieces of our experiences and then reconstruct them to create plausible, but not necessarily accurate, accounts of what happened."[160] The constructed nature of episodic memory may constitute an additional obstacle to the attempt at diffusing repressed urges by bringing to light the associated memory traces. It does not, however, affect our theory, which does not require that the memory traces that guide human activity have to embody *episodic* memories.

Finally, let us consider the following hypothetical situation: A repressed memory has been truly recovered and the associated urge been diverted. However, the disappearance of this "threat" disrupts a delicately structured equilibrium. Recall that the whole psyche consists of a large number of memory traces, many of which are united in the main unit, while the others constitute a number of smaller units. The main unit and the other units keep each other in a delicate equilibrium in which the main unit uses free tension to counter the urges associated with those other units. Recall further that the reality assessment of the main unit is co-determined by the memory traces of the unpleasant experiences that accompanied the repression of various urges. A similar situation may prevail between the various trace units, especially those which can be activated by similar stimuli and yet seek expression in mutually incompatible ways. We may then assume that urges excited by "stronger" trace units reserve part of their tension for block-

---

1997; 1999): "We have underestimated the development of the explicit memory system for facts and events in infants because we usually test the explicit memory system by asking people questions, which are answered with words. Obviously preverbal infants cannot tell us whether they consciously recollect a particular event. But recently researchers have found ways to test infants by getting them to kick when they recognize the repetition of events, and they can remember them."

[160] Marshall, 2007: 39; see further Addis, Wong & Schacter, 2007.

ing urges excited by their "weaker" competitors, only to be blocked themselves by the tension at the disposal of the main unit. The resulting equilibrium between numerous units constitutes character, i.e., the configuration of stable traits which might be defined as the organization of inner conflicts.[161] This organization is in danger of collapsing when one of its constituent elements is removed. In concrete terms, a repressed trace unit which has so far been held in check by a neighboring trace unit that is now being integrated into the main unit may constitute a new threat to the equilibrium of the whole. These various factors are most easily and efficiently dealt with by renewed repression of the trace that comes up for integration, or rather: by interrupting and, as far as possible, undoing the integration that is taking place. This is possible because the recovered memory trace does not disappear through being integrated in the main unit. The memory trace is still there, ready to take on once again the emotional charge from which it was believed to have been freed. In such cases a successful psychotherapy can be undone by the tendency of the whole to resist disturbances to the equilibrium in place.[162]

---

[161] Cp. Freud, "Character and anal erotism" (1908; SE IX p. 175): "the permanent character-traits are either unchanged prolongations of the original instincts, or sublimations of those instincts, or reaction-formations against them."

[162] See in this connection what Freud said about the mechanisms of defence ("Analysis terminable and interminable", 1937; SE XXIII p. 237-38): "[They] become fixated in his ego. They become regular modes of reaction of his character, which are repeated throughout his life whenever a situation occurs that is similar to the original one. This turns them into infantilisms, and they share the fate of so many institutions which attempt to keep themselves in existence after the time of their usefulness has passed. [...] the defensive mechanisms directed against former danger recur in the treatment as *resistances* against recovery." In 1914 Freud stated ("Remembering, repeating and working-through"; SE XII p. 155): "I have often been asked to advise upon cases in which

§4 A "Complete Cure"

Our investigation so far has yielded a provisional outline of how the human mind functions. This outline is sketchy: it omits far more than it includes.[163] Nevertheless, it is precise enough to be useful for our present purposes. We will use it in discussing the claims of the early Buddhist texts which constitute our point of departure. For this purpose, we will address the question: What conditions will have to be fulfilled for a "complete psychotherapeutic cure" to be possible? This question does not so much concern the practical limits of psychotherapy as the limits imposed by our theory.

A complete psychotherapeutic cure would comprise the full integration of all repressed memory traces into the main unit. In ordinary circumstances such integration is prevented by the repression of certain memory traces, which involves the recruitment of tension by the main unit to counteract the discharge of the connected urges. These urges can sometimes be identified in a therapeutic context by discovering the memories to which they are attached. We have, however, seen that this method is hindered by the virtually limitless capacity of the main unit to construct fantasies, including those which correspond to repressed contents. Moreover, many urges are not associated with episodic memories. In these cases the search for memories cannot lead to the intended result. These diffi-

---

the doctor complained that he had pointed out his resistance to the patient and that nevertheless no change had set in; indeed, the resistance had become all the stronger, and the whole situation was more obscure than ever. [...] One must allow the patient time to become more conversant with this resistance with which he has now become acquainted, to *work through* it, to overcome it, by continuing, in defiance of it, the analytic work [...]"

[163] Some of its most serious shortcomings will be remedied below.

culties could be avoided if there were a more direct method to identify and confront urges, i.e. one which does not exclusively depend upon the reconstruction of repressed memories. We will come back to this issue below.

To reach a complete psychotherapeutic cure (supposing for the time being that such a thing can exist), at least three requirements will have to be fulfilled:

(i) To begin with, the level of (bodily) tension of the patient will have to be reduced to an absolute minimum. We have seen that psychotherapies often create therapeutic environments free from disturbing elements. A peaceful consulting room and a non-judgmental therapist are factors that contribute to the right "atmosphere" (not to speak of the transference, considered indispensable in psychoanalytic treatments). This environment is of necessity temporary, and will soon be replaced by the habitual environment of the patients. In between therapeutic sessions, they will have to go back to work, look after their family, or be involved in ordinary life in other ways. As a consequence, the level of tension which the main unit reserves for "anticipating the future" will not drop below a certain threshold. For our patients, too, life goes on.

There are, then, obvious limits to the degree to which the therapeutic environment can be optimized for patients who wish to continue their life in society. However, we are at present not bound by practical considerations of this kind. We are exploring the question what environment would be ideal for therapy to have optimal effect. The answer should now be clear. For optimal effect patients should not return to "ordinary life" in between therapeutic sessions; they should abstain from "anticipating the future" and avoid all situations which might in any way raise the standby level of bodily tension. This last requirement has a surprising but important consequence:

§4 A "Complete Cure"

for optimal effect the patient should be alone, even without a therapist. The presence of all other human beings, including that of a therapist, will inevitably raise the level of tension kept in reserve by the patient's main unit (which will in that case have to anticipate social interaction with those human beings).[164]

(ii) A second requirement is *a method of directly identifying urges* without having to know beforehand the repressed memories with which they are associated. It is true that such a method will also bring up repressed memories, for the specific manifestation of an urge is determined by the associated memory trace. However, since the identification concerns urges rather than memories, the creation of imitation memories by the main unit can no longer stand in the way of therapeutic success. The absence of episodic memories will also no longer constitute a problem.

Existing psychotherapies often identify repressed thought contents on the basis of partially successful attempts of the associated urges to express themselves. Freud's famous example of the President of the Lower House of Austrian Parliament can illustrate this.[165] This gentleman, being faced with the prospect of a particularly turbulent session, mistakenly pronounced it *closed* rather than opened. His mistake revealed his hidden wish to avoid the session that was about to take place. An outside observer depends on such slips and other communicable features to gain access to the repressed material of the

---

[164] Being alone, too, can produce anxiety in certain people. The Buddhist texts are aware of this; see Appendix 1 of Part II §6.

[165] Freud, *The Psychopathology of Everyday Life* (1901; SE VI p. 59). One might object that this example does not concern the expression of *repressed* thought contents, since we may assume that the President was well aware of his wish to avoid the session. The example may not, therefore, be perfect, but it must do for expository purposes.

patient. In the special case we are considering, the patient is alone with himself and is his own observer. He does not therefore depend on communicable features alone and may use signals that are accessible only to himself. He does not have to analyze the defenses that have let him down, but may look for direct, if private, manifestations of the repressed urges. For this to succeed, he may prevent them from finding any outlet, not by mustering supplementary tension to keep them repressed, but in an altogether different way. The following considerations will show how this can be done.

Consciousness does not accompany all the activities initiated by the main unit. Many routine activities take place without conscious awareness. These activities are not repressed (i.e., linked to repressed memories or images). We rather remain unaware of them because consciousness can "follow" only a limited number of activities at a time and leaves routine activities to an "automatic pilot".[166] This is the selective role of *attention*, which we discussed above. The "automatic pilot," which is responsible for activity carried out without awareness normally accomplishes its task satisfactorily. People can ride a bicycle without being aware of all the movements this involves; they can speak their language without consciously constructing each sentence; and so on. However, it is during these non-consciously performed (but non-repressed) activities that repressed urges are most likely to succeed in finding expression. To take the example of the President of the Lower House of Austrian Parliament, referred to above, his slip (a "Freudian slip") gave expression to the secret and unavowed wish to avoid this session. It occurred in the middle of his opening remarks, a speech activity which is normally left at least in part to the "automatic pilot". This illustration shows how repressed

---

[166] Automaticity is particularly prominent in social interaction. For a survey of this phenomenon, see Bargh, 2007.

§4 A "Complete Cure"

urges use non-conscious but unrepressed activities to push for discharge. It also suggests that, had the President of the Lower House of Parliament decided to pronounce his words slowly and consciously, paying full attention to each and every one of them, he would not then have made his slip. This may reflect a general rule. Even routine activities, if and when carried out with full awareness, do not provide opportunities for repressed urges to express themselves.[167]

Repressed urges, then, find outlets in the middle of automated activities, i.e., activities that are not conscious even though they are not connected with repressed material. Automated activities can be reduced to a minimum or even completely avoided by someone who applies awareness to all of his actions. It requires that all activity be reduced to a minimum, and that what remains be slowed down to the extent possible.[168] This can be achieved, for example, by sitting down and directing one's attention at the few activities that remain, such as breathing. This may not be a very practical course of action for patients who have jobs and other responsibilities in society, but the hypothetical patient we are considering has already done away with all this. Nothing therefore prevents us from pursuing our reflections.

---

[167] One is reminded of the surgeon with Tourette's syndrome described by Oliver Sacks (1995: 73 ff.), whose tics and iterations are only interrupted by periods of intense attention, which include operating upon patients and flying an airplane; and of Nick Van Bloss, a pianist with severe Tourette's syndrome, whose tics stop the moment he begins to play (*The Observer*, 12 April 2009). Equally interesting is the case of patients with obsessive compulsive disorder described by Schwartz & Begley (2002, chapter two); Buddhism-inspired mindful awareness allowed these patients to avoid being overwhelmed by their obsessions, and in due course to refocus their attention on other things. The same technique appears to be effective against Tourette's syndrome and depression (chapter seven).

[168] On the "sluggishness of consciousness", see Wegner, 2002: 56 f.

Our hypothetical patient, having completely given up all forms of anticipating the future and having parted ways with all human beings including his therapist, has now reduced his activities to the few he can be fully aware of. What happens to his repressed urges? In an ideal environment, one that provides no stimuli whatsoever (and in which our patient somehow succeeds in directing his fantasy life away from "dangerous" thoughts), we must assume that these urges will not be excited. But they will not disappear either. In new situations where stimuli are again present the repressed urges will reappear, and little or no therapeutic progress will have been made. Urges, however, are not only excited by external stimuli. Traces can be activated by consciously directed fantasies; the associated urges will then be put in a state of excitation. We had occasion to point out that the states of excited urges are bodily states, *emotions* in the terminology of Damasio. These bodily states will be mapped and the result of this mapping will be *feelings*. Feelings are the unmistakable signs that allow our patient to identify his urges, including repressed urges. Our patient may experiment upon himself by exploring which fantasies evoke which feelings. The resulting knowledge will be useful at a later stage. For the time being he has no instrument to overcome the repression. He does, however, have a way to find out the "location" of repressed urges.

I will argue below, on the basis of the evidence of our early Buddhist texts, that there is an instrument to overcome repression. At this point it is sufficient to assume its existence, if only for argument's sake. Granting this, we have to address the question: What further requirement may there be to accomplish a complete psychotherapeutic cure? There is one indeed: the third item on our list.

§4 A "Complete Cure"

(iii) As was explained above, incomplete psychotherapeutic cures are in danger of being of short duration. They disturb the equilibrium that exists between the different entities that make up the mind, i.e., the main unit and other (repressed) trace units. This danger threatens our hypothetical patient, and the extraordinary measures he has taken so far do not immunize him from it. Relapse is possible, or even likely, until the mind in its entirety has been dealt with. Any remaining repressed trace units may push the mind back into its former equilibrium. Unmodified warning signals in the main unit against "dangerous" (i.e., repressed) thought contents may do the same.[169] As a result, a complete psychotherapeutic cure will have to be brought about in as short a time as possible, preferably in *one single therapeutic session*. In this way a new equilibrium will be established which is more stable than the earlier one. In this new equilibrium no forces remain which could push the mind back into an earlier state.

The above speculations about a complete psychotherapeutic cure have called into existence a hypothetical patient capable of bringing it about. This patient differs in numerous ways from the average patient undergoing psychotherapy. He abandons his therapist and all other living company. He discards all projects for the future definitively. He reduces his activity to only such deeds as he can carry out with full awareness. And then, with all these preliminaries successfully in place, he brings about his complete psychotherapeutic cure in one single session.

---

[169] In view of the fact that formerly charged trace units have a tendency to take on those emotional charges once again, it is conceivable that it will be necessary, not just to allow repressed memories access to consciousness, but also to use this consciousness to "reconsolidate" them, i.e., change them.

Needless to say, this description does not fit any patients known to psychotherapists. It does, however, fit the ideal Buddhist practitioner depicted in the early texts.[170] These texts also suggest that the instrument which can overcome repression is *absorption°*.[171] We will see below that absorption is a particularly intensive form of concentration which is combined with optimally reduced bodily tension.[172] Absorption plays a role at levels two, three and four of the four levels of meditation that are usually distinguished in the Buddhist texts. At the most advanced level, the fourth, the ideal Buddhist practitioner brings about the transformation which, as will be argued below, corresponds to our complete psychotherapeutic cure.

How does absorption fit into the theory of the human mind constructed above? Absorption is intense concentration. This, in its turn, is a form of attention. Attention can be directed at, or away from sensory input and memory traces. It is impor-

---

[170] See Appendix 1 of Part II §1, §2, §4, §5. The early Buddhist tradition is unanimous in its claim that the Buddha reached his goal at the end of one single session, which lasted one night.

[171] See Appendix 1 of Part II §1, with my commentary.

[172] Absorption is a form of "effortless attention" (Bruya, 2010); see esp. Dormashev, 2010: 310 f. Cp. Austin, 1998: 71: "during rare moments, [...] meditators may [...] make a major shift into an extraordinarily different mode. It is a shift that carries the properties of clarity, persistence, and concentration far beyond their ordinary limits. Now, as attention transforms itself, [...] it reaches that state called *absorption*. [...] Absorptions convey the sense of being held, transfixed, and riveted. It is a process during which extra, concentrated energy involuntarily infuses the act of attention." See further Austin, 2006: 313 ff. It is legitimate to ask whether the combination of intense concentration (conceivably resulting from terror) with drop of blood pressure and reduced bodily tension explains the so-called "near-death experiences" frequently recorded in the literature, which in that case may have to be explained in terms of deep absorption. Indeed, Blanke & Dieguez (2009: 314, with references to further literature) point out that "[p]eople with [near-death experience] ... score higher than control subjects on absorption ...".

§4 A "Complete Cure"

tant to note that for attention to be directed at some things it will be *withdrawn* from others.[173] Attention withdrawn from memory traces ensures that these will not be activated (or will be less activated). When attention is withdrawn from sensory input, it prevents this input from activating memory traces. Either way no urges will be excited.

This leaves the question: What is the absorption referred to in the Buddhist texts directed *at*? The answer is that absorption can but is not obliged to have an object. Like attention, of which it is a more intense variant, absorption can occur without being directed at anything in particular. The concentration of a fearful person who finds him- or herself in a dark and isolated place is not initially directed at anything in particular.[174] A suspect sound or a moving shadow may give it a focus. This shows that it did not have one before. It appears indeed that the faculty of attention in humans can be used without being wholly directed at any specific object. Some of the neurological literature reviewed above supports this.[175]

How does absorption overcome repression? Imagine that our patient has successfully entered into a state of absorption. As long as it lasts, no memory traces will be activated and no urges will be excited. (An exception may have to be made for the memory traces and associated urges to which our patient decides to direct his attention (or part of it).)[176] Assuming

---

[173] Cf. Part I §2, above.

[174] This is at the same time an example of a conscious state that is not intentional in the philosophical sense: "An example of a conscious state that is not intentional is the sense of anxiety that one sometimes gets when one is not anxious about anything in particular but just has a feeling of anxiousness" (Searle, 2004: 97).

[175] See note 152, above.

[176] A further exception may have to be made for "independent" urges such as hunger. The Buddhist texts insist that these urges must be appeased as far as possible before a successful "treatment" can be under-

that our patient has reduced the standby level of his bodily tension to an absolute minimum, he now finds himself in an ideal situation to explore his urges and the memories to which they are attached. Urges will announce themselves as feelings if and when the mind, in this concentrated state, imagines an object or event related to them and thus activates the relevant trace unit. The urges will announce themselves in the usual manner (though weakly) by bringing about the appropriate bodily states (the emotions). These in their turn will be perceived as feelings in the mind. The low degree of excitation of the urge, resulting from the low degree of activation of the corresponding memory trace, deprives it of all danger. It cannot manifest itself, for example in bodily activity. The minimal level of standby bodily tension ensures that the conditions for repression are not fulfilled. As a result, the trace unit can be integrated into the main unit, and the associated urge diffused.

The situation so far described may be compared to a successful therapeutic session. But where the psychotherapy stops (at least for that day), our ideal patient continues. He repeats the process with respect to *all* of his urges, one after the other. He discovers his urges with the help of his feelings, because feelings are indicators of bodily emotions. Once all of the remaining urges have been dealt with, the result will be the complete psychotherapeutic cure which we set out to explore.

---

taken. See Appendix 1 of Part II §3.

§5 The Theory Adapted

At this point we must turn to the question: What must human psychology be like for a complete psychotherapeutic cure to be possible?

Freud held that conflict is inherent in the human mind.[177] If this were true, no amount of therapy would ever be able to resolve all conflicts. Our reading of the Buddhist texts leads to a different view. If we assume with those texts that a complete therapeutic cure is possible, conflict cannot be inherent in the human mind. Let us consider the consequences of this position.

Freud postulated the existence of some mutually opposed drives or instincts which he thought are behind the activities

---

[177] In his "The psycho-analytic view of psychogenic disturbance of vision" (1910; SE XI p. 214), for example, Freud speaks of "the undeniable opposition between the instincts which subserve sexuality, the attainment of sexual pleasure, and those other instincts, which have as their aim the self-preservation of the individual — the ego-instincts." Later on, in *Beyond the Pleasure Principle* (1920; SE XVIII pp. 3-64), the Death instinct is posited as being in fundamental and irreducible opposition to the Life instinct; in *Civilization and its Discontents* (1930; SE XXI pp. 59-145) it is in conflict with Eros. A curious passage in this last book (SE XXI pp. 78-79) plays with the idea that suffering may be reduced or even eliminated by "killing off the instincts": "Just as a satisfaction of instinct spells happiness for us, so severe suffering is caused us if the external world lets us starve, if it refuses to state our needs. One may therefore hope to be freed from a part of one's sufferings by influencing the instinctual impulses. This type of defence against suffering is no longer brought to bear on the sensory apparatus; it seeks to master the internal sources of our needs. The extreme form of this is brought about by killing off the instincts, as is prescribed by the worldly wisdom of the East and practised by Yoga. If it succeeds, then the subject has, it is true, given up all other activities as well — he has sacrificed his life; and, by another path, he has once more only achieved the happiness of quietness."

of the mind. Leaving *his* ideas aside, it will be useful to recall that *our* theory distinguishes two kinds of urges.[178]

There are, on the one hand, the "independent" urges, exemplified by hunger. These urges can "announce" their excitation on their own by activating the associated memory traces. Hunger will make itself felt whether or not we see, smell or think about food. On the other hand, there are urges that cannot by themselves activate memory traces and are therefore only "known" when some extraneous factor activates their memory traces. These are the "dependent" urges, for their nature depends on the memory traces with which they are associated. They are excited when the organism is confronted with an object or event which on an earlier occasion accompanied discharge. This confrontation can be external (through perception) or internal (through thought or imagination). If no such confrontation takes place, urges of this kind will remain "dormant". Unlike independent urges, the nature of dependent urges is entirely determined by the past experiences of the individual concerned.

This distinction between two kinds of urges is significant. In the case of hunger and other independent urges, one may assume that we have some idea as to their real nature. The urge of hunger requires food to find its discharge, no matter the memory traces with which it may be associated in any particular individual. We assume that we know the nature of hunger, and we may be right in this.[179] However, no such assumption

---

[178] Panksepp (1998: 168) pleads for an even more drastic reduction: "In the old psychological terminology, the bodily need detection systems of the brain were thought to generate 'drives', but the use of that concept has diminished as we have come to realize that such a broad abstract *intervening variable* cannot be credibly linked to unitary brain processes." About pleasure the same author states (p. 184): "Perhaps many stimuli can converge on a single pleasure system."

[179] Note that hunger in itself does not "aim" at food, unless memory

§5 The Theory Adapted

is justified in the case of urges that are only known through their associated memory traces. These memory traces provide the urges with an "aim", but this aim is entirely dependent upon earlier experiences of satisfaction. It would therefore be a mistake to depict these urges anthropomorphically as drives that pursue their own specific aims irrespective of the memory traces with which they have become associated. We are thus confronted with the question: What are the conditions for discharge of dependent urges? What is their real nature?

This question inevitably lead us to the topic of sexuality. Sexuality presents itself in many different forms and pursues many different objects and aims. Therefore it is difficult to determine its nature. The form it takes in an adult is largely determined by earlier experiences, many of them belonging to childhood. It is tempting to think of the development of sexuality in an individual in "Darwinian" terms: Out of the innumerable ways in which this urge can be satisfied, those which have met with early experiences of satisfaction are selected. The adult is no longer able to choose out of the innumerable possibilities that were open in childhood, for the urge is now indissociably connected with a relatively limited number of memory traces.

Sexuality is entitled to special attention in this study since *getting rid of thirst*, which is dealt with in the third Noble Truth of the early Buddhist texts, includes getting rid of sexual desire. Given that the form which sexuality takes is (co-)determined by the specific memory traces of satisfaction in each individual, we wish to know what all these experiences of satisfaction have in common.

We find ourselves face to face with the question in what the sexual urge consists (supposing for the time being that there is such a thing). In contradistinction to hunger, it would be a mistake to assume that this urge really looks for satisfaction in

---

traces have provided it with that aim.

one specific way, say, in "normal" adult heterosexual activity. The many ways in which this urge expresses itself in different people suggests something quite different, viz., that there are many ways in which this urge can find discharge. Children, to use the Freudian expression, are "polymorphously perverse": "a disposition to perversions is an original and universal disposition of the human sexual instinct and [...] normal sexual behaviour is developed out of it as a result of organic changes and psychical inhibitions occurring in the course of maturation".[180]

What, then, is the sexual urge? What do all the ways in which it finds discharge, whether perverse or otherwise, have in common? Freud seemed to think that they have nothing in common: "the sexual instinct itself must be something put together from various factors, and [...] in the perversions it falls apart, as it were, into its components. [...] [T]he sexual instinct of adults arises from a combination of a number of impulses of childhood into a unity, an impulsion with a single aim."[181]

How does sexual satisfaction take place in children? Freud proposed the following answer:[182]

> Satisfaction arises first and foremost from the appropriate sensory excitation of what we have described as erotogenic zones. It seems probable that any part of the skin and any sense-organ — probably, indeed, *any* organ — can function as an erotogenic zone, though there are some particularly marked erotogenic zones whose excitation would seem to be secured from the very first by certain

---

[180] Freud, in the "Summary" of his *Three Essays on the Theory of Sexuality* (1905; SE VII p. 231).

[181] Ibid. (SE VII p. 231-232). On October 9, 1918, Freud wrote to his friend Oskar Pfister: "Aber mit der Sexualtheorie? Was fällt Ihnen denn ein, die Zerlegung des Sexualtriebes in Partialtriebe zu bestreiten, wozu die Analyse uns jeden Tag nötigt?" (Freud & Meng, 1963: 62)

[182] Ibid. (SE VII p. 232-233).

§5 The Theory Adapted

organic contrivances. It further appears that sexual excitation arises as a byproduct, as it were, of a large number of processes that occur in the organism, as soon as they reach a certain degree of intensity, and most especially of any relatively powerful emotion, even though it is of a distressing nature.

One can forgive Freud for not finding much that these different sources of sexual satisfaction have in common.[183] He continued saying: "The excitations from all these sources are not yet combined; but each follows its own separate aim, which is merely the attainment of a certain sort of pleasure." And he concluded his book on sexuality with the words:[184]

> The unsatisfactory conclusion [...] that emerges from these investigations of the disturbances of sexual life is that we know far too little of the biological processes constituting the essence of sexuality to be able to construct from our fragmentary information a theory adequate to the understanding alike of normal and of pathological conditions.

Freud used here the expression *essence of sexuality*, as if he still believed that there should be something that unites these "biological processes".[185] But clearly he did not know what it was. And yet, the list of sources of infantile sexuality which he pro-

---

[183] In "Instincts and their vicissitudes" (1915; SE XIV pp. 109-140) Freud states, similarly, that "the sexual instincts [...] are numerous, emanate from a great variety of organic sources, act in the first instance independently of one another and only achieve a more or less complete synthesis at a late stage."

[184] SE VII p. 243.

[185] He also refers to these as "various factors" and "components", as well as "a number of impulses".

vided in the same book contains one item that may contain a key to the answer. Consider the following passage:[186]

> Finally, it is an unmistakable fact that *concentration of the attention* upon an intellectual task and intellectual strain in general produce a concomitant sexual excitation in many young people as well as adults.

At first sight this is a very strange item in the list. What could an intellectual task or an intellectual strain have in common with more recognizable forms of sexual activity?[187] A closer look reveals that they do have something in common, namely, *concentration of the attention*. This is arguably the *only* feature which *all* sources of sexual satisfaction have in common. Note in this connection that the passage quoted above contains the phrase: "sexual excitation arises as a byproduct, as it were, of a large number of processes that occur in the organism, *as soon as they reach a certain degree of intensity*" (my emphasis). Concentrated attention appears to be inseparable from sexual excitation.

Freud did not notice this, no doubt because *concentration* and *attention* play no important role in his psychology. This is a pity, for we have already discovered that these notions are vital if we wish to make psychological sense of the early Buddhist texts. We now see that these same notions may help us to arrive at a deeper understanding of the nature of certain urges.

In brief, the thesis presented here is as follows. Certain experiences are undergone in the specific states of concentration

---

[186] Ibid. (SE VII p. 204); my emphasis.

[187] Cp. Cioffi's (1998: 48) scathing remarks about the sexual nature of abstract ideas: "it is difficult to imagine what associations to proportional representation, the single tax, states rights, or the axiom of extensionality could warrant their being recognised as disguised manifestations of sexual impulses." In the thesis to be presented here there is no need for such associations.

§5 The Theory Adapted

which we call *absorption*. Absorption is experienced as pleasurable, for reasons that will be explained below.[188] Sexuality is pleasurable because, and to the extent that, it is experienced in a state of absorption.[189]

It must here be observed that the memory trace produced by absorption does not primarily record the state of absorption but rather the object or event experienced in this state.[190] This object or event will activate the memory trace on future occasions. The activated memory trace aims the accompanying urge toward a renewed experience of this object or event rather than toward the more immediate cause of the initial pleasure, namely, the state of absorption. The search for pleasure (whether sexual or other) will henceforth be guided by such memory traces.

Our hypothetical patient, who has undergone a complete psychotherapeutic cure, will have integrated all of his urges. His reality assessment, moreover, will "know" that the state of absorption rather than the renewed experience of objects or events provides satisfaction. This cannot fail to affect his behavior. We will discuss this below. First we have to answer two questions: Why is absorption experienced as pleasurable? And how does our ideal patient gain satisfaction through absorption, whereas most ordinary people do not succeed in doing so? To answer these questions, we have to dedicate more thought to absorption.

---

[188] It is important to keep in mind that not all states of concentration are experienced as pleasurable; see below.

[189] The more specifically *sexual* aspect of sexual pleasure will be discussed below.

[190] Memory does more to distort the past experience: "What we learn from the past is to maximize the qualities of our future memories, not necessarily of our future experience." (Kahneman, 2011: 381). The memory of contextual details depends on the lateral prefrontal cortex; its maturation does not occur until early adulthood (Ofen et al., 2007).

§6 The Theory Refined

The question why concentration may (but does not have to) be experienced as pleasurable is easy to answer in terms of our theory. We have postulated that the fundamental principle of mental activity is the "search" for reduced bodily tension. Events that bring this about are experienced as pleasurable while those that raise bodily tension are experienced as unpleasurable. There are various ways in which bodily tension can be reduced. Concentration is one of them.

We know that attention implies relative deactivation of certain memory traces. Deactivation of memory traces means reduced excitation of the associated urges. If this leads to a reduced *overall* level of bodily tension (which is not always the case), the resulting experience will be pleasurable. *Absorption* is the term we reserve for intense concentration accompanied by a reduced overall level of bodily tension.

Our theory also explains why all concentration is not experienced as pleasurable. It is true that concentration may reduce the level of bodily tension connected with deactivated memory traces. However, it increases the level of excitation of the urges associated with the memory traces that *are being* selected. These selected traces may excite their associated urges so strongly that the result is an overall rise in the level of bodily tension. Moreover, the overall level of bodily tension must often be increased to provide enough extra tension for concentration to be possible.

This last observation is in agreement with common experience. There are tasks that require concentration yet are far from pleasurable. In such cases it is likely that the task at hand is not sufficiently inspiring to facilitate the withdrawal of attention from competing concerns. Additional bodily tension

§6 *The Theory Refined*

is then recruited to make concentration possible. The overall level of bodily tension will not be lower but rather higher than before. The attention mustered in such situations is most commonly due to an act of will.

Common experience also teaches us that the concentration that accompanies dangerous and frightening situations is not pleasurable. In such cases the state of concentration is not due to an act of will but rather evoked by an involuntary assessment of the situation. These states of concentration, too, are accompanied by a general mobilization of extra bodily tension. The overall result is that the total amount of bodily tension rises rather than falls — hence the displeasure.[191]

Other experiences from daily life illustrate the agreeable effects that certain states of concentration can have. Music lovers experience pleasure when they listen to their favorite composer in an appropriate setting. The reasons why the music is capable of absorbing a large part of their attention are no doubt connected with their personal life history. The result of this absorption is that the excitation of unconnected urges will be reduced. In balance there will be an overall reduction of bodily tension, so that the net result will be pleasure.[192] The pleasure

---

[191] Practitioners of high-risk sports, amateurs of horror films, and others with similar inclinations fall in a separate category; see below.

[192] Interestingly, for some of Oliver Sacks's patients, music-induced pleasure culminates in epileptic seizures. So G. G.: "His seizures start with or are preceded by a special state of intense, involuntary, almost forced attention or listening. In this already altered state, the music seems to grow more intense, to swell, to take possession of him, and at this point he cannot stop the process, cannot turn off the music or walk away from it. Beyond this point he retains no consciousness or memory, though various epileptic automatisms, like gasping and lipsmacking, ensue." Another patient, Silvia N., was freed from similar seizures through surgical intervention. "Mrs. N. is delighted, of course, by her cure. But she is occasionally nostalgic, too, for some of her epileptic experiences — like the 'gates of heaven', which seemed to take her to a place unlike

will be most exquisite if the surroundings ask for minimal attention. Even the most beautiful music can become a source of displeasure if listened to, or rather heard, in demanding circumstances.[193]

In certain stressful occupations such as high-risk sports or fairground joyrides, the net result may still be pleasure. In such cases the amount of attention absorbed by the situation is so great that little remains for other concerns. The release of tension following the most threatening episodes accounts for the resultant experience of pleasure. In these cases the concentration of attention is not normally due to an act of will.

Recall now that the form of concentration referred to in the early Buddhist texts is different from the one known from daily experience. To begin with, it does not use bodily tension specially generated for this purpose. Rather, it uses the (already lowered) standby level of bodily tension. The result is the kind of concentration we call absorption.

The absorption referred to in the Buddhist texts is not directed at an object. The texts use a special expression: "signless-absorption-of-mind"°. Our theory predicts that absorption will *always* give rise to pleasure if it is not directed at an object, for such absorption *only* reduces bodily tension and does not excite any urges.

We turn to the next question: If absorption brings pleasure without effort (no bodily tension needs to be generated to make it possible), why should anyone bother to search for

---

anything she had ever experienced before." (Sacks, 2007: 27, 29). On the potentially religious dimension of music, see note 38, above. On the sometimes orgasmic nature of epilectic seizures, see Komisaruk, Beyer-Flores & Whipple, 2008: 103. For the role of expectation in listening to music, see Huron, 2006.

[193] This analysis is not likely to be valid without adjustment for all the different ways in which people listen to music, or for all types of music.

§6 The Theory Refined

pleasure in any other way? Why is this most efficient method to obtain satisfaction systematically ignored?

The two answers to this question complement each other. The first one is straightforward: Absorption does not figure prominently in memory traces.[194] Memory traces record primarily objects and events that are associated with experiences of satisfaction, not states of absorption. Since the kind of absorption we are concerned with is not associated with any objects or events, it has no "sign" by which it might be remembered. (This is no doubt the reason why it is called "signless-absorption-of-mind"° in the early Buddhist texts). Certain events — music, high-risk sports, etc. — induce states of intense attention; "signless" absorption differs from them in that it does not come about on its own but is voluntarily evoked.

The second answer, the complement of the first, is as follows. It is only after childhood that people may obtain enough knowledge of their own mind to be able to explore its possibilities.[195] Meanwhile, the available bodily tension has been taken up by numerous memory traces that have accumulated over the years and by actual concerns ("anticipations of the future"). These factors resist attempts at withdrawal of attention so that concentration becomes difficult. Only the concentration that focuses on matters privileged by those memory traces and actual concerns will not be resisted (or will be less resisted). Indeed, most forms of voluntary concentration depend on a prior increase in bodily tension. They are therefore experienced as unpleasurable. The "royal road" to pleasure through voluntary absorption, without prior increase in bodily tension,

---

[194] See below for a more precise statement.

[195] See note 190, above. Note that victims of traumatic experiences, including children, may accidentally "find this place" (i.e., a state of absorption) as a way to escape from their torment; Maldonado & Spiegel, 1998, esp. p. 64.

is closed off. One can only gain access to it through a special stratagem. The preparatory practices described in the Buddhist texts are to be understood as such a stratagem. They make access to pleasure through "signless absorption" possible.[196]

We can reformulate the preceding paragraphs as follows. Our point of departure is the presupposition that a diffuse, all-purpose bodily tension accompanies normal states of wakefulness.[197] The level of this diffuse tension may vary. Absorption can reduce it. Most "normal" forms of concentration increase it. Accepting the presence of such a diffuse, all-purpose bodily tension is not problematic in terms of our theory. In an earlier chapter we had to assume its existence in order to explain that the main unit has tension available to resist repressed urges. Much of this tension may result from the simultaneous activation of numerous distinct memory traces. Its employment is guided by the main unit's reality assessment. It can thus be used in the immediate service of a goal pursued at any particular moment by the main unit. It can also be used to resist repressed urges. No matter what the details may be, this diffuse general-purpose tension exists. Lowering its level will give rise to pleasure. Certain states of concentration, most notably the one we call absorption, can play a role in this. In the course of an individual's growth and development, ever more bodily

---

[196] Many so-called mystics have and had access to absorption, and left testimonies as to the pleasure that accompanies it; see Appendix 2 of Part II, below.

[197] Cp. Freud in *The Ego and the Id* (1923; SE XIX p. 44): "It will be noticed [...] that [...] we have tacitly made [an] assumption which deserves to be stated explicitly. We have reckoned as though there existed in the mind — whether in the ego or in the id — a displaceable energy, which, indifferent in itself, can be added to a qualitatively differentiated erotic or destructive impulse, and augment its total cathexis. Without assuming the existence of a displaceable energy of this kind we can make no headway." Freud's *energy* corresponds to our *tension*.

§6 The Theory Refined

tension is bound up with specific tasks. As a result, concentration in a normal adult can draw upon a mere fraction of the bodily tension that is present. Thus, concentration will usually have to marshal additional bodily tension to be at all possible. The pleasurable effect of voluntary concentration will thus be much reduced. Indeed, it may disappear altogether, or become unpleasure. The potential link between specific states of concentration and pleasure remains therefore unknown to most people. And yet, if concentration succeeds in reducing the overall level of bodily tension, it will be experienced as pleasure.

Many situations, then, are pleasurable because we experience them in a state of absorption (more precisely: on account of the drop in bodily tension that results from absorption). The source of pleasure in these cases is the state of absorption and not those particular situations themselves. This means that many of the aims we pursue in life, guided as we are by our memory traces, are fundamentally *mis*-guided.[198] We strive to repeat situations connected with earlier experiences of satisfaction where these situations were not the real cause of satisfaction. In extreme cases this may associate pleasure with otherwise painful or dangerous situations. This explains the fact (a fact which puzzled Freud) that sexuality can find expression in many different ways, some of them painful.[199]

---

[198] Cp. Schooler & Mauss, 2010: 251: "[W]hy, if flow states are so positive, do people not seek them out more reliably. ... the answer to this question seems relatively straightforward. People fail to seek out flow experiences because they lack meta-awareness about the fact that such experiences are the most positive." For more on *flow*, see Appendix 2 of Part II, below.

[199] For Freud's own (more recent) attempt to solve the riddle of the association of pleasure with pain, see his "The economic problem of masochism" (1924; SE XIX pp. 155-170).

The Buddhist texts present absorption as one of two sources of pleasure. The first stage-of-meditation° is described as manifesting "rapture and pleasure born of seclusion°", while the second has "rapture and pleasure born of absorption".[200] We know that reduction of bodily tension is the real source of pleasure; it underlies all its manifestations. The Buddhist "rapture and pleasure born of seclusion°" is due to a reduction of tension unaccompanied by absorption: it is brought about by avoiding situations that activate memory traces. The second stage-of-meditation° reduces bodily tension further through absorption. In this way it adds to the "rapture and pleasure" of the person concerned.

The Buddhist texts distinguish between "sensual pleasures" and "pleasure that has nothing to do with sensual pleasures and unwholesome states".[201] It is easy to understand this difference in terms of our theory. "Sensual pleasures" are pleasures obtained through the intermediary of activated memory traces. "Pleasure that has nothing to do with sensual pleasures and unwholesome states" is the pleasure derived directly from seclusion and absorption.

The importance of the practices that precede absorption in the Buddhist texts will now be clear. Mindfulness° and seclusion, in particular, bring down bodily tension (and in this way lead to "rapture and pleasure born of seclusion"). Without them, concentration can only minimally deactivate the memory traces from which attention is withdrawn and absorption will not be possible. Once the field has been prepared by the practice of mindfulness and seclusion, these traces can be deactivated. "Rapture and pleasure born of absorption" can then be attained.

---

[200] Appendix 1 of Part II §1(10-11).
[201] E.g. Appendix 1 of Part II §3.

§7 *Sexuality and Sublimation*

Let us return to our ideal patient. He has used his feelings (which are signs of bodily states) to identify the "location" of his urges, including his repressed urges. Absorption is the way to overcome repression. Overcoming repression normally means: integrating the associated memory trace into the main unit. To our ideal patient the process presents itself differently. Memory traces retain features of situations that accompanied satisfaction. They guide their associated urges toward an attempted repetition of those situations. Our ideal patient knows that these memory traces are fundamentally "mistaken". However, recalled memories can be modified; they can be corrected. Our ideal patient can carry out the corrections by recalling these memories while in a state of absorption. In this state his level of bodily tension will be extremely low. The memory traces will now "recognize" that the remembered pleasure was due to the lowering of bodily tension; even greater pleasure can be obtained by lowering bodily tension further by means of absorption. Integration of the modified memory trace meets with no opposition: being modified, it will not be accompanied by the same urge.

§7 Sexuality and Sublimation

The explanation proposed here of certain urges (the "dependent" urges) is meant to throw light on a variety of behaviors, among these sexual behavior. The present theory explains how and why sexual behavior can take many different forms. It is less clear why it should cover sexual behavior in the narrow sense. Why should sexual intercourse be the more or less regular outcome of the search for reduced bodily tension?

The human mind is not a blank slate, nor was it one at birth or conception.[202] Hereditary factors are involved in its formation. These hereditary factors will push certain developments in one direction rather than another, with the result that specific individuals are programmed to have inclinations of one kind rather than another. This much must be granted, and we cannot but hope that further research will tell us more about the mechanisms set in motion by these constitutional factors.[203]

---

[202] See on this Pinker, 2002; Plotkin, 2007.

[203] Many evolutionary psychologists adhere to the "massive modularity thesis", in which "our cognitive architecture resembles a confederation of hundreds or thousands of functionally dedicated computers (often called modules)" (Tooby & Cosmides, 1995: xiii); these modules "embody 'innate knowledge' about the problem-relevant parts of the world" (Tooby & Cosmides, 1992: 59). This thesis is inconsistent with what we now know about the formation of the brain; Buller, 2005: 127 ff. See further Ramachandran, 2012: 362: "... MVF [mirror visual feedback] ... radically changes our theoretical views on brain function. The "old" view, based on the MIT model, postulates that the brain consists of a number of hierarchically organised, largely isolated "modules" (e.g., for vision and touch). Each module performs some computation on the input, makes some aspect of the information explicit, and passes it on to the next and so on. The modules are hard-wired at birth and don't talk much to each other. Our work with MVF (causing "paralysed hands" to move painlessly) and "remapping" of S1 in amputees and the work of Candy McCabe, Pat Wall, Peter Halligan, M. Sumitani, Alvaro Pascual-Leone, Mike Merzenich, John Kaas, and others in the last decade suggest a radical revision of our views on brain function; that it isn't a serial hierarchical bucket brigade. Each module, far from being hardwired, is in a constant state of dynamic equilibrium with the environment it is immersed in (e.g., deafferentation leads to the rapid emergence of referred sensations accompanying changes in brain topography) — changing connections online in response to changing environmental needs. And instead of being insulated, the modules interact profoundly with each other (MVF psychophysics and brain imaging); interact back and forth with the skin, muscles and bones (as demonstrated using MVF in CRPS [complex regional pain syndrome]); and indeed, interact with

§7 Sexuality and Sublimation

It is possible to think of our present study as an investigation into the limits of environmental conditioning. If we regard certain psychotherapies as attempts at partial deconditioning, the Buddhist texts we are examining may then be taken as testimonies with regard to how far deconditioning can go. It would be premature and unhelpful to postulate in this study more than a minimum of hereditary factors, i.e., factors that resist deconditioning altogether. While granting the importance of such factors, we have to continue to use a model that leaves them as much as possible out of consideration. These factors are bound to announce their presence at the point where our theory reaches the limits of its explanatory power.

This takes us back to our question, "Why should the search for reduction of bodily tension so often lead to sexual behavior?"[204] Most manifestations of sexuality — even in Freud's broad understanding of this term — are connected with the body, and with certain of its parts in particular: the sexual organs and other erotogenic zones. These are all areas that are well endowed with sensory nerves.[205] It is tempting to

---

other brains (mirror neurons)! Modules do exist of course, especially for sensations ... and aspects of memory acquisition (hippocampus), but for most brain tissue current analogies — including the computer metaphor — are grossly off the mark."

[204] Shared features of orgasms and mystical experiences have been pointed out by Newberg and D'Aquili (2001: 125), as reported in Horgan, 2003: 86-87. See also Parrinder, 1976: 169-174.

[205] See, e.g., Komisaruk, Beyer-Flores & Whipple, 2006: 22; 228 f. These same authors further observe (p. 223-24): "it seems that while the genital system is particularly well-organized to mediate the orgasmic process, other body systems evidently manifest at least some of the same properties and, consequently, under appropriate stimulus conditions and sensitization may exhibit comparable activity." Klein, 2002/2006: 138: "If the size of the individual organs were commensurate with the space given them in the brain, the penis and the vagina could easily outweigh the entire upper body."

surmise that this relatively strong presence of sensory nerves, along with the rather large surface of the brain associated with them,[206] explains to at least some extent why these body areas become so easily the object of intense attention. Besides that, the genital organs in adults can produce pleasure of the highest intensity accompanying the discharge of sexual substances (as Freud put it).[207] The genital organs present themselves in this way as the primary focus of sexual satisfaction. "Pleasure

---

[206] Interestingly, Ramachandran & Blakeslee (1998: 35 f.) report a case of a person who enjoyed sex more after the amputation of his foot. The reason proposed is that the genitals are next to the foot in the body's brain maps; the amputation resulted in an expansion of the brain surface related to the genitals, at the expense of the brain surface that used to be connected with the foot and which served no purpose any longer. The amputee did indeed experience his orgasm in his "phantom foot".

[207] The question why, in terms of our theory, the discharge of sexual substances should be accompanied by pleasure, is intriguing, and the fact that "it may well be that the larger part of the orgasm-correlated secretion [...] is due to concurrent opioid release within the brain" (Panksepp, 1998: 243; cp. Komisaruk, Beyer-Flores & Whipple, 2006: 153 f.) may give a clue to an answer; Georgiadis & Kortekaas (2010: 190) speak of "the recent idea that, neurochemically, pleasure, but not motivation, may be subserved primarily by opioid mechanisms ... Opiates presumably stimulate oxytocin release ..., which, in turn, has been shown to enhance orgasmic pleasure ..." See further below. Note also that during women's orgasms, according to the findings of Gert Holstege as reported in *New Scientist* (25 June 2005 p. 14), brain activity decreases in the amygdala, the hippocampus, and many more areas (similar findings for both men and women in Georgiadis et al., 2009: decreased activity in the medial temporal lobe, most notably in the right amygdala and left fusiform gyrus); Georgiadis (2007) reports on ejaculation-related deactivations throughout the pre-frontal cortex in human males; can this be interpreted as highly selective attention, leaving out most other concerns? The filtering of irrelevant information in attention tests is preceded by activity in the prefrontal cortex and basal ganglia, particularly in the globus pallidus; McNab & Klingberg, 2007.

§7 Sexuality and Sublimation

of the highest intensity" means "greatest reduction of bodily tension".

These thoughts about the development of sexual behavior must be looked upon as hypothetical. They may nevertheless help to explain why the pleasure generated by specific states of attention will often give rise to a preoccupation with the erotogenic zones as specific sources of pleasure, and with the genitals in particular.

Another question, parallel to the preceding one but wider in its scope, is: "Why should the search for reduced bodily tension lead to any activities at all, whether of a sexual or non-sexual nature?" Using psychoanalytical terminology, such activities include those covered by the expression *sublimation*. Strictly speaking, this expression is less appropriate in the context of our theory, for it recognizes no primitive sexual instinct that can be "lifted up" (Latin *sublimatus*). Nevertheless we will continue to use this expression.

In terms of our theory, activities are undertaken when appropriate memory traces are activated. A memory trace retains the memory of an earlier experience of satisfaction, and the activity inspired by an activated memory trace aims at repeating that experience. This activity is not always successful: it does not always lead to renewed satisfaction. The (unrepressed) memory traces of unsuccessful activities will, over time, be replaced by traces of activities that *do* lead to renewed satisfaction.

This leaves us with the following. Initial experiences of satisfaction produce memory traces which induce the organism to repeat the earlier activities. These memory traces weaken or disappear if their activities do not lead to renewed satisfaction. Satisfaction is therefore a precondition not only for the initial registration of a memory trace, but *also* for its continued presence in the mind. The question now is: what satisfaction do the repeated activities (including "sublimated" ones) provide? If they are just misguided attempts to repeat an experience of satisfaction that belongs to the past and is henceforth definitely out of reach, no renewed satisfaction should be expected from them.

Our theory obliges us to look *not only* for the satisfaction that created the memory trace in the first place, *but also* for the satisfaction that the activity engendered by it produces later on. As we have said, satisfaction (or pleasure) results from a reduction of the level of bodily tension. We must conclude that sublimated activity, too, lowers the level of bodily tension. But why should sublimated activity give rise to pleasure at all? In terms of our earlier example: Why should music lovers who listen to their favorite composer experience pleasure?

A part of the answer to this question has already been given. Music lovers listening to their favorite composer experience pleasure because the music puts them in a state of absorption *now*. This state of absorption takes attention away from other memory traces and reduces the bodily tension connected with them. Our music lovers will, of course, be well advised to listen to their music in surroundings that deactivate other memory traces as far as possible, e.g., in a concert hall or in the tranquility of their home. Why does the music put them in a pleasure-providing state of absorption? The question is not how our music lovers acquired their specific taste to begin with.[208] We start our present exploration from the assumption that appropriate memory traces have been formed and are henceforth present in their mind. These memory traces link the music to earlier experiences of satisfaction. Why should this same music lead to renewed satisfaction when it is heard again?

These questions bring us to an aspect of the human mind that we have not yet covered. An activated memory trace of an

---

[208] See on this Levitin, 2006: 223 ff.

§7 Sexuality and Sublimation

earlier experience of satisfaction attracts the attention of the mind: the greater the satisfaction remembered (and therefore promised) by the memory trace, the more attention it attracts. More attention means deeper absorption. Absorption produces pleasure because it reduces the overall level of bodily tension. Our music lovers now experience a new pleasure which is due to their *present* absorption and not to some kind of hypothetical transfer of earlier pleasure. They may be tempted to believe that this exquisite pleasure is due to some features of the music they are listening to. From a psychological point of view, our reflections suggest that this is not the case.

It is not necessary to postulate that the satisfaction of the remembered event was as great as, or greater than the satisfaction accompanying its present memory. Certain memories demonstrate the opposite. Marcel Proust's *À la recherche du temps perdu* contains a famous example:

> [My mother] sent for one to those squat, plump little cakes called "petites madeleines", which look as though they had been moulded in the fluted valve of a scallop shell. And soon, mechanically, dispirited after a dreary day with the prospect of a depressing morrow, I raised to my lips a spoonful of the tea in which I had soaked a morsel of the cake. No sooner had the warm liquid mixed with the crumbs touched my palate than a shudder ran through me and I stopped, intent upon the extraordinary thing that was happening to me. An exquisite pleasure had invaded my senses, something isolated, detached, with no suggestion of its origin. And at once the vicissitudes of life had become indifferent to me, its disasters innocuous, its brevity illusory — this new sensation having had on me the effect which love has of filling me with a precious essence; or rather this essence was not in me, it *was* me. I had ceased now to feel mediocre, contingent,

mortal. Whence could it have come to me, this all-powerful joy? I sensed that it was connected with the taste of the tea and the cake, but that it infinitely transcended those savours, could not, indeed, be of the same nature.

[...]

I began [...] to ask myself what it could have been, this unremembered state which brought with it no logical proof, but the indisputable evidence, of its felicity, its reality, and in whose presence other states of consciousness melted and vanished.

[...]

Undoubtedly what is thus palpitating in the depths of my being must be the image, the visual memory which, being linked to the taste, is trying to follow it into my conscious mind.

[...]

And suddenly the memory revealed itself. The taste was that of the little piece of madeleine which on Sunday mornings [...], when I went to say good morning to her in her bedroom, my aunt Léonie used to give me, dipping it first in her own cup of tea or tisane.[209]

Jonah Lehrer (2007: 88) reminds us that the remembered event was probably much less pleasurable than its recall: "After all, when Marcel was actually a child in Combray, eating madeleines to his heart's content, all he wanted was to escape his small town. But once he escaped, Marcel incessantly dreamed of recovering the precious childhood that he had so wantonly squandered. This is the irony of Proustian nostalgia: it remembers things as being far better than they actually were." It is of course possible that we are confronted here with a screen

---

[209] Proust, 1913/1981: 48-50.

memory behind which deeper (and presumably more satisfying) memories hide. There is no need to take a position in this matter. It seems safer to restate that present pleasure is not the result of a transfer of past pleasure. Proust's present pleasure was determined, not by the pleasure that accompanied the remembered event, but by the degree of absorption he experienced while remembering it.[210]

§8 The Result of a "Complete Cure"

Let us return to our ideal patient and see in what state the transformations described so far have left him. If our thesis regarding the true nature of "dependent" urges is correct, we will be obliged to expand the notion of a "complete psychotherapeutic cure". Such a cure will still integrate all repressed memory traces into the main unit as well as redirecting the associated urges. It will however do more than that. It will also change the reality assessment of the individual memory traces and of the main unit as a whole. Before the "complete cure", the organism, guided by its memory traces, would aim to repeat earlier experiences of satisfaction. After the "complete cure", it will still aim to repeat earlier experiences of satisfaction, but the memory traces will be changed: it will thus no longer be

---

[210] Linden (2011: 135) speaks of a "minor miracle": "when pleasure and associative learning are mixed ..., a minor miracle ... takes place. Now behaviorally compelling stimuli don't have to be intrinsically pleasurable, like sex of food, or artificially pleasurable, like drugs. Any sound, smell, sight, or memory can become associated with pleasure and can thereby become pleasurable in its own right." On p. 148 Linden mentions again the "ability to feel pleasure from arbitrary rewards" and wonders whether "these rewards [are] really entirely arbitrary" or if there is "some common theme or quality that runs through them?" If the theory here presented is correct, the "common theme or quality" that runs through "arbitrary rewards" is absorption.

guided by the same memory traces. Perhaps it would be better to say that the same memory traces now survive in a reinterpreted, and therefore modified form. The memory traces now "know" that they recall satisfaction only because the objects and events remembered were accompanied by states of reduced bodily tension often brought about by absorption, with the result that the organism will now try to reestablish such states directly and will abandon the pursuit of worldly aims. It will be able to do so because the obstacles to absorption, i.e. all those factors that demand the maintenance of a high level of standby tension, will now have disappeared.[211]

One consequence of the above must be emphasized. A person who has undergone a "complete cure" will no longer have sexual desire of any kind. This conclusion becomes inevitable once we accept that sexuality in its various manifestations is among the urges that are not intrinsically directed at specific objects and activities. Objects and activities come to play a role because the mind has the tendency of keeping a record of objects and activities rather than of the states which are the real causes of satisfaction. The idea that ideal patients might achieve a complete therapeutic cure and find themselves without sexual interests and needs fully agrees, of course, with the early Buddhist texts. Indeed, getting rid of desire, including sexual desire, is presented as the key to all other aims.

The theory we constructed allows for an internal arrangement of the mind in which desire is absent (rather than being suppressed, repressed, kept in check, or sublimated). The

---

[211] The question as to why the historical Buddha bothered to preach his message after his enlightenment, rather than remaining in his newly acquired state of peace, occupied the early Buddhist tradition; see Bareau, 1963: 135 ff. It also poses a challenge to the theory here presented. The question whether the Buddha still had desires was also discussed in the medieval Buddhist tradition, and has attracted the attention of modern scholars; see Franco, 2012.

§8 The Result of a "Complete Cure"

Buddhist texts which are at the basis of this study, and whose testimony we have accepted as our working hypothesis, state in no uncertain terms that such an arrangement of the mind can be brought about and that it was actually brought about at least once.

The same applies to all desires in the broadest sense of the term. Those who have successfully undergone the treatment described in the preceding pages will no longer be attached to the objects and events represented in their memory traces. As a result, they will not be attached to any people, things or states of affairs. A partial exception will have to be made for what we have called "independent" urges, such as hunger and thirst, and for bodily discomfort and disturbance, including illness. These will still influence the persons concerned. However, protection against these can be obtained by entering into a state of absorption. This is what the historical Buddha is reported to have done when suffering from physical ailments caused by old age.[212] This is also what our theory predicts.[213]

---

[212] See Appendix 1 of Part II §8.

[213] People may not feel pain in involuntary states of absorption, too: "One has to pay attention to pain for it to hurt" (Spiegel & Spiegel, 2004: 309). See, e.g., the testimony of 'A' as reproduced in Laski, 1961: 418-19: "Last night as I was walking home from the station I had one of those strange experiences of 'rising upward within oneself', of 'coming inwardly alive'. As it happens, I can remember the comparatively trivial beginnings of it. A minute or so after I had left the station, I was attacked, though not severely, by the indigestion which is always liable to recur when I have been working particularly hard. I thought to myself, though I suppose not in so many words, 'I could separate myself from this pain [...]' Even as I thought this the pain disappeared; that is, it was in some way left behind [...] and the sensation of 'rising up within' began." There is, furthermore, considerable anecdotal evidence that even severe pain can be "forgotten" when attention is deviated or otherwise occupied: "[O]verwhelming and serious injury is sometimes accompanied by a surprising absence of pain perception until hours after the injury occurred. This traumatic dissociation has been observed in vic-

To conclude, I add a few specifications about pleasure. Pleasure is experienced when the level of bodily tension is reduced. It is therefore associated with the transition from one state to another. Once bodily tension *has* been reduced and a more or less stable state of low tension *has* been reached, there should be no experience of pleasure. This agrees with the description of the fourth stage-of-meditation° in the Buddhist texts as having "neither-pain-nor-pleasure and purity of mindfulness due to equanimity".[214] The same characterization should apply to any stable state of low tension, including the more or less regular states of those who have done a "complete therapy". If our theory is correct, the outcome of a "complete therapy" will be a state of permanent mental peace and not necessarily a state of permanent bliss.

We have occasionally referred to neurological research in connection with our psychological theory. We return to it to ask a very hypothetical question, which may be presented graphically as follows. Suppose that, by some miracle, the brain of the historical Buddha had been preserved and could be studied by brain specialists.[215] Would they find anything noteworthy?

If we base ourselves on the testimony of the earliest sources, we can state with confidence that nothing like an "enlighten-

---

tims of natural disasters, combat, and motor vehicle accidents." (Spiegel & Spiegel, 2004: 309; see further Wall, 1999: 4 ff.) Note further that Grahek (2007: 40 & passim) argues that "pain, when stripped of [all its affective, cognitive, and behavioral components], loses all its representational and motivational force. It comes to nothing in the sense that it is no longer a signal of threat or damage for the subject, and doesn't move (*emotio*) his mind and body in any way." On persistent posttraumatic dissociation, see note 133, above.

[214] See Appendix 1 of Part II §1(13).

[215] One thinks, of course, of Einstein, the bizarre odyssey of whose brain is described in Abraham, 2001.

§8 The Result of a "Complete Cure"

ment bump" would be found in this brain.[216] It is true that brain plasticity, even in adults, is now a recognized phenomenon.[217] It is also true that meditation may bring about lasting changes in the brain.[218] However, the early sources are categorical about the duration of the process responsible for the decisive modification in the mind of the historical Buddha: only one night.[219] This is far too short a period to allow for extensive modifications in the brain.

In spite of this, we may take it for granted that changes in the mind are paralleled by changes in its neuronal substrate. In other words, we may expect the brain of the Buddha to distinguish itself in some respects from the brains of people who have not effected the "complete cure". We may, however, feel skeptical about the possibility of finding and identifying the distinctive features during an autopsy with the tools presently available.[220]

The situation might be different if the Buddha's functioning brain could be observed. Recall that Edelman and Tononi put forward the hypothesis that some of the *splinter cores* which they found in the functioning brain beside and independently of their *dynamic core* may correspond to the unconscious, i.e. to our repressed trace units. Our theory, in combination with their hypothesis, suggests that in the Buddha's brain these splinter cores might have become integrated into the dynam-

---

[216] The cranial bump on early statues of Bodhisattvas (= Buddhas-to-be°) may represent a head-cloth covering a hair-bun; the bump was subsequently added to statues of the Buddha, too. See Falk, 2012.

[217] Schwartz & Begley, 2002; Begley, 2007; Doidge, 2007.

[218] See Begley, 2007: 212 ff.

[219] It is almost superfluous to add that this decisive modification followed preliminary activities which took much longer.

[220] For a discussion of the neurobiological consequences of psychotherapeutic interventions, see Etkin et al., 2005.

ic core. In other words, no splinter cores might be found in that brain. All this is, of course, pure speculation. Yet it can be stated with confidence that the psychological changes brought about by the process described in the early Buddhist texts must leave traces in the brain.

Summary and Concluding Reflections

The result of the preceding investigation can be summarized as follows. The mind is motivated by the search for pleasure. It is guided in this by memories of earlier experiences of pleasure. However, the mind does not "know" why earlier experiences were pleasurable; it is simply programmed to retain objects and events that accompanied those earlier experiences. Its search for pleasure becomes in this way a search to recreate situations that accompanied earlier experiences of pleasure. This does not always lead to renewed pleasure.

Discharge of bodily tension is experienced as pleasure. Since the mind does not "know" this, it can be led astray by its memories. The activities it undertakes to recreate pleasurable situations, however, may in themselves be pleasurable. These activities, too, will then be remembered and added to the store of memories on which the mind draws in determining future behavior. This store of memories will become immense and will be different for each individual, depending in important measure on their different experiences.

All individuals have in common that their motivational structure is not based on a correct evaluation of what constitutes pleasure. If discharge of bodily tension could be brought about directly and, at the same time, if all memories could be "convinced" that the features they retain are not the "right" ones, the end result would be a human being with a radically different motivational structure. Such a human being would no longer have the same desires as others. Its principal remaining desire would be to bring about discharge of bodily tension in this direct manner, which amounts to saying that it is free from normal desire in any of its forms.

This hypothetical person has much in common with the practitioner who has successfully followed the process described in the oldest Buddhist texts, instantiated in the historical Buddha. Most notably, both are without desire.

The Buddhist texts enumerate two direct methods to bring about discharge of bodily tension. One is complete disengagement from human society. The other is mental absorption. Once our hypothetical person has succeeded in "convincing" his memories that the features he associates with pleasure are not the "right" ones, he has also succeeded in disengaging himself from human society. His only remaining "desire" will be to enter into profound absorption.

"Convincing" all memory traces that they do not remember the "right" things and that they promise pleasure where little or none is to be had, is more easily said than done. In order to understand how this goal can be attained, our "top-down" presentation must now make place for a "bottom-up" summary of the inner workings of the human mind.

The mind contains a large number of *memory traces*, usually combined into *trace units* (also called *secondary traces*) of various sizes. Trace units are associated with bodily *urges*, whose direction is determined by "their" trace units. Trace units are *activated* by a confrontation with the objects or events whose memories they embody or by thoughts or fantasies about them. Activated trace units put the associated urges into a state of *excitation*. The degree of activation of the trace units determines the degree of excitation of the associated urges.

The memory traces that we are concerned with here record earlier experiences of *pleasure*. Pleasure is experienced when the overall level of bodily *tension* is reduced. The overall level of bodily tension is largely the result of the simultaneous excitation of numerous urges to various degrees.

Summary and Concluding Reflections

The level of excitation of urges is directly related to the degree of activation of the corresponding trace units. This degree of activation is not exclusively determined by the objects and events that present themselves to the organism (whether through sensory input, memory or imagination). *Attention* plays a major role. The more attention is directed at one object, event, or mental content, the less remains for others. Attention aimed at one thing implies attention withdrawn from another. Attention withdrawn means reduced activation of the trace units concerned, and reduced excitation of the associated urges. In favorable circumstances, appropriately directed attention generates a globally reduced level of bodily tension, and therefore a pleasurable experience. This happens most significantly in the kind of attention called *absorption*.

Activated memory traces of earlier satisfaction tend to generate attention and may in this way produce *renewed satisfaction*.

Trace units (or secondary traces) are the result of the *integration* of (primary and/or secondary) memory traces. Memory traces along with their associated urges embody *reality assessments*. Through them the associated urges "know" how to attain satisfaction. Larger trace units embody more encompassing reality assessments than their constituent traces.

Distinct trace units may be activated simultaneously, thus putting different urges in a state of simultaneous excitation. This can result in conflict. Such a conflict is resolved if the trace units concerned integrate into a larger trace unit. The reality assessment of this larger trace unit will either choose between the courses of action of the integrated traces or choose a new one that provides optimal satisfaction to all the excited urges.

If there are obstacles to the mutual integration of trace units, the strongest one may use part of its available bodily tension to block the urges associated with the others. Mutual integration can then be prevented through withdrawing attention from the weaker trace units and directing it elsewhere. Conflicts like these normally oppose the largest trace unit of all, the *main unit*, to other trace units which are then designated *repressed*. Repression will leave a trace in the main unit which blocks future access to the repressed trace unit.

The numerous trace units of the mind — i.e., one main unit and many repressed trace units — keep each other in a more or less delicate *equilibrium*. Attempts to integrate repressed trace units into the main unit — strictly speaking these are renewed attempts, subsequent to the initial one that failed and therefore led to repression — meet in this way with resistance. In order to succeed, they have to establish a new equilibrium between the various forces that are active in the mind.

In spite of the many practical difficulties that oppose the integration of repressed trace units and their urges, theoretically there is no limit to this process: theoretically nothing stands in the way of a main unit in which *all* trace units and their urges are integrated.

In practice this goal may be attained by means of the overall reduction of bodily tension. In the case of independent urges, such as hunger, the reduction of tension is linked to specific activities, such as eating. In the case of dependent urges, two factors can bring it about:

(i) Reduced activation of the memory traces that are responsible for the excitation of the associated bodily urges. This happens typically when, and to the extent that, people can separate themselves from their social surroundings and the associated expectations.

(ii) Absorption. Absorption withdraws attention from (many or all) memory traces and further reduces in this way their activation and the excitation of the associated urges.

Summary and Concluding Reflections

Because the mechanism of repression depends on the availability of bodily tension, access to repressed memory traces can be obtained once bodily tension is reduced to an absolute minimum through these two means: social isolation and absorption. Repressed memories can be localized through the systematic exploration of feelings, which are the sign-posts of bodily tension.

The theory presented does more than providing space for the mental possibilities recorded in the early Buddhist texts. It also presents a coherent picture, if ever so rudimentary, of the nature of many "ordinary" mental events. The fact that it proposes an explanation both for the initial motivation that makes human beings tick and for the motivation that keeps them ticking may count among its more specific virtues.

These are factors that plead in favor of the theory. However, they do not prove that it is correct, i.e., true to reality.[221] To make progress in that direction, we need to know whether, and to what extent the theory can be tested. Can it be confronted with experimental situations that might confirm, refute or refine it, or that might call for other adaptations? It does not really matter whether the experiments concerned belong to the realm of psychology, neurology, physiology, or perhaps to some other domain, as long as they can test the theory or some aspect of it.

Since I do not myself have the means and expertise required to set up experiments of this kind, it may be useful to enumerate some of the assumptions underlying the theory, and some of its consequences, so that a skilled experimenter may be able to put them to the test. First of all, there is the assumption that

---

[221] In striving to describe how the mind really works, we are elaborating a theory rather than a model, which is a metaphor or analogy of what really happens.

attention behaves as if it is of a more or less constant and finite quantity: attention has to be withdrawn from one place in order to be directed elsewhere. Does attention really follow such a rule, even approximately? Experimental research confirms that directed attention has to compete with the general state of arousal of the organism, but the issue may not be completely settled.[222] Secondly, there is the further assumption that a bodily tension exists which follows a twofold rule: (i) fluctuations in the total amount of tension determine the pleasure a person experiences, and (ii) the constituent urges of this tension compete with each other. Does such a tension exist, and is it measurable? Is it perhaps possible to "translate" these levels of tension into degrees of arousal that belong to the seeking system discussed earlier?[223] Thirdly, there are the claims about

---

[222] Coull (2005: 51-52) states: "Electrophysiological recordings in monkeys have shown that *phasic* LC (i.e., locus coeruleus, JB) firing to targets [...] actually varies according to the *tonic* LC activity (equivalent to the state of arousal of the animal) and has corresponding effects on attentional performance [...] This pattern of activity follows an inverted U-shaped curve whereby too low or too high a state of tonic LC firing, or arousal, alters phasic LC firing and, consequently, impairs performance. Optimal performance corresponds to an intermediate state of tonic LC discharge or arousal." This would at first sight seem to agree with our theory where higher and intermediate states of arousal are concerned, but not in low states of arousal. However, the fact that outer objects do not attract focused attention in monkeys (and perhaps humans) when their overall state of arousal is low, does not need to imply that no attention is available in that state.

[223] Cp. Panksepp, 1998: 167: "Existing evidence suggests that the seeking system is under the control of internal *homeostatic* receptor systems that detect various bodily imbalances." On p. 168, this same author makes a remark which suggests that bodily tension may be measurable: "At a physiological level, increased arousal can be measured by the intensification of reflexes as well as neural changes." Kaplan (2004: 550) goes further and introduces a comparison with an early notion of Freud: "In his earliest efforts to formulate a psychology, Freud postu-

Summary and Concluding Reflections

the relationship between absorption and pleasure, and the possibility of attention without an object. At the time of writing, I have not found many scientific studies that deal with these claims,[224] but mystical literature and affirmations of practitioners of certain forms of meditation support them.[225] The claimed existence of trace units different from the main unit (and different from the Freudian *system of the unconscious* and Id) might also permit experimental verification.[226] The claim, furthermore, that much of human (and perhaps animal?) motivation does not depend on inbuilt instincts that pursue their own goals, but rather on urges whose direction is fully or largely determined by memory traces, gives rise to interesting questions. What would happen if certain memory traces were suppressed? It appears possible to prevent memory traces from reconsolidating by chemical means, at least in rats.[227] Our the-

---

lated a quantitative factor, which, in *Project for a Scientific Psychology* [...] he designated Q. This quantitative factor may be roughly translated as a physical energic factor. It has been compared to the seeking system theorized by Panksepp [...]"

[224] Note however the following: "It is possible the brain does not have distinct neuronal signals related to attention and reward expectation." (Maunsell, 2004: 264). In human beings, one of the physical characteristics of concentration called up "at will" (i.e., without reward expectation) is increased pupil size; cp. Kahneman, 1973: 19, referring to Libby et al. 1973. Pupil dilation also accompanies other mental phenomena such as decision-taking and excitation (see *New Scientist* of 6 March 2010, p. 11; Bradley et al., 2008), but this may find its explanation in the fact that those other phenomena are themselves accompanied by states of increased concentration.

[225] On the relationship between absorption and pleasure, see Appendix 2 of Part II. On the possibility of attention without object, see above, esp. note 152.

[226] See the remarks made above in connection with the "splinter cores" of Edelman and Tononi.

[227] Miller & Marshall, 2005; Lee et al., 2005.

ory suggests that such procedures might deeply interfere with the motivational life of the organism concerned. Rigorous testing of the theory seems therefore possible in principle.

There are further questions of a more theoretical nature. How do the rudimentary reality assessments of memory traces give rise to the more sophisticated reality assessment of a trace unit and ultimately of the main unit? Is there a way to visualize this process without introducing *homunculi*, i.e., anthropomorphic elements which shift rather than solve the problem?[228] And what is the exact relationship between feelings and "acting out"? Is it true, as our theory suggests, that acting out emotions reduces or even annuls the corresponding feelings?[229] Once again, we can only hope that future research will answer these questions.

Recall that our theory distinguishes two different ways in which pleasure can be attained: reduction of tension brought about by the removal of sources of tension (the Buddhist "rapture and pleasure born of seclusion") and absorption ("rapture and pleasure born of absorption"). There is only one ultimate source of pleasure, to be sure, viz. the reduction of the overall

---

[228] It may be useful here to refer back to note 120, above.

[229] Cf. James, 1890: II: 466: "Manifesting an emotion, so far from increasing it, makes it cease. Rage evaporates after a good outburst [...] *During* the manifestation the emotion is always felt." There is also an obvious parallel in the alternative between *repeating* and *remembering* to which Freud draws attention, for example in his "Remembering, repeating and working-through" (1914; SE XII p. 150: "the patient does not *remember* anything of what he has forgotten and repressed, but *acts* it out. He reproduces it not as a memory but as an action; he *repeats* it, without, of course, knowing that he is repeating it.") Note that Klein (2002/2006: 42) warns against the "widely held psychological conviction" according to which people "will be free of their anger if they express it, that theirs tears will release their pain"; referring to publications by Mallick & McCandless (1966) and Tavris (1989), he considers this belief "no truer than the flat earth".

level of bodily tension. The two ways to achieve this are nevertheless quite different. This raises the question: Do these two have their counterparts in the two chemical agents that are often associated with pleasure, viz. opioids and dopamine (cf. Panksepp, 1998: 184)? About opioid systems Panksepp states (1998: 386 n. 94): "The general pleasure produced by brain opioid systems may be related to an interesting effect that can be produced by high doses of externally administered opioids — a quieting of the body that at its most extreme takes the form of catalepsy: When animals are given high doses of opiates, their bodies become rigidly 'waxy', so that one can mold them into almost any shape. Perhaps a mild form of this type of immobility characterizes animals that have no regulatory imbalances — ones that are completely satisfied." Dopamine presents a puzzle to him (1998: 385 n. 88): "[...] it remains unclear what type of neuropsychic reinforcing event is mediated by dopamine. Does the induced psychological process resemble consummatory pleasure or some other form of desirable psychic arousal? The present position is that the psychological state is akin to a generalized desire or reward-seeking urge rather than any type of pleasure that typically accompanies consummatory acts. Generally, this is in accord with the most common subjective reports from human subjects, which indicate that what is being experienced are feelings of positive energization, arousal, power, effectiveness, and being on top of things." The crucial expressions in this passage are "consummatory pleasure" and "some other form of desirable psychic arousal." It is the latter which is to be associated with dopamine.[230] A more recent study confirms this (Burgdorf &

---

[230] LeDoux's following inference therefore would appear to be mistaken (2002: 246): "Dopamine was believed to be the chemical of pleasure. However, [...] dopamine is [...] more involved in anticipatory behaviors (looking for food or drink or a sexual partner) than in consummatory

Panksepp, 2006: 183-84): "There appear to be at least two distinct classes of PA [positive affect, JB] states represented in the brain, with separate but overlapping neuroanatomical substrates. An appetitive PA system, devoted [in rats, JB] to foraging and reward-seeking, associated in part with the effects of psychostimulants such as cocaine and amphetamine is dependent in part on the ventral striatal dopamine system. A nearby PA system involved in processing sensory pleasure such as pleasurable touch and hedonic tastes involves the opiate and GABA system in the ventral striatum and orbital frontal cortex." The link between dopamine and attention appears to be well established.[231]

Critics of our theory will justifiably ask how biological evolution could ever have produced this kind of mind. Human beings are biological organisms and the product of biological evolution. The mechanism governing this process is known in principle and consists in the elimination, by natural selection,

---

responses (eating, drinking, having sex). But being hungry or thirsty is unpleasant. Pleasure, to the extent it is experienced [...], would not come during the anticipatory state but instead during consummation. Since dopamine is involved only in the anticipatory phase, and not in the consummatory phase, its effects (at least in the case of primary need states) cannot be explained in terms of pleasure."

[231] See, e.g., Rolls, 1999: 191 ff.; here one finds a possible explanation as to how dopamine could play an important role in setting the sensitivity of the response selection function there specified (which presumably corresponds to what we call *attention*). Austin (1998: 200-01) refers to experiments which suggest that dopamine helps sustain *goal-directed* behaviors, and then suggests "that [dopamine] can normally enter in to influence our several mechanisms of attention". See further LeDoux, 2002: 189-90; Rolls, 2005: 312 ff.; Leyton, 2010. On the question of the relation between pleasure on the one hand and dopamine and opioids on the other, see also Katz, 2006: §§3.2 and 3.3, with references to further literature.

Summary and Concluding Reflections

of features that reduce fitness. An essential ingredient of fitness is procreation. In human beings as in many other organisms, this is inseparable from sexuality. A "sexual instinct" of one sort or another would therefore seem to be a fundamental necessity.[232] Without it, reproduction might be seriously compromised. Organisms that are deficient in this respect should soon be selected away. How then is it possible that human beings have no sexual instinct in the strict sense? And what selection pressure could replace a clear, goal-oriented sexual instinct with the mechanism presented in our theory? The need for food is represented in the human mind by a clear, goal-oriented drive,[233] viz. hunger. Why then is sexuality not similarly represented?

This criticism is valid but can be answered without great difficulty. If our theory is correct, human beings do indeed not have a clear, goal-oriented sexual instinct.[234] However, for the

---

[232] Rolls (2005: 41 ff.) argues "that emotions are states elicited by goals (rewards and punishers), and that this is part of an adaptive process by which genes can specify the behaviour of the animal by specifying goals for behaviour rather than fixed responses." If our present theory is correct, not even the goals for certain types of human behavior have been specified by genes (or at any rate not fully), and yet this does not endanger the survival of the species. About sexuality, Rolls states (p. 360): "Sexual behaviour is an interesting type of motivated behaviour to compare with feeding and drinking. For both feeding and drinking, there are internal signals such as plasma glucose or cellular dehydration related to homeostatic control that set the levels of food or water reward in order to produce the appropriate behaviour. *In the case of sexual behaviour, there are no similar short-term homeostatic controls.*" (my emphasis, JB)

[233] Strictly speaking, hunger in our theory is not a "goal-oriented" drive, but a drive that can only be satisfied in a small number of ways (primarily eating).

[234] Even theoretically this is not necessarily a disadvantage, for postulating an instinct does not explain much. Rose (2005: 114), having enumerated nine different meanings of the word 'instinct', observes:

vast majority of mankind this does not make the slightest difference. The number of people who have overcome their sexual urges through insight into their underlying motivational structure and by bringing about the appropriate changes is minuscule: there is indeed only one *ex hypothesi* "certain" example; further examples are uncertain.[235] The negative effect of natural selection on the development from a straightforward sexual instinct (that presumably once existed in evolutionary history) to the mechanism expressed in our theory is therefore negligible.

The positive effect, on the other hand, may have been considerable. The fact that sexual reproduction is only one of the many possible outcomes of the motivational mechanism of the human mind — however important it is — has opened up almost limitless objects of human motivation. These include the sexual "perversions" as well as all of those activities and interests that are sometimes united under the banner of sublimation. Most if not all of human culture may in this way result from the absence of an exclusively sexual instinct, i.e. one that is programmed to serve only the purpose of reproduction. Reproduction does take place, but the very fact that the motivational energy underlying sexuality is not completely consumed by this aim has allowed humanity to create an ever more favorable environment for its offspring. The survival value of the transition from pure sexual instinct to the more flexible mechanism described in our theory is therefore not in question. The

---

"The problem with all of these ... senses of the word is that they lack explanatory power. Rather, they assume what they set out to explain, that is, an autonomous developmental sequence. They are thus as empty as Molière's famous burlesque explanation of sleep as being caused by a 'dormative principle.'"

[235] The case we are studying must be strictly distinguished from the wide-spread human tendency toward asceticism, including sexual restraint.

Summary and Concluding Reflections

question by what trajectory through the fitness landscape (a trajectory of the type "climbing Mount Improbable")[236] a presumably earlier sexual instinct could make place for the situation described in our theory, must for the time being remain unanswered.

We have seen that the theory presented here is open to experimental tests, at least in principle. The treasure announced at the beginning of this study can therefore be evaluated. Let us hope that this will be done soon and that this value will turn out to be sufficient to justify the effort made. If it is, readers are free to form their own judgment about the value of the map, i.e., the working hypothesis from which we started. They may be reminded that there is no logically compelling reason to accept the working hypothesis even if it has led to a valuable result. Indeed, there can be no logical objection to using it like Wittgenstein's ladder, which can be discarded once one has reached a higher level.

---

[236] Dawkins, 1996.

Appendix 1: The Main Texts with a Psychological Commentary

This Appendix presents the most important passages from the early Buddhist texts that specify the positions which we have attributed to them.[237] They are taken from the version of the Buddhist canon that has been preserved in the language called Pali. Other old versions have been preserved in Chinese translation, and fragments in other languages. The differences between these versions are interesting for the philologist but without significance for our investigation. Use has been made of existing translations, which have been slightly adjusted so as to avoid the employment of Indian expressions where this is not absolutely necessary and to assure consistency in the translation of key terms.

§1 The Path of Liberation as a Whole

The most general presentation of the Buddhist method is contained in a long passage that occurs on numerous occasions in the early texts (perhaps twenty or thirty times in the discourses preserved in Pali). It describes in most general terms the effect which the teaching of a Buddha (here called Tathagata) can have on an ideal follower. The passage reads as follows:[238]

---

[237] For details about the philological work which underlies my understanding of the early canonical texts, the reader is advised to refer to the first part of my *Buddhist Teaching in India* (2009).

[238] *The Middle Length Discourses of the Buddha: A new translation of the Majjhima Nikaya*, original translation by Bhikkhu Nanamoli, translation edited and revised by Bhikkhu Bodhi, Wisdom Publications, Bos-

Appendix 1: The Main Texts, with a Psychological Commentary

1. Here a Buddha appears in the world, accomplished, fully enlightened, perfect in true knowledge and conduct, sublime, knower of worlds, incomparable leader of persons to be tamed, teacher of gods and humans, enlightened, blessed. He teaches this world with its gods, its Maras, and its Brahmas, this generation with its recluses and brahmins, its princes and its people, what he has himself realised with direct knowledge. He propounds the Dhamma[239] good in the beginning, good in the middle, and good in the end, with the right meaning and phrasing, and he reveals a holy life that is utterly perfect and pure.

2. A householder or householder's son or one born in some other clan hears that Dhamma. On hearing the Dhamma he acquires faith in the Buddha. Possessing that faith, he considers thus: 'Household life is crowded and dusty; life gone forth is wide open. It is not easy, while living in a home, to lead the holy life utterly perfect and pure as a polished shell. Suppose I shave off my hair and beard, put on the yellow robe, and go forth from the home life into homelessness.' On a later occasion, abandoning a small or a large fortune, abandoning a small or a large circle of relatives, he shaves off his hair and beard, puts on the yellow robe, and goes forth from the home life into homelessness.

3. Having thus gone forth and possessing the monk's training and way of life, abandoning the killing of living beings, he abstains from killing living beings; with rod and weapon laid aside, gentle and kindly, he abides

---

ton, 1995, pp. 272 ff. This translates *Majjhima Nikaya* I p. 179 ff. I have added my own numbering in order to facilitate cross-reference.

[239] Dhamma = the teaching of the Buddha.

compassionate to all living beings. Abandoning the taking of what is not given, he abstains from taking what is not given; taking only what is given, expecting only what is given, by not stealing he abides in purity. Abandoning incelibacy, he observes celibacy, living apart, abstaining from the vulgar practice of sexual intercourse.

4. Abandoning false speech, he abstains from false speech; he speaks truth, adheres to truth, is trustworthy and reliable, one who is no deceiver of the world. Abandoning malicious speech, he abstains from malicious speech; he does not repeat elsewhere what he has heard here in order to divide [those people] from these, nor does he repeat to these people what he has heard elsewhere in order to divide [these people] from those; thus he is one who reunites those who are divided, a promoter of friendships, who enjoys concord, rejoices in concord, delights in concord, a speaker of words that promote concord. Abandoning harsh speech, he abstains from harsh speech; he speaks such words as are gentle, pleasing to the ear, and loveable, as go to the heart, are courteous, desired by many and agreeable to many. Abandoning gossip, he abstains from gossip; he speaks at the right time, speaks what is fact, speaks on what is good, speaks on the Dhamma and the Discipline; at the right time he speaks such words as are worth recording, reasonable, moderate, and beneficial.

[...]

5. He becomes content with robes to protect his body and with almsfood to maintain his stomach, and wherever he goes, he sets out taking only these with him. Just as a bird, wherever it goes, flies with its wings as its only burden, so too the monk becomes content with robes to protect his body and with almsfood to maintain his stomach, and

wherever he goes, he sets out taking only these with him. Possessing this aggregate of noble virtue, he experiences within himself a bliss that is blameless.

6. On seeing a form with the eye, he does not grasp at its signs and features. Since, if he left the eye faculty unguarded, evil unwholesome states of covetousness and grief might invade him, he practises the way of its restraint, he guards the eye faculty, he undertakes the restraint of the eye faculty. On hearing a sound with the ear [...] On smelling an odour with the nose [...] On tasting a flavour with the tongue [...] On touching a tangible with the body [...] On cognizing a mental property with the mind, he does not grasp at its signs and features. Since, if he left the mind faculty unguarded, evil unwholesome states of covetousness and grief might invade him, he practises the way of its restraint, he guards the mind faculty, he undertakes the restraint of the mind faculty. Possessing this noble restraint of the faculties, he experiences within himself a bliss that is unsullied.

7. He becomes one who acts in full awareness° when going forward and returning; who acts in full awareness when looking ahead and looking away; who acts in full awareness when flexing and extending his limbs; who acts in full awareness when wearing his robes and carrying his outer robe and bowl; who acts in full awareness when eating, drinking, consuming food, and tasting; who acts in full awareness when defecating and urinating; who acts in full awareness when walking, standing, sitting, falling asleep, waking up, talking, and keeping silent.

8. Possessing this aggregate of noble virtue, and this noble restraint of the faculties, and possessing this noble mindfulness° and full awareness, he resorts to a secluded

resting place: the forest, the root of a tree, a mountain, a ravine, a hillside cave, a charnel ground, a jungle thicket, an open space, a heap of straw.

9. On returning from his almsround, after his meal he sits down, folding his legs crosswise, setting his body erect, and establishing mindfulness° before him. Abandoning covetousness for the world, he abides with a mind free from covetousness; he purifies his mind from covetousness. Abandoning ill will and hatred, he abides with a mind free from ill will, compassionate for the welfare of all living beings; he purifies his mind from ill will and hatred. Abandoning sloth and torpor, he abides free from sloth and torpor, percipient of light, mindful and fully aware; he purifies his mind from sloth and torpor. Abandoning restlessness and remorse, he abides unagitated with a mind inwardly peaceful; he purifies his mind from restlessness and remorse. Abandoning doubt, he abides having gone beyond doubt, unperplexed about wholesome states; he purifies his mind from doubt.

10. Having thus abandoned these five hindrances, imperfections of the mind that weaken wisdom, quite secluded from sensual pleasures, secluded from unwholesome states, he enters upon and abides in the first stage-of-meditation°, which is accompanied by applied and sustained thought, with rapture° and pleasure° born of seclusion. [...]

11. Again, with the stilling of applied and sustained thought, a monk enters upon and abides in the second stage-of-meditation°, which has self-confidence and singleness of mind without applied and sustained thought, with rapture° and pleasure° born of absorption. [...]

12. Again, with the fading away as well of rapture°, a monk abides in equanimity, and mindful and fully aware, still feeling pleasure° with the body, he enters upon and abides in the third stage-of-meditation°, on account of which the noble ones announce: 'He has a pleasant abiding who has equanimity and is mindful.' [...]

13. Again, with the abandoning of pleasure° and pain, and with the previous disappearance of joy and grief, a monk enters upon and abides in the fourth stage-of-meditation°, which has neither-pain-nor-pleasure and purity of mindfulness due to equanimity. [...]

[...]

14. When his concentrated mind is thus purified, bright, unblemished, rid of imperfection, malleable, wieldy, steady, and attained to imperturbability, he directs it to knowledge of the destruction of the taints. He understands as it actually is: 'This is suffering'; [...] 'This is the origin of suffering'; [...] 'This is the cessation of suffering'; [...] 'This is the way leading to the cessation of suffering'; [...] 'These are the taints'; [...] 'This is the origin of the taints'; [...] 'This is the cessation of the taints'; [...] 'This is the way leading to the cessation of the taints'.

[...]

15. When he knows and sees thus, his mind is liberated from the taint of sensual desire, from the taint of being, and from the taint of ignorance. When it is liberated there comes the knowledge: 'it is liberated'. He understands: 'Birth is destroyed, the holy life has been lived, what had to be done has been done, so that I will not return here.'

This passage presents in brief all the elements that the aspirant must practice. Buddhist candidates for liberation, like the ideal patient described in the main text, withdraw from all human company. By abandoning home and property, they are no longer involved in social life. By abstaining from killing living beings, giving up the possession of arms and renouncing all forms of human interaction including sexual intercourse, they minimalize the opportunities for social emotions. Instead they practice a form of passive compassion, presumably an emotion that facilitates the lowering of bodily arousal. Also the attempt to promote friendship and concord rather than their opposites where intercourse with other human beings is unavoidable is to serve the goal of calming body and mind.

These practices do not promote "Buddhist morality", and therefore a vision of society. Rather their aim is to calm body and mind. The level of (bodily) tension is in this way reduced as far as possible, as a precondition for the psychological work that is to come. Once that stage is achieved, the practice of awareness° and mindfulness° in all circumstances follows. This practice is more than simply preliminary: it accompanies all following stages up to and including the transformation that will reward the candidate's efforts. The psychological significance of awareness and mindfulness is that the candidate will only carry out activities of which he is fully aware. As a result, repressed urges (which often slip through in the middle of automated activities) cannot find expression. As a result, they will attract attention as feelings whenever they are excited.

Mental peace is crucial to the final stages of the path, the so-called four stages-of-meditation°. The first of these may come about of its own when total seclusion from outer forms of stimulation has been achieved. This is confirmed by another passage, which we will consider below (§3).

Appendix 1: The Main Texts, with a Psychological Commentary

From the second stage onward, absorption comes to play a central role. The "rapture and pleasure" of the second stage are "born of absorption". Absorption is not mentioned in connection with the third stage, but a "concentrated mind" reappears in the fourth. We must assume that absorption characterizes all these stages.

We have discussed the role that absorption plays in the economy of the mind in the main text. Absorption withdraws attention from the tasks to which it is habitually assigned, among them resisting repressed urges. This opens up the way to dealing with those urges.

Beside this global presentation of the path to liberation, there are presentations of its elements. Some of these elements are explicitly mentioned in the above global presentation, others are new. We will look at a selection of them.

§2 Guiding One's Thoughts

Among the preparatory practices, training one's mind to focus on certain thoughts rather than others plays an important role. Some autobiographical remarks attributed to the Buddha deal with the issue:[240]

> Monks, before my enlightenment, while I was still only an unenlightened Buddha-to-be°, it occurred to me: "Suppose that I divide my thoughts into two classes." Then I set on one side thoughts of sensual desire, thoughts of ill will, and thoughts of cruelty, and I set on the other side thoughts of renunciation, thoughts of non-ill will, and thoughts of non-cruelty.

---

[240] *The Middle Length Discourses of the Buddha* (as above), pp. 207 ff. This translates *Majjhima Nikaya* I p. 114 ff.

As I abided thus, diligent, ardent, and resolute, a thought of sensual desire arose in me. I understood thus: "This thought of sensual desire has arisen in me. This leads to my own affliction, to others' affliction, and to the affliction of both; it obstructs wisdom, causes difficulties, and leads away from Nibbana." When I considered: "This leads to my own affliction," it subsided in me; when I considered: "This leads to others' affliction," it subsided in me; when I considered: "This leads to the affliction of both," it subsided in me; when I considered: "This obstructs wisdom, causes difficulties, and leads away from Nibbana," it subsided in me. Whenever a thought of sensual desire arose in me, I abandoned it, removed it, did away with it.

As I abided thus, diligent, ardent, and resolute, a thought of ill will arose in me [...] a thought of cruelty arose in me. I understood thus: "This thought of cruelty has arisen in me. This leads to my own affliction, to others' affliction, and to the affliction of both; it obstructs wisdom, causes difficulties, and leads away from Nibbana." When I considered thus [...] it subsided in me. Whenever a thought of cruelty arose in me, I abandoned it, removed it, did away with it.

Monks, whatever a monk frequently thinks and ponders upon, that will become the inclination of his mind. If he frequently thinks and ponders upon thoughts of sensual desire, he has abandoned the thought of renunciation to cultivate the thought of sensual desire, and then his mind inclines to thoughts of sensual desire. If he frequently thinks and ponders upon thoughts of ill will [...] upon thoughts of cruelty, he has abandoned the thought of

Appendix 1: The Main Texts, with a Psychological Commentary

non-cruelty to cultivate the thought of cruelty, and then his mind inclines to thoughts of cruelty.

[...]

As I abided thus, diligent, ardent, and resolute, a thought of renunciation arose in me. I understood thus: "This thought of renunciation has arisen in me. This does not lead to my own affliction, or to others' affliction, or to the affliction of both; it aids wisdom, does not cause difficulties, and leads to Nibbana. If I think and ponder upon this thought even for a night, even for a day, even for a night and day, I see nothing to fear from it. But with excessive thinking and pondering I might tire my body, and when the body is tired, the mind becomes disturbed, and when the mind is disturbed, it is far from absorption." So I steadied my mind internally, quieted it, brought it to singleness, and concentrated it. Why is that? So that my mind should not be disturbed.

As I abided thus, diligent, ardent, and resolute, a thought of non-ill will arose in me [...] a thought of non-cruelty arose in me. I understood thus: "This thought of non-cruelty has arisen in me. This does not lead to my own affliction, or to others' affliction, or to the affliction of both; it aids wisdom, does not cause difficulties, and leads to Nibbana. If I think and ponder upon this thought even for a night, even for a day, even for a night and day, I see nothing to fear from it. But with excessive thinking and pondering I might tire my body, and when the body is tired, the mind becomes disturbed, and when the mind is disturbed, it is far from absorption." So I steadied my mind internally, quieted it, brought it to singleness, and concentrated it. Why is that? So that my mind should not be disturbed.

Monks, whatever a monk frequently thinks and ponders upon, that will become the inclination of his mind. If he frequently thinks and ponders upon thoughts of renunciation, he has abandoned the thought of sensual desire to cultivate the thought of renunciation, and then his mind inclines to thoughts of renunciation. If he frequently thinks and ponders upon thoughts of non-ill will [...] upon thoughts of non-cruelty, he has abandoned the thought of cruelty to cultivate the thought of non-cruelty, and then his mind inclines to thoughts of non-cruelty.

It is easy to see that one class of thoughts — thoughts of sensual desire, thoughts of ill will, and thoughts of cruelty — is likely to activate memory traces that excite urges. The other class — thoughts of renunciation, thoughts of non-ill will, and thoughts of non-cruelty — will excite no urges. The preference for the second class of thoughts has less to do with morality than with the aim which is crucial for someone who is to make progress on the path, namely reducing the level of tension. The justification of this preference from the point of view of psychological theory is that when memory traces are reactivated, they become more strongly entrenched and in this way gain prominence in the mind.[241]

---

[241] On a neuro-physiological level this may be an example of Hebb's law, according to which "cells that fire together, wire together", thus transforming short-term memories into long-term ones which are then further consolidated; see Solms & Turnbull, 2002: 145 f. Interestingly, Hebb's law was already proposed, long before Hebb, by Freud in his *Project for a Scientific Psychology* (SE I pp. 281-397), written in 1895 but not published until 1950; see Pribram & Gill, 1976: 65.

Appendix 1: The Main Texts, with a Psychological Commentary

§3 Avoiding Hunger

There are urges that do not go away when they are not thought about. One example is hunger. However much we train ourselves to avoid thinking about food, sooner or later hunger will manifest itself. This is why a distinction must be made between urges that announce themselves only when the corresponding memory traces are activated, and others that can present themselves independently. In its manifestation, hunger is as dependent upon "its" memory traces as any other urge. Nevertheless, there is a difference: hunger does not have to wait for the activation of its memory traces. An independent urge can itself activate its memory traces (the memories of earlier satisfaction).

Practitioners who wish to bring down the level of excitation of all of their urges may not easily succeed in removing hunger through mental means. Since they aim at eliminating disturbing factors, we may expect them to appease hunger and thirst by eating and drinking. While this may seem self-evident to a modern reader, it was far from self-evident in the ascetically inclined period in which Buddhism arose. This will be clear from the passage to be presented below.

The description of the path of liberation examined above does not deal with hunger and thirst. The reason may well be that facing hunger and thirst was not among the virtues cultivated in the early Buddhist tradition. However, the issue is dealt with in certain autobiographic remarks attributed to the Buddha. According to the passages concerned, the Buddha-to-be° had unsuccessfully tried various methods to reach his goal before he found the correct one. These unsuccessful methods included abstinence from food as well as various painful practices. His discovery of the correct method is indissociably linked to his decision to partake of food again and to end his painful practices. The following passage describes how this supposedly happened. The speaker is, once again, the Buddha, who has just recounted his failed attempts to use those alternative methods:[242]

> I considered: "I recall that when my father the Sakyan was occupied, while I was sitting in the cool shade of a rose-apple tree, quite secluded from sensual pleasures, secluded from unwholesome states, I entered upon and abided in the first stage-of-meditation°, which is accompanied by applied and sustained thought, with rapture° and pleasure° born of seclusion. Could that be the path to enlightenment?" Then, following on that memory, came the realisation: "That is the path to enlightenment."
>
> I thought: "Why am I afraid of that pleasure° that has nothing to do with sensual pleasures and unwholesome states?" I thought: "I am not afraid of that pleasure° since it has nothing to do with sensual pleasures and unwholesome states."
>
> I considered: "It is not easy to attain that pleasure° with a body so excessively emaciated. Suppose I ate some solid food — some boiled rice and bread." And I ate some solid food — some boiled rice and bread. [...]
>
> Now when I had eaten solid food and regained my strength, then quite secluded from sensual pleasures, secluded from unwholesome states, I entered upon and abided in the first stage-of-meditation°, which is accompanied by applied and sustained thought, with rapture° and pleasure° born of seclusion.

---

[242] *The Middle Length Discourses of the Buddha* (as above), p. 340. This translates *Majjhima Nikaya* I p. 246 f.

Appendix 1: The Main Texts, with a Psychological Commentary

This passage confirms the importance of "silencing" hunger. Judging by this passage, hunger and physical discomfort were the final obstacles in the way of the future Buddha; he had presumably met all other preconditions.

There is another reason why this passage is important. It presents the first stage-of-meditation° as something that may occur naturally, at least in certain people. The Buddha's childhood memory, whatever its historical value, suggests that certain people may attain this stage while totally relaxed and on their own. Its precondition is seclusion. This is not surprising, for our ideal patient, too, realized this when he withdrew from the world and from his therapist.

§4 Awareness

Section 7 of the description of the path to liberation deals with awareness. Practitioners must practice it both during their ordinary daily occupations and when undertaking the sitting practice that leads to profound meditation. This section occurs several times in the old canon. Here is a different passage dealing with awareness:[243]

> Again, monks, when walking, a monk understands: "I am walking"; when standing, he understands: "I am standing"; when sitting, he understands: "I am sitting"; when lying down, he understands: "I am lying down"; or he understands accordingly however his body is disposed.

---

[243] *The Middle Length Discourses of the Buddha* (as above), pp. 146. This translates *Majjhima Nikaya* I p. 56-57.

§5 Mindfulness

A particularly important element of the path of liberation is the mindfulness° practiced once the practitioner has taken up a seated position with the intention of traversing the last stages of the path. A detailed account is found in the following selection of passages, taken from the discourse called "The Foundations of Mindfulness":[244]

> Monks, this is the direct path for the purification of beings, for the surmounting of sorrow and lamentation, for the disappearance of pain and grief, for the attainment of the true way, for the realisation of Nibbana — namely, the four foundations of mindfulness.
>
> What are the four? Here, monks, a monk abides contemplating the body as a body, ardent, fully aware, and mindful, having put away covetousness and grief for the world. He abides contemplating feelings as feelings, ardent, fully aware, and mindful, having put away covetousness and grief for the world. He abides contemplating mind as mind, ardent, fully aware, and mindful, having put away covetousness and grief for the world. He abides contemplating mind-objects as mind-objects, ardent, fully aware, and mindful, having put away covetousness and grief for the world.
>
> And how, monks, does a monk abide contemplating the body as a body? Here a monk, gone to the forest or to the root of a tree or to an empty hut, sits down; having folded his legs crosswise, set his body erect, and

---

[244] *The Middle Length Discourses of the Buddha* (as above), pp. 145 ff. This translates *Majjhima Nikaya* I p. 55 ff. The selection of passages from this rather long discourse has been guided by considerations explained in Bronkhorst, 1985, p. 309 ff.

Appendix 1: The Main Texts, with a Psychological Commentary

established mindfulness in front of him, ever mindful he breathes in, mindful he breathes out. Breathing in long, he understands: "I breathe in long"; or breathing out long, he understands: "I breathe out long." Breathing in short, he understands: "I breathe in short"; or breathing out short, he understands: "I breathe out short." He trains thus: "I shall breathe in experiencing the whole body"; he trains thus: "I shall breathe out experiencing the whole body." [...]

[...]

And how, monks, does a monk abide contemplating feelings as feelings? Here, when feeling a pleasant feeling, a monk understands: "I feel a pleasant feeling"; when feeling a painful feeling, he understands: "I feel a painful feeling"; when feeling a neither-painful-nor-pleasant feeling, he understands: "I feel a neither-painful-nor-pleasant feeling." When feeling a worldly pleasant feeling, he understands: "I feel a worldly pleasant feeling"; when feeling an unworldly pleasant feeling, he understands: "I feel an unworldly pleasant feeling"; when feeling a worldly painful feeling, he understands: "I feel a worldly painful feeling"; when feeling an unworldly painful feeling, he understands: "I feel an unworldly painful feeling"; when feeling a worldly neither-painful-nor-pleasant feeling, he understands: "I feel a worldly neither-painful-nor-pleasant feeling"; when feeling an unworldly neither-painful-nor-pleasant feeling, he understands: "I feel an unworldly neither-painful-nor-pleasant feeling."

[...]

And how, monks, does a monk abide contemplating mind as mind? Here a monk understands mind affected by lust as mind affected by lust, and mind unaffected by lust as mind unaffected by lust. He understands mind affected by hate as mind affected by hate, and mind unaffected by hate as mind unaffected by hate. He understands mind affected by delusion as mind affected by delusion, and mind unaffected by delusion as mind unaffected by delusion. He understands contracted mind as contracted mind, and distracted mind as distracted mind. He understands exalted mind as exalted mind, and unexalted mind as unexalted mind. He understands surpassed mind as surpassed mind, and unsurpassed mind as unsurpassed mind. He understands concentrated mind as concentrated mind, and unconcentrated mind as unconcentrated mind. He understands liberated mind as liberated mind, and unliberated mind as unliberated mind.

[...]

And how, monks, does a monk abide contemplating mind-objects as mind-objects? Here a monk abides contemplating mind-objects as mind-objects in terms of the five hindrances. And how does a monk abide contemplating mind-objects as mind-objects in terms of the five hindrances? Here, there being sensual desire in him, a monk understands: "There is sensual desire in me"; or there being no sensual desire in him, he understands: "There is no sensual desire in me"; and he also understands how there comes to be the arising of unarisen sensual desire, and how there comes to be the abandoning of arisen sensual desire, and how there comes to be the future non-arising of abandoned sensual desires."

There being ill will in him [...] There being sloth and torpor in him [...] There being restlessness and remorse in him [...] There being doubt in him, a monk understands: "There is doubt in me"; or there being no doubt in him,

Appendix 1: The Main Texts, with a Psychological Commentary

he understands: "There is no doubt in me"; and he understands how there comes to be the arising of unarisen doubt, and how there comes to the abandoning of arisen doubt, and how there comes to be the future non-arising of abandoned doubt.
[...]

Our psychological investigation shows that mindfulness serves a double purpose. First of all, it limits all activity to conscious activity (in so far as this is possible). This prevents repressed urges from finding expression during these sessions even if the associated memory traces are activated. As a result these urges will give rise to feelings; this is the second function of mindfulness. Feelings and the state of body and mind in general are the object of attention during this exercise. Mindfulness, according to this understanding, permits practitioners to locate their repressed urges.

The role which mindfulness plays in attaining absorption is explained in the following passage, which also emphasizes the need of "investigating and examining with wisdom" the state of mindfulness. This is essential if practitioners are to locate their repressed urges.[245]

> Monks, on whatever occasion a monk abides contemplating the body as a body, ardent, fully aware, and mindful, having put away covetousness and grief for the world — on that occasion unremitting mindfulness is established in him.[246] [...]

---

[245] *The Middle Length Discourses of the Buddha* (as above), pp. 946 ff. This translates *Majjhima Nikaya* III p. 85 ff.

[246] The same is repeated with regard to feelings, mind, and mind-object.

Abiding thus mindful, he investigates and examines that state with wisdom and embarks upon a full inquiry into it. [...]

In one who investigates and examines that state with wisdom and embarks upon a full inquiry into it, tireless energy is aroused. [...]

In one who has aroused energy, unworldly rapture arises. [...]

In one who is rapturous, the body and the mind become tranquil. [...]

In one whose body is tranquil and who feels pleasure°, the mind becomes concentrated. [...]

He closely looks on with equanimity at the mind thus concentrated. [...]

§6 Fear of Being Alone

One of the difficulties which a person who leaves human company has to face is fear, especially at night. Overcoming such fear has to be a priority if the remainder of the training is to succeed. The following passage, which is autobiographical in character, depicts the Buddha-to-be° confronting fear:[247]

> On one occasion the Blessed One was living at Savatthi in Jeta's Grove, Anathapindika's Park. Then the brahmin Janussoni went to the Blessed One and exchanged greetings with him. When this courteous and amiable talk was finished, he sat down at one side and said: "Master

---

[247] *The Middle Length Discourses of the Buddha* (as above), pp. 102-104. This translates *Majjhima Nikaya* I p. 16 ff.

Gotama, when clansmen have gone forth from the home life into homelessness out of faith in Master Gotama, do they have Master Gotama for their leader, their helper, and their guide? And do these people follow the example of Master Gotama?"

"That is so, brahmin, that is so. When clansmen have gone forth from the home life into homelessness out of faith in me, they have me for their leader, their helper, and their guide. And these people follow my example."

"But, Master Gotama, remote jungle-thicket resting places in the forest are hard to endure, seclusion is hard to practise, and it is hard to enjoy solitude. One would think the jungles must rob a monk of his mind, if he has no concentration."

"That is so, brahmin, that is so. Remote jungle-thicket resting places in the forest are hard to endure, seclusion is hard to practise, and it is hard to enjoy solitude. One would think the jungles must rob a monk of his mind, if he has no concentration. Before my enlightenment, while I was still only an unenlightened Buddha-to-be°, I too considered thus: 'Remote jungle-thicket resting places in the forest are hard to endure, seclusion is hard to practise, and it is hard to enjoy solitude. One would think the jungles must rob a monk of his mind, if he has no concentration.'
[...]
"I considered thus: 'There are the specially auspicious nights of the fourteenth, the fifteenth,[248] and the eighth

---

[248] Fourteenth or fifteenth night = new moon night.

of the fortnight.²⁴⁹ Now what if, on such nights as these, I were to dwell in such awe-inspiring, horrifying abodes as orchard shrines, woodland shrines, and tree shrines? Perhaps I might encounter that fear and dread.' And later on, such specially auspicious nights as the fourteenth, the fifteenth, and the eighth of the fortnight, I dwelt in such awe-inspiring, horrifying abodes as orchard shrines, woodland shrines, and tree shrines. And while I dwelt there, a wild animal would come up to me, or a peacock would knock off a branch, or the wind would rustle the leaves. I thought: 'What now if this is the fear and dread coming?' I thought: 'Why do I dwell always expecting fear and dread? What if I subdue that fear and dread while keeping the same posture that I am in when it comes upon me?' While I walked, the fear and dread came upon me; I neither stood nor sat nor lay down till I had subdued that fear and dread. While I stood, the fear and dread came upon me; I neither walked nor sat nor lay down till I had subdued that fear and dread. While I sat, the fear and dread came upon me; I neither walked nor stood nor lay down till I had subdued that fear and dread. While I lay down, the fear and dread came upon me; I neither walked nor stood nor sat down till I had subdued that fear and dread."

This passage deals with an authentic practical problem that solitary practitioners had to deal with. Although it is not very specific in explaining how they should deal with it, it is clear that they were not to avoid situations in which fear and dread might arise. If fear and dread did arise, the practitioner was not to cede to panic. In such situations, the practitioners should remain concentrated. The passage is especially instructive in

---

²⁴⁹ Eighth night = half-moon night.

Appendix 1: The Main Texts, with a Psychological Commentary

that it shows concern for certain practical difficulties that had not been mentioned in the description of the path as a whole. Since our outline of a psychological theory does not deal with fear, we can draw no conclusions about this emotion in particular.[250] What this passage does show is how practitioners are advised to deal with strong emotions in general. Rather than being affected by them, the practitioner observes them while they come and go. Once again, concentration is a key element in preventing that one be "robbed of one's mind".

This passage also illustrates how the practitioner, by not avoiding objectively dangerous situations, abandons all forms of "anticipating the future". Anticipating the future is responsible for the raised level of bodily tension that stands in the way of a "complete psychotherapeutic cure". Ideal practitioners, we learn from this passage, do away with it in all situations, including those that are potentially threatening to their well-being and survival.

§7 Who Succeeds?

A discussion between the Buddha and a brahmin called Ganaka Moggallana begins by presenting the instructions that the Buddha gives to his disciples in similar terms to those

---

[250] It is however tempting to recall that certain neuro-scientists recognize a fear system in the brain, beside the seeking system mentioned earlier. And just as Buddhist meditational practice may make use of the fact that the seeking system can be dissociated from its objects, i.e., from what it is seeking, is it conceivable that the Buddhist practice here described uses the fact that "the representational (or 'object') aspect of the [fear] system is left largely a blank, to be filled in by early experience" (Solms and Turnbull, 2002: 134; cp. Panksepp, 1998: 213 ff., LeDoux, 1996: 161 ff.)?

used for the path to liberation examined in § 1, above. It then continues:[251]

> When this was said, the brahmin Ganaka Moggallana asked the Blessed One: "When Master Gotama's disciples are thus advised and instructed by him, do they all attain Nibbana, the ultimate goal, or do some not attain it?"
>
> "When, brahmin, they are thus advised and instructed by me, some of my disciples attain Nibbana, the ultimate goal, and some do not attain it."
>
> "Master Gotama, since Nibbana exists and the path leading to Nibbana exists and Master Gotama is present as the guide, what is the cause and reason why, when Master Gotama's disciples are thus advised and instructed by him, some of them attain Nibbana, the ultimate goal, and some do not attain it?"
>
> "As to that, brahmin, I will ask you a question in return. Answer it as you choose. What do you think, brahmin? Are you familiar with the road leading to [the city] Rajagaha?"
>
> "Yes, Master Gotama, I am familiar with the road leading to Rajagaha."
>
> "What do you think, brahmin? Suppose a man came who wanted to go to Rajagaha, and he approached you and said: 'Venerable sir, I want to go to Rajagaha. Show me the road to Rajagaha.' Then you told him: 'Now, good man, this road goes to Rajagaha. Follow it for a while and

---

[251] *The Middle Length Discourses of the Buddha* (as above), pp. 877 ff. This translates *Majjhima Nikaya* III p. 4 ff.

Appendix 1: The Main Texts, with a Psychological Commentary

you will see a certain village, go a little further and you will see a certain town, go a little further and you will see Rajagaha with its lovely parks, groves, meadows, and ponds.' Then, having been thus advised and instructed by you, he would take a wrong road and would go to the west. Then a second man came who wanted to go to Rajagaha, and he approached you and said: 'Venerable sir, I want to go to Rajagaha.' Then you told him: 'Now, good man, this road goes to Rajagaha. Follow it for a while [...] and you will see Rajagaha with its lovely parks, groves, meadows, and ponds.' Then, having been thus advised and instructed by you, he would arrive safely in Rajagaha. Now, brahmin, since Rajagaha exists and the path leading to Rajagaha exists and you are present as the guide, what is the cause and reason why, when those men have been thus advised and instructed by you, one man takes a wrong road and goes to the west and one arrives safely in Rajagaha?"

"What can I do about that, Master Gotama? I am one who shows the way."

"So too, brahmin, Nibbana exists and the path leading to Nibbana exists and I am present as the guide. Yet when my disciples have been thus advised and instructed by me, some of them attain Nibbana, the ultimate goal, and some do not attain it. What can I do about that, brahmin? The Buddha is one who shows the way."

It is clear from this passage that not all of the disciples of the Buddha reached the highest goal, the "complete psychotherapeutic cure". It appears rather that the Buddhist tradition looked upon people who had reached the goal as being exceptional. They were held to be so special, in fact, that the names of the first disciples who succeeded in reaching the goal, and that of the last to do so after receiving instruction from the Buddha have been recorded.[252] Those who had not succeeded are said to have included Ananda, the Buddha's favorite personal attendant. A legend makes up for this embarrassing situation by claiming that Ananda, very conveniently, did reach the goal — just in time to participate in some important communal activities.[253] We can conclude from this that the tradition was far from certain about the number of people who had reached the goal and had the tendency to assign this attribute to highly respected members of the community.

§8 The Liberated Person

We pointed out in the main text that the Buddha was purportedly free from psychological suffering but not free from physical suffering. This observation is based on the assumption that the distinction between these two kinds of suffering is clear and free from ambiguity — an assumption that is far from obvious. It will be interesting to consider some passages that may elucidate the relationship between the two. We first consider the words in which the Buddha is believed to have announced his approaching end to his favorite disciple, Ananda:[254]

> Ananda, I am now old, worn out, venerable, one who has traversed life's path, I have reached the term of life, which is eighty. Just as an old cart is made to go by being held together with straps, so the Buddha's body is kept going by

---

[252] See Bareau, 1963: 190 ff.; 1970-71: II: 114 ff.
[253] EncBuddh s.v. Ananda (6), Fasc. I, 4 p. 532.
[254] *The Long Discourses of the Buddha: A translation of the Digha Nikaya*, translated from the Pali by Maurice Walshe, Wisdom Publications, Boston, 1987, p. 245. This translates *Digha Nikaya* II p. 100.

Appendix 1: The Main Texts, with a Psychological Commentary

being strapped up. It is only when the Buddha withdraws his attention from outward signs, and by the cessation of certain feelings, enters into the signless-absorption-of-mind°, that his body knows comfort.

This passage presents the remedy against bodily pain which our theory has led us to expect. Withdrawal of attention from all sensory input, including pain, through objectless ("signless") absorption of the mind is exactly what our theory would have predicted as an appropriate method to avoid physical suffering.[255] To be sure, this method does not cure the body: the Buddha is reported to have pronounced these words a short time before his demise.

In numerous passages the Buddha is depicted as spending his afternoons in seclusion. Some of these show that he spent this time in absorption. One example is the visitor who wishes to speak to him but is told by the attendant, who is a woman, that the Buddha has withdrawn in seclusion. The visitor responds: "Well, then, lady, when the Blessed Lord rises from his absorption, please tell him what I have said."[256] Another passage speaks of absorption as the state in which the Buddha constantly abides; it then continues by admitting that he sometimes sleeps during the day.[257]

---

[255] Not surprisingly, the absorption responsible for aesthetic enjoyment affects pain thresholds; de Tommaso et al., 2008.

[256] *The Long Discourses of the Buddha* (as above), p. 324 (modified). This translates *Digha Nikaya* II p. 271.

[257] *The Middle Length Discourses of the Buddha* (as above), p. 342. This translates *Majjhima Nikaya* I p. 249.

Appendix 2: Absorption and Pleasure in Mysticism and Meditation

Expressions such as *joy, rapture* or *ecstasy* are frequent in descriptions of mystical and meditative experiences. So are words like *absorption, concentration* and *attention*. This shows that experiences corresponding to the former set of words often accompany states corresponding to the latter. The two sets are not, however, always presented as being inherently connected. This was to be expected, for we have seen that the mind associates experiences primarily with objects and events. This is how they are remembered, but this is also the way in which they are experienced. It is not surprising, therefore, that states of deep absorption, which are experienced as being different from "ordinary" states of consciousness, are frequently said to give access to a different, higher reality.[258] The joy, rapture or ecstasy that accompany them are variously interpreted, very often as characteristics of the "real" self that perceives the "higher" reality. There is also a tendency to attribute less significance to joy, rapture and ecstasy than to the knowledge that mystical states presumably provide. This is illustrated by the following citations.

In his *The Varieties of Religious Experience* (1902), William James discusses "the deliciousness of some of [the] states [of the 16th century mystic Saint Teresa, which] is spoken of as too extreme to be borne, and as verging on bodily pain." James adds the following commentary (1902: 398): "To the medical mind these ecstasies signify nothing but suggested and imitated hypnoid states, on an intellectual basis of superstition, and a corporeal one of degeneration and hysteria. Undoubtedly these pathological conditions have existed in many and possibly all the cases, but that fact tells us nothing about the

---

[258] For more on this, see the first study in this book, Part I above.

Appendix 2: Absorption and Pleasure in Mysticism and Meditation

value for knowledge of the consciousness which they induce." A full century later, John Horgan (2003: 7) still attributes crucial importance to knowledge: "Certain mystics describe their experience as a form of ecstatic forgetfulness or self-dissolution rather than of knowing. To my mind, however, a sense of absolute knowledge is the *sine qua non* of mystical experiences; this noetic component transforms them into something more than transient sensations."

In spite of the disinclination on the part of modern investigators to attribute significance to the pleasure felt in mystical and meditative states, reports about them abound. Careful researchers have taken note of this. The following examples must suffice to illustrate this.

Abraham H. Maslow is famous for the "peak-experiences" which he studied primarily in living subjects. He holds that these peak-experiences are "the very beginning, the intrinsic core, the essence, the universal nucleus of every known high religion" (Maslow, 1964: 19); there is no need to discuss this claim here. Maslow provides a list of attributes of reality as perceived in peak-experiences (which may also be seen, he adds, as a list of the irreducible, intrinsic values of this reality). This list contains 14 items (truth, goodness, beauty, wholeness, etc.). According to Maslow, it should be distinguished from another list which enumerates the attitudes or emotions of the "peaker" toward this cognized reality and its attributes. This second list contains, among others, joy, rapture, bliss, and ecstasy.[259] Indeed, "the peak-experience is only good and desirable" (Maslow, 1968: 81). Concentration comes up, too (Maslow, 1964: 60): "In the cognition that comes in peak-experiences, characteristically the percept is exclusively and fully attended to. That is, there is tremendous concentration of a kind which does not normally occur." This confirms *both* that a state of deep con-

---
[259] Maslow, 1964: 91-94.

centration accompanies these experiences *and* that these experiences tend to be directed at objects and events. Elsewhere Maslow calls this state "total attention", and adds that it is "very much akin to fascination or complete absorption" (Maslow, 1968: 74). Elsewhere again he distinguishes two kinds of peak-experiences, in the second of which "fascination occurs, and in which there is an extreme narrowing of consciousness down to the particular percept [...] and in which the rest of the world is totally forgotten [...] This is when there is so much absorption and fascination with the percept, and everything else in the world is so much forgotten that there is a felt transcenden[c]e [...]" (Maslow, 1971: 243). Maslow does not say that the exceptional state of concentration is *responsible* for the experiences and that it *causes* the joy that is experienced, but he provides all the elements that allow us to consider this possibility.

Like Maslow, Mihaly Csikszentmihalyi has studied optimal experience in ordinary life. "The optimal state of inner experience," he states (2002: 6), "happens when psychic energy — or attention — is invested in realistic goals [...] The pursuit of a goal brings order in awareness because a person must concentrate attention on the task at hand and momentarily forget everything else." He calls this flow experience. Flow experience gives rise to enjoyment, because one is able to concentrate on what one is doing, and one acts with a deep but effortless involvement that removes from awareness the worries and frustrations of everyday life (p. 49). Indeed, "one of the most frequently mentioned dimensions of the flow experience is that, while it lasts, one is able to forget all the unpleasant aspects of life. This feature of flow is an important by-product of the fact that enjoyable activities require a complete focusing of attention on the task at hand — thus leaving no room in the mind for irrelevant information." (p. 58) In optimal experience "concentration is so intense that there is no attention left over to

Appendix 2: Absorption and Pleasure in Mysticism and Meditation

think about anything irrelevant, or to worry about problems" (p. 71).[260]

The title of B. Alan Wallace's recent book — *The Attention Revolution: Unlocking the power of the focused mind* (2006) — leaves no doubt as to the importance of attention in the (Buddhist) meditative states he cultivates, teaches and studies. Just before achieving the state called shamatha, Wallace tells us (p. 156), there is "an extraordinary sense of physical bliss, which then triggers an equally exceptional experience of mental bliss. This rush of physical and mental rapture is transient, which is a good thing, for it so captivates the attention that you can do little else except enjoy it. Gradually it subsides and you are freed from the turbulence caused by this intense joy. Your attention settles down in perfect stability and vividness." Elsewhere in the same book (p. 81) Wallace informs us that "the 'natural state' of the mind, according to Buddhist contemplatives, is characterized by the three qualities of bliss, luminosity, and nonconceptuality."[261] Wallace believes this to be one of the most remarkable discoveries ever made concerning the nature of consciousness, but other interpretations are possible. A possible causal link between attention (concentration, absorption) and bliss (rapture, joy) receives no attention in Wallace's book, but it might provide an equally good if not better explanation.

Evelyn Underhill's *Mysticism* (1911) is a classic in the study of "European mysticism from the beginning of the Christian era to the death of Blake" (its subtitle). In a chapter on "Ecstasy and rapture" we read (p. 358): "Nearly all the great contempla-

---

[260] Cp. Seligman, 2003: 111: "It is the total absorption, the suspension of consciousness, and the flow that the gratifications produce that defines liking these activities [...] Total immersion, in fact, blocks consciousness, and emotions are completely absent."

[261] Similarly Wallace, 2012: 68-69.

tives [...] describe as a distinct, and regard as a more advanced phase of the spiritual consciousness, the group of definitely ecstatic states in which the concentration of interest on the Transcendent is so complete, the gathering up and pouring out of life on this one point so intense, that the subject is more or less entranced, and becomes, for the time of the ecstasy, unconscious of the external world." Underhill is clearly of the opinion that concentration and ecstasy go together. However, true to the usual prejudice in most studies of mysticism and related phenomena, she does not consider the one (concentration) to be the cause of the other (ecstasy). The perception of reality that accompanies such states is far more important, in her opinion (p. 359): "The induced ecstasies of the Dionysian mysteries, the metaphysical raptures of the Neoplatonists, the voluntary or involuntary trance of Indian mystics and Christian saints — all these, however widely they may differ in transcendental value, agree in claiming such value, in declaring that this change in the quality of consciousness brought with it a valid and ineffable apprehension of the Real." She does not perceive the importance of ecstasy: "The ecstasy is merely the psycho-physical condition which accompanies it." We have already seen that the emphasis on the object or event experienced ("the Real" in this case) at the expense of the state in which this experience takes place (absorption) is a predisposition of the human mind. In the present investigation the emphasis lies elsewhere, namely, on the link between states of deep concentration and joy. Underhill's studies confirm that there is such a link.

Marghanita Laski's book *Ecstasy* (1961) draws attention to withdrawal ecstasies that frequently precede intensity ecstasies (chapter IV). In her concluding chapter she describes the relationship between these two (p. 369): "Ecstatic experiences may be divided into two kinds according to the manner in

Appendix 2: Absorption and Pleasure in Mysticism and Meditation

which they are approached. One manner, which I have called withdrawal and which involves a more or less gradual loss of normal perceptions, I have noted only in passing. Withdrawal experiences [...] may sometimes turn into the other kind of experience which I have called intensity experience; indeed I think it probable that all intensity experiences begin by being, to no matter how slight a degree, withdrawal ones." Both bring delight. Although Laski herself does not connect intensity experiences with the kind of concentration we call absorption, her material is compatible with it.[262] Furthermore, her two kinds of ecstasy — withdrawal ecstasy and intensity ecstasy — naturally assimilate to the two kinds of pleasure we have distinguished in the main text: pleasure resulting from the reduction of tension brought about by the removal of its sources (the Buddhist "rapture and pleasure born of seclusion") and pleasure resulting from absorption ("rapture and pleasure born of absorption").

Only the second of these two is referred to by Felicitas D. Goodman (1988a: 11) where she speaks about possession: "In order for the switch from the ordinary perceptual state to the ecstatic one to take place, people first of all have to prepare physically. ... But mainly, people need to concentrate. Trained practitioners do that as a matter of course; others have to learn it."

---

[262] In the literary texts that are part of the material on which her study is based, for example, we find statements like "I was absorbed; [...] I was exalted" (p. 402; from Richard Jefferies's *The Story of My Heart*); "It is the strangest sensation for the mind to fix itself in the contemplation of one single natural thing [...] Fixed on one, all things become supernaturally distinct and detailed." (p. 402; from Margiad Evans' *Autobiography*); "my sharpened but converging senses" (p. 414; from Jacquetta Hawkes' *Man on Earth*); "I was totally absorbed in prayer. [...] the joyful ground shone with purple light." (p. 417; from Ovid).

Appendix 3: Psychology and Free Will

For the investigation carried out in Part II we needed a psychological theory in which experiential terms had a place. This was the only way to make sense of the claims which we had accepted as working hypothesis. This appendix will argue that the use of such a psychological theory brings an unexpected advantage: while working within the framework of such a theory we do not need to worry about questions relating to determinism and free will.

The Oxford Handbook of Free Will observes that the problem of free will and necessity (or determinism) is "perhaps the most voluminously debated of all philosophical problems."[263] This should not surprise us. This abstruse philosophical problem is directly related to a conviction that most of us share, and that was well formulated by William James: "the whole feeling of reality, the whole sting and excitement of our voluntary life, depends on our sense that in it things are *really being decided* from one moment to another, and that it is not the dull rattling off of a chain that was forged innumerable ages ago."[264] And yet, one of the tasks which science sets out to address is precisely finding the rules governing "the rattling off of a chain forged innumerable ages ago". Abandoning the idea that there are such rules comes close to abandoning the hope of studying human beings scientifically.

This is not the place to review the different ways in which scholars, scientists and philosophers try to solve the problem.[265]

---

[263] Kane, 2002: 3, citing Matson, 1987: I: 158. Dennett (1984: 2), commenting on this claim, states: "Any philosopher ought to feel at least a little embarrassed that with so much work so little progress has been made."

[264] James, 1890: I: 453.

[265] *The Oxford Handbook of Free Will* (Kane, 2002), already mentioned,

Appendix 3: Psychology and Free Will

James himself was inclined to a spiritual solution. Others have tried to capitalize on the presumed discovery that nature itself in its fundamental functioning does not seem to be governed deterministically.[266] Others again have argued that the almost infinite complexity of processes in the human brain offer us something as good as free will, even if it is not quite the real thing.[267]

Many psychologists do not waste time on this question. They may be willing to grant that we have the *feeling* of free will, and may try to explain why. They are not willing to assign a causal role to this feeling in the mechanism that governs our behavior. They present a variety of arguments and experimental finding to prove *The Illusion of Conscious Will*.

This, incidentally, is the title of a book by the psychologist Daniel M. Wegner (2002). It will be useful to consider the position he puts forward. Conscious will, he points out (p. 67), "is not a direct perception of [the] relation [between thought and action] but rather a feeling based on the causal inference one makes about the data that do become available to

---

provides a useful presentation of the main positions. See also Fischer et al., 2007.

[266] This remains far from certain. Almost a century after its creation, the indeterministic nature of quantum physics is regularly challenged. See the review articles in *New Scientist* of 22 March 2008, 28 March 2009 and 2 August 2012, and the cover story of 30 April 2011 ("End of uncertainty: Goodbye Heisenberg. Hello quantum certainty?"). Another difficulty with this approach is how undetermined, i.e. random, processes can be supposed to account for free will.

[267] See, e.g., Dennett, 2003: 225: "I claim that the varieties of free will I am defending are worth wanting precisely because they play all the *valuable* roles free will has been traditionally invoked to play. But I cannot deny that the tradition also assigns properties to free will that my varieties lack. So much the worse for tradition, say I." *The Varieties of Free Will Worth Wanting* is the subtitle of an earlier book by Dennett (1984).

consciousness — the thought and the observed act." "The experience of will ... is the way our minds portray their operations to us, not their actual operation. Because we have thoughts of what we will do, we can develop causal theories relating those thoughts to our actions on the basis of priority, consistency, and exclusivity. We come to think of these prior thoughts as intentions, and we develop the sense that the intentions have causal force even though they are actually just previews of what we may do." (p. 96). It follows, Wegner thinks, that conscious will is an *epiphenomenon*: "Just as compass readings do not steer the boat, conscious experiences of will do not cause human actions" (p. 318).

James's conviction that things are *really being decided* by us from one moment to another will find little comfort in Wegner's position. He thought that this conviction is incompatible with the other one according to which reality is "the dull rattling off of a chain that was forged innumerable ages ago." Wegner, too, thinks that these two are incompatible. In reality they are not. For Wegner, the *real* action takes place in the brain, or in the unconscious mind. There is there no place for conscious will. Seen this way, this is a mere epiphenomenon with no causal role to play. However, Wegner's conclusion is the outcome of his prior decision as to what psychology is all about. The decision that the real action is confined to the brain, or to processes that remain below the surface, cannot but exclude conscious activities from the causal chain. It follows from such an apriori decision that all the decisions we take, including difficult ones which require much thought (as opposed to the lifting of a finger which figures so prominently in Wegner's experiments), are no real decisions at all.

Wegner's position has to face some serious difficulties. If, as he claims, conscious will is an illusion, an epiphenomenon that plays no role in determining our behavior, then the elements that go into the making of conscious will, ultimately pleasure and pain, play no such role either. This raises the question why evolution has provided us with those experiences to begin with. The obvious answer — viz. that pursuing pleasure and avoiding pain bring evolutionary rewards — is impossible to maintain if those experiences cannot even in principle influence behavior.[268]

If, unlike Wegner and so many others, we opt for a psychology which includes experiential elements, James's incompatibility disappears. In that case, our decisions *can* have a causal effect, for the simple reason that our decisions are part of the causal chains which our psychology seeks to uncover. This choice does not introduce indeterminism, to be sure. The causal chains of this new psychology are as deterministic as any. "Free" choices are determined by prior events, whatever their precise nature. Yet the main demand of those who insist on the acceptance of free will, their conviction that their decisions are "real" and have causal efficacy, is now fulfilled. As some recent researchers have correctly pointed out: "determinism does not imply that our deliberations and conscious purposes are causally irrelevant to what we do".[269] The difficult and painful decisions we sometimes have to make are not just the feelings that accompany processes which are beyond our ken and control.

---

[268] Compare the opening sentence of Jeremy Bentham's *Introduction to the Principles of Morals and Legislation*: "Nature has placed mankind under the governance of two sovereign masters, *pain* and *pleasure*. It is for them alone to point out what we ought to do, as well as to determine what we shall do." (cited Kahneman, 2011: 377) Note further that pleasure and pain are "multiply realizable": "They can ... be embodied in highly diverse kinds of physical-chemical processes and substrates." (Deacon, 2012: 29)

[269] Nahmias, Coates & Kvaran, 2007: 220.

On the contrary, these decisions are the way in which a fundamentally deterministic process unfolds.[270]

Introducing experiential notions into psychology as functional elements (rather than as accompanying epiphenomena) means abandoning (at least for the time being) the attempt to explain human behavior in terms of ultimately physical and chemical processes. This is a step other sciences have taken before, so it should not count as an obstacle.[271] Evolutionary biology, to take an example, does not and cannot provide the insights we expect from it if it refuses to think of phenotypes as opposed to genotypes.[272] A full account of the molecular processes in organisms is unlikely to clarify why certain species

---

[270] Similar remarks could be made about intellectual effort. To cite Mary Midgley: "When Einstein has just solved a difficult problem, his reasoning cannot be explained by giving even the most accurate account of the actions of his neurons. To suggest that their actions were its real cause would mean that they did the work on their own and told him about it afterwards. Anyone who has tried leaving such work to their neurons will agree that this story is improbable." (letter to *New Scientist*, 3 January 2009)

[271] An extensive literature has developed around the question of different levels of explanation, and the related issue of reductionism; see e.g. McCauley, 2007; Looren de Jong, 2002; Hofstadter, 2007: 37 ff. An important concept here is "emergence" — the notion that important kinds of organization may emerge in systems of many interacting parts, but not follow in any way from the properties of those parts. See the various contributions in Clayton & Davies, 2006. For a sophisticated attempt to explain mind from matter, see Deacon, 2012.

[272] "Because the genotype is asymmetrically dependent on the phenotype with respect to natural selection ..., it is the phenotype that offers the best causal explanation of reproductive success ... . The phenotypic level has a causal efficacy and explanatory legitimacy of its own, even if the phenotype is determined by the genotype (among other things). Identifying phenotypic traits is not a merely heuristic, free-for-all, essentially void kind of explanation, but rather, it taps real causal factors in an organism's chances of survival." (Schouten & Looren de Jong, 2004: 312)

Appendix 3: Psychology and Free Will

survive and others don't. The biologist has to think simultaneously on different levels if progress is to be made.

A different yet comparable situation may prevail in the study of human psychology. If we wish to make headway, we have to find place for conscious experiences, not as by-products, but as functional elements of the theory to be constructed.[273] This is not quite as radical as it may seem at first sight. Goal-directed activity, requiring cognitive maps and goal-seeking, is known from living organisms of all levels of complexity.[274]

This is not the occasion to enter into the details of this fundamental discussion. It should however be clear that much is gained by including experiential notions as functional terms into psychology. This is indeed the position here taken. One of its immediate rewards, as we have seen, is that the so-called problem of Free Will loses its fangs. More precisely put, once the causal role that conscious will can play is acknowledged, the so-called problem of free will is no more than an abstruse philosophical problem that, even if it could be given a precise

---

[273] Philosophers will be inclined to invoke the help of emergence; see note 271, above. "Materialist theories of mind ... seek to do justice to two compelling but apparently incompatible scruples. One is that ours is a physical world, everything happening within it open to physical explanation. The other is that mindedness is a matter of causal significance, that it makes a causal difference that there are minds. The more we feel the pull of one of these scruples, the more mysterious becomes the other. A robust commitment to physicalism leaves the mind looking like an epiphenomenal by-product of natural processes, a causally inert shadow. But a view of the mind as possessing aetiological autonomy threatens to re-enchant the physical world with supernatural causes and effects. The attraction of emergentism is that it offers a way to escape the dilemma. An emergentist tries to prise free the soundly motivated scruples about the dependence and autonomy of the mental from too-rigid theory, to see the problems as symptoms of the fact that an insight has been poorly encoded in doctrine." (Ganeri, 2011: 696-697).

[274] See note 120, above.

formulation (which I doubt), will no longer deserve the attention it receives from specialists and non-specialists alike.

Technical Terms and their Sanskrit and Pali Equivalents

English translation	Sanskrit	Pali
awareness	saṃprajanya	sampajañña
Buddha-to-be	bodhisattva	bodhisatta
absorption	samādhi	samādhi
mindfulness	smṛti	sati
pleasure	sukha	sukha
rapture	prīti	pīti
signless-absorption-of-mind	animitta cetaḥ-samādhi	animitta ceto-samādhi
stage-of-meditation	dhyāna	jhāna
thirst	tṛṣṇā	taṇhā

Abbreviations

EncBuddh   *Encyclopaedia of Buddhism*, ed. G. P. Malalasekera, vol. 1 ff., Colombo 1961 ff.

SE   *The Standard Edition of the Complete Psychological Works of Sigmund Freud*, translated from the German under the general editorship of James Strachey, 24 volumes, London: The Hogarth Press

BIBLIOGRAPHY

Abraham, Carolyn (2001): *Possessing Genius. The Bizarre Odyssey of Einstein's Brain*. Cambridge: Icon Books. 2005.

Addis, Donna Rose; Wong, Alana T. & Schacter, Daniel L. (2007): "Remembering the past and imagining the future: Common and distinct neural substrates during event construction and elaboration." *Neuropsychologia* 45(7), 1363-1377.

Alper, Harvey P. (ed.)(1989): *Understanding Mantras*. Albany: State University of New York Press.

Alper, Harvey P. (1989a): "Introduction." = Alper, 1989: 1-14.

Ansermet, François & Magistretti, Pierre (2004): *À chacun son cerveau. Plasticité neuronale et inconscient*. Paris: Odile Jacob.

Ansermet, François & Magistretti, Pierre (2010): *Les énigmes du plaisir*. Paris: Odile Jacob.

Ansermet, François & Magistretti, Pierre (2010a): "Quel inconscient?" = Magistretti & Ansermet, 2010: 195-199.

Arbib, Michael A. (2003): "The evolving mirror system: a neural basis for language readiness." = Christiansen & Kirby, 2003: 182-200.

Arbib, Michael A. (2005): "From monkey-like action recognition to human language: An evolutionary framework for neuro-linguistics." *Behavioral and Brain Sciences* 28, 105-167.

Arbib, Michael A. & Bickerton, Derek (ed.)(2010): *The Emergence of Protolanguage: Holophrasis vs compositionality*. Amsterdam - Philadelphia: John Benjamins.

Atran, Scott (1998): "Folk biology and the anthropology of science: Cognitive universals and cultural particulars." *Behavioral and Brain Sciences* 21, 547-609.

Austin, James H. (1998): *Zen and the Brain. Toward an understanding of meditation and consciousness*. Cambridge, Massachusetts & London, England: MIT.

Austin, James H. (2006): *Zen-Brain Reflections. Reviewing recent developments in meditation and states of consciousness.* Cambridge, Massachusetts & London, England: MIT.

Bareau, André (1963): *Recherches sur la biographie du Buddha dans les Sutrapitaka et les Vinayapitaka anciens. De la quête de l'éveil à la conversion de Sariputra et de Maudgalyayana.* Paris: Adrien-Maisonneuve.

Bareau, André (1970-71): *Recherches sur la biographie du Buddha dans les Sutrapitaka et les Vinayapitaka anciens. II. Les derniers mois, le parinirvana et les funérailles.* Two Volumes. Paris: Adrien-Maisonneuve.

Bargh, John A. (ed.)(2007): *Social Psychology and the Unconscious. The automaticity of higher mental processes.* New York and Hove: Psychology Press.

Barney, Stephen A.; Lewis, W. J.; Beach, J. A. & Berghof, Oliver (tr.) (2006): *The Etymologies of Isidore of Seville.* Cambridge University Press.

Baron-Cohen, Simon (1995): *Mindblindness. An essay on autism and theory of mind.* Cambridge, Massachusetts – London, England: MIT Press.

Beckman, Gary (2005): "The limits of credulity." *Journal of the American Oriental Society* 125, 343-352.

Begley, Sharon (2007): *Train your Mind, Change your Brain. How a new science reveals our extraordinary potential to transform ourselves.* New York: Ballantine Books.

Bennett, Maxwell; Dennet, Daniel; Hacker, Peter & Searle, John (2007): *Neuroscience and Philosophy. Brain, Mind, and Language.* New York: Columbia University Press.

Benson, Ophelia & Stangroom, Jeremy (2006): *Why Truth Matters.* London & New York: Continuum.

Bentall, Richard P. (2003): *Madness Explained. Psychosis and Human Nature.* Penguin.

Bickerton, Derek (2003): "Symbol and structure: a comprehensive framework for language evolution." = Christiansen & Kirby, 2003: 77-93.

Bibliography

Bickerton, Derek (2007): "Language evolution: a brief guide for linguists." *Lingua* 117(3), 510-526.

Bickerton, Derek (2009): *Adam's Tongue. How humans made language, how language made humans.* New York: Hill and Wang.

Bickerton, Derek (2010): "But how did protolanguage actually *start*?" = Arbib & Bickerton, 2010: 167-174.

Biello, David (2007): "Searching for God in the brain." *Scientific American* October 3, 2007.

Blanke, Olaf & Dieguez, Sebastian (2009): "Leaving body and life behind: Out-of-body and near-death experience." *The Neurology of Consciousness: Cognitive Neuroscience and Neuropathology.* Ed. Steven Laureys & Giulio Tononi. London: Academic Press. Pp. 303-325.

Bloch, Jules (1950): *Les inscriptions d'Asoka.* Traduites et commentées. Paris: Les Belles Lettres.

Bloom, Paul (2010): *How Pleasure Works. The new science of why we like what we like.* London: The Bodley Head.

Boden, Margaret A. (2006): *Mind as Machine. A history of cognitive science.* Oxford: Clarendon Press. 2 vol.

Böhl, Felix (1991): "Die etymologische Namensdeutung in der rabbinischen Literatur." *Discours étymologique.* Actes du Colloque international organisé à l'occasion du centenaire de la naissance de Walther von Wartburg. Edités par Jean-Pierre Chambon et Georges Lüdi, avec la collaboration de Hans-Martin Gauger, Frank Lestringant, Georges Pinault (Max Niemeyer Verlag, Tübingen 1991). Pp. 161-172.

Borch-Jacobsen, Mikkel & Shamdasani, Sonu (2012): *The Freud Files. An inquiry into the history of psychoanalysis.* Cambridge University Press.

Boroditsky, Lera (2001): "Does language shape thought?: Mandarin and English speakers' conceptions of time." *Cognitive Psychology* 43, 1-22.

Boyd, Brian (2009): *On the Origin of Stories. Evolution, cognition, and fiction.* Cambridge, Massachusetts & London, England: The Belknap Press of Harvard University Press.

Boyer, Pascal & Liénard, Pierre (2006): "Why ritualized behavior? Precaution systems and action parsing in developmental, pathological and cultural rituals." *Behavioral and Brain Sciences* 29, 1-56.

Bradley, Margaret M.; Miccoli, Laura; Escrig, Miguel A. & Lang, Peter J. (2008): "The pupil as a measure of emotional arousal and autonomic activation." *Psychophysiology* 45, 602-607.

Bremner, J. Douglas & Marmar, Charles R. (ed.)(1998): *Trauma, Memory, and Dissociation*. Washington, DC & London, England: American Psychiatric Press.

Brockman, John (ed.)(2007): *What Is Your Dangerous Idea? Today's Leading Thinkers on the Unthinkable*. London: Harper Perennial.

Bronkhorst, Johannes (1984): "Nirukta, Unadi Sutra, and Astadhyayi." *Indo-Iranian Journal* 27, 1-15.

Bronkhorst, Johannes (1985): "Dharma and Abhidharma." *Bulletin of the School of Oriental and African Studies* 48 (1985), pp. 305-320.

Bronkhorst, Johannes (2001): "Etymology and magic: Yaska's Nirukta, Plato's Cratylus, and the riddle of semantic etymologies." *Numen* 48, 2001, 147-203.

Bronkhorst, Johannes (2009): *Buddhist Teaching in India*. Boston: Wisdom Publications.

Bronkhorst, Johannes (2010): "Ritual, holophrastic utterances, and the symbolic mind." *Ritual Dynamics and the Science of Ritual. Volume I: Grammar and morphologies of ritual practices in Asia*. Ed. Axel Michaels and Anand Mishra. Wiesbaden: Harrassowitz. Pp. 159-202.

Bronkhorst, Johannes (2011): *Buddhism in the Shadow of Brahmanism*. Leiden – Boston: Brill. (Handbook of Oriental Studies 2/24.

Brugger, Peter (2012): "The tell-tale brain: Unlocking the mystery of human nature." *Cognitive Neuropsychiatry* 17(4), 351-358.

Brunet, Alain; Orr, Scott P.; Tremblay, Jacques; Robertson, Kate; Nader, Karim & Pitman, Roger K. (2008): "Effect of post-retrieval propranolol on psychophysiologic responding during subsequent script-driven traumatic imagery in post-traumatic stress disorder." *Journal of Psychiatric Research* 42(6), 503-506.

Bibliography

Bruya, Brian (ed.)(2010): *Effortless Attention. A new perspective in the cognitive science of attention and action.* Cambridge, Massachusetts & London, England: A Bradford Book, The MIT Press.

Buller, David J. (2005): *Adapting Minds. Evolutionary Psychology and the persistent quest for human nature.* Cambridge, Massachusetts – London, England: A Bradford Book, MIT Press.

Burgdorf, Jeffrey & Panksepp, Jaak (2006): "The neurobiology of positive emotions." *Neuroscience and Biobehavioral Reviews* 30, 173-187.

Burton, David (2004): *Buddhism, Knowledge and Liberation: A Philosophical Study.* Aldershot, England & Burlington, USA: Ashgate.

Buser, Pierre (2005): *L'inconscient aux mille visages.* Paris: Odile Jacob.

Cammann, Schuyler (1962): *Substance and Symbol in Chinese Toggles. Chinese Belt Toggles from the C. F. Bieber Collection.* Philadelphia: University of Pennsylvania Press.

Candland, Douglas Keith (1993): *Feral Children and Clever Animals. Reflections on human nature.* New York – Oxford: Oxford University Press.

Cardeña, Etzel; Lyn, Stephen Jay & Krippner, Stanley (ed.)(2000): *Varieties of Anomalous Experience: Examining the scientific evidence.* Washington, DC : American Psychological Association.

Carter, Rita (2008): *Multiplicity. The New Science of Personality.* London: Little, Brown.

Chagnon, Napoleon A. (1968): *Yanomamö: The fierce people.* New York etc.: Holt, Rinehart and Winston.

Christiansen, Morton H. & Kirby, Simon (ed.)(2003): *Language Evolution.* Oxford: Oxford University Press.

Cioffi, Frank (1998): *Freud and the Question of Pseudoscience.* Chicago and La Salle: Open Court.

Clark, David H. & Stephenson, F. Richard (1977): *The Historical Supernovae.* Oxford etc.: Pergamon Press.

Clayton, N. S.; Correia, S. P. C.; Raby, C. R.; Alexis, D. M.; Emery, N. J. & Dickinson, A. (2008): "Response to Suddendorf & Corballis (2008): in defence of animal foresight." *Animal Behaviour* 76, e9-e11.

Clayton, Philip & Davies, Paul (ed.)(2006): *The Re-Emergence of Emergence. The emergentist hypothesis from science to religion*. Oxford University Press.

Cohen, Jon (2007): "The world through a chimp's eyes." *Science* 316, 44-45.

Cole, M. (2006): "Culture and cognitive development in phylogenetic, historical and ontogenetic perspective." *Handbook of Child Psychology, vol. 2: Cognition, Perception and Language*. 6th edition. Ed. W. Damon & D. Kuhn. Wiley, Chichester. (not seen)

Correia, Sérgio P. C.; Dickinson, Anthony & Clayton, Nicola S. (2007): "Western scrub-jays anticipate future needs independently of their current motivational state." *Current Biology* 17, 856-861.

Coull, Jennifer T. (2005): "Psychopharmacology of human attention." = Itti et al., 2005: 50-56.

Crews, Frederick (ed.)(1998): *Unauthorized Freud. Doubters confront a legend*. Harmondsworth: Penguin Books.

Crow, T. J. (1991): "The origins of psychosis and 'The Descent of Man.'" *British Journal of Psychiatry* 159 (suppl. 14), 76-82.

Crow, T. J. (1995): "A Darwinian approach to the origins of psychosis." *British Journal of Psychiatry* 167, 12-25.

Crow, Tim J. (1998): "Nuclear schizophrenic symptoms as the key to the evolution of modern *homo sapiens*." *From Brains to Consciousness? Essays on the new sciences of the mind*. Ed. Steven Rose. Princeton, New Jersey: Princeton University Press. Pp. 137-153.

Csikszentmihalyi, Mihaly (1996): *Creativity. Flow and the psychology of discovery and invention*. New York: HarperPerennial.

Csikszentmihalyi, Mihaly (2002): *Flow. The Classic Work on How to Achieve Happiness*. Revised and updated edition. London etc.: Rider.

Damasio, Antonio R. (1994): *Descartes' Error: Emotion, Reason and the Human Brain*. New York: Grosset/Putnam.

Damasio, Antonio (1999): *The Feeling of What Happens. Body, Emotion and the Making of Consciousness*. London: Vintage, 2000.

Damasio, Antonio (2003): *Looking for Spinoza. Joy, Sorrow and the Feeling Brain*. William Heinemann. Reprint: Vintage, London etc. 2004.

Damasio, Antonio (2010): *Self Comes to Mind*. New York: Pantheon Books.

Dawkins, Richard (1996): *Climbing Mount Improbable*. Viking. Reprint: Penguin Books, London etc., 1997.

Deacon, Terrence (1997): *The Symbolic Species. The co-evolution of language and the human brain*. Harmondsworth: Penguin Books.

Deacon, Terrence W. (2003): "Universal Grammar and semiotic constraints." = Christiansen & Kirby, 2003: 111-139.

Deacon, Terrence W. (2003a): "Multilevel selection in a complex adaptive system: the problem of language origins." *Evolution and Learning: The Baldwin Effect Reconsidered*. Ed. Bruce H. Weber & David J. Depew. Cambridge, Massachusetts – London, England: MIT Press. Pp. 81-106.

Deacon, Terrence W. (2012): *Incomplete Nature: How mind emerged from matter*. New York – London: W. W. Norton.

Deacon, Terrence & Cashman, Tyrone (2009): "The role of symbolic capacity in the origins of religion." *Journal for the Study of Religion, Nature and Culture* 3(4), 490-517.

Deady, Denis K.; Law Smith, Miriam J.; Kent, J. P. & Dunbar, R. I. M. (2006): "Is priesthood an adaptive strategy? Evidence from a historical Irish population." *Human Nature* 17(4), 393-404.

Dehaene, Stanislas (2011): "Signatures of consciousness." *The Mind*. Ed. John Brockman. New York etc.: Harper Perennial. Pp. 217-238.

Dehaene, Stanislas; Changeux, Jean-Pierre; Naccache, Lionel; Sackur, Jérôme & Sergent, Claire (2006): "Conscious, preconscious, and subliminal processing: a testable taxonomy." *Trends in Cognitive Sciences* 10(5), 204-211.

Dehaene, Stanislas & Naccache, Lionel (2001): "Towards a cognitive neuroscience of consciousness: basic evidence and a workspace framework." *Cognition* 79, 1-37.

Dennett, Daniel C. (1984): *Elbow Room. The Varieties of Free Will Worth Wanting*. New York: Oxford University Press.

Dennett, Daniel C. (1991): *Consciousness Explained*. Boston etc.: Little, Brown and Company.

Dennett, Daniel C. (2003): *Freedom Evolves*. London: Allen Lane.

Dennett, Daniel C. (2005): *Sweet Dreams. Philosophical Obstacles to a Science of Consciousness*. Cambridge, Massachusetts & London, England: The MIT Press.

de Tommaso, Marina; Sardaro, Michele & Livrea, Paolo (2008): "Aesthetic value of paintings affects pain thresholds." *Consciousness and Cognition* 17(4), 1152-1162.

Deutscher, Guy (2005): *The Unfolding of Language. The evolution of mankind's greatest invention*. London: Random House.

Deutscher, Guy (2010): *Through the Language Glass. How words colour your world*. London: William Heinemann.

Diamond, Jared (1992): *The Third Chimpanzee: The evolution and future of the human animal*. Toronto: HarperCollins.

Doidge, Norman (2007): *The Brain That Changes Itself. Stories of personal triumph from the frontiers of brain science*. London: Penguin.

Donald, Merlin (2001): *A Mind So Rare. The evolution of human consciousness*. New York & London: W. W. Norton.

Dormashev, Yuri (2010): "Flow experience explained on the grounds of an activity approach to attention." = Bruya, 2010: 287-333.

Doyère, Valérie; Debiec, Jacek; Monfils, Marie-H.; Schafe, Glenn E. & LeDoux, Joseph E. (2007): "Synapse-specific reconsolidation of distinct fear memories in the lateral amygdala." *Nature Neuroscience* 10(4), 414-416.

Dufresne, Todd (2003): *Killing Freud. Twentieth-century culture and the death of psychoanalysis*. London – New York: Continuum.

Dufresne, Todd (2007): *Against Freud. Critics talk back*. Stanford University Press.

Duyvendak, J. J. L. (1942): "Further data bearing on the identification of the Crab Nebula with the supernova of 1054 A.D., part I. The ancient oriental chronicles." *Publications of the Astronomical Society of the Pacific* 54, 91-94.

Bibliography

Edelman, Gerald M. (1992): *Bright Air, Brilliant Fire. On the matter of the mind.* New York: Basic Books.

Edelman, Gerald M. (2004): *Wider than the Sky. The phenomenal gift of consciousness.* London: Penguin Books.

Edelman, Gerald M. (2006): *Second Nature. Brain science and human knowledge.* New Haven and London: Yale University Press.

Edelman, Gerald M. & Tononi, Giulio (2000): *A Universe of Consciousness. How matter becomes imagination.* New York: Basic Books. (The same book has been brought out by Penguin Books under the title *Consciousness*.)

Eissler, K. R. (1969): "Irreverent remarks about the present and future of psychoanalysis." *International Journal of Psychoanalysis* 50, 461-471.

Eliade, Mircea (1986): *Histoire des croyances et des idées religieuses. 3. De Mahomet à l'âge des Réformes.* Paris: Payot.

Etkin, Amit; Pittenger, Christopher; Polan, H. Jonathan & Kandel, Eric R. (2005): "Toward a neurobiology of psychotherapy: basic science and clinical applications." *Journal of Neuropsychiatry and Clinical Neuroscience* 17, 145-158.

Evans, Jonathan St. B. T. (2008): "Dual-processing accounts of reasoning, judgment, and social cognition." *Annual Review of Psychology* 59, 255-278.

Everett, Daniel (2012): *Language: The Cultural Tool.* London: Profile Books.

Eysenck, Michael W. (1982): *Attention and Arousal. Cognition and Performance.* Berlin – Heidelberg - New York: Springer.

Falk, Harry (2012): "Small-scale Buddhism." = Voegeli et al., 2012: 491-517.

Fischer, John Martin; Kane, Robert; Pereboom, Derk & Vargas, Manuel (2007): *Four Views on Free Will.* Malden, MA etc.: Blackwell.

Flanagan, Owen (2011): *The Bodhisattva's Brain. Buddhism naturalized.* Cambridge, Massachusetts & London, England: The MIT Press.

Ford, Brian J. (2009): "On intelligence in cells: the case for whole cell biology." *Interdisciplinary Science Review* 34(4), 350-365.

Forman, Robert K. C. (1990): *The Problem of Pure Consciousness. Mysticism and philosophy*. New York – Oxford: Oxford University Press.

Forman, Robert K. C. (1999): "What does mysticism have to teach us about consciousness?" *Models of the Self*. Ed. S. Gallagher & J. Shear. Thorverton, Devon: Imprint Academic. Pp. 361-377.

Franco, Eli (2012): "Once again on the desires of the Buddha." = Voegeli et al., 2012: 229-245.

Franke, William (2007): *On What Cannot Be Said. Apophatic discourses in philosophy, religion, literature, and the arts*. Volume 1: Classic formulations; volume 2: Modern and contemporary transformations. Notre Dame, Indiana: University of Notre Dame Press.

Freeman, Walter J. (1999): *How Brains Make up their Minds*. London: Phoenix. 2000.

Freud, Ernst L. & Meng, Heinrich (ed.)(1963): *Sigmund Freud, Oskar Pfister, Briefe 1909-1939*. Frankfurt am Main: S. Fischer.

Frosh, Stephen (2006): *For and Against Psychoanalysis*. 2nd edition (first edition 1997). London and New York: Routledge.

Ganeri, Jonardon (2011): "Emergentisms, ancient and modern." *Mind* 120 (479, July 2011), 671-703.

Garner, Aleena R.; Rowland, David C.; Hwang, Sang Youl; Baumgaertel, Karsten; Roth, Bryan L.; Kentros, Cliff & Mayford, Mark (2012): "Generation of a synthetic memory trace." *Science* 335, 1513-1516.

Gay, Peter (1988): *Freud. A life for our time*. Anchor Books, New York, 1989.

Gellman, Jerome (2005): "Mysticism." *The Stanford Encyclopedia of Philosophy* (Spring 2005 Edition). Ed. Edward N. Zalta. URL = http://plato.stanford.edu/archives/spr2005/entries/mysticism/

Georgiadis, Janniko R. & Kortekaas, Rudie (2010): "The sweetest taboo: functional neurobiology of human sexuality in relation to pleasure." = Kringelbach & Berridge, 2010: 178-201.

Bibliography

Georgiadis, Janniko R.; Simone Reinders, A. A. T.; Van der Graaf, H. C. E.; Paans, Anne M. J. & Kortekaar, Rudie (2007): "Brain activation during human male ejaculation revisited." *NeuroReport* 18(6), 553-557.

Georgiadis, Janniko R.; Simone Reinders, A. A. T.; Paans, Anne M. J.; Renken, Remco & Kortekaar, Rudie (2009): "Men versus women on sexual brain function: prominent differences during tactile genital stimulation, but not during orgasm." *Human Brain Mapping* 30, 3089-3101.

Gershuny, Beth S. & Thayer, Julian F. (1999): "Relations among psychological trauma, dissociative phenomena, and trauma-related distress: a review and integration." *Clinical Psychology Review* 19(5), 631-657.

Gleitman, Lila & Papafragou, Anna (2005): "Language and thought." *The Cambridge Handbook of Thinking and Reasoning*. Ed. Keith J. Holyoak & Robert G. Morrison. New York: Cambridge University Press. Pp. 633-661.

Gomez, Lavinia (2005): *The Freud Wars. An introduction to the philosophy of psychoanalysis*. London and New York: Routledge.

Goodman, Felicitas D. (1988): *Ecstasy, Ritual, and Alternate Reality*. Bloomington & Indianapolis: Indiana University Press.

Goodman, Felicitas D. (1988a): *How about Demons? Possession and Exorcism in the Modern World*. Bloomington & Indianapolis: Indiana University Press.

Grace, George W. (1987): *The Linguistic Construction of Reality*. London etc.: Croom Helm.

Grahek, Nikola (2007): *Feeling Pain and Being in Pain*. Second edition. Cambridge, Massachusetts & London, England: A Bradford Book / The MIT Press.

Greenfield, Patricia M.; Keller, Heidi; Fuligni, Andrew & Maynard, Ashley (2003): "Cultural pathways through universal development." *Annual Review of Psychology* 54, 461-490.

Hacking, Ian (1995): *Rewriting the Soul. Multiple personality and the sciences of memory*. Princeton, New Jersey: Princeton University Press.

Henderson, John B. (1984): *The Development and Decline of Chinese Cosmology*. New York: Columbia University Press.

Herman, David (2003): "Stories as a tool for thinking." *Narrative Theory and the Cognitive Sciences*. Ed. David Herman. Stanford: CSLI Publications. Pp. 163-192.

Hinüber, Oskar von (2006): "Everyday life in an ancient Indian Buddhist monastery." *Annual Report of the International Research Institute for Advanced Buddhology* (Soka University, Tokyo) 9 (2005), 3-31.

Hirstein, William (2005): *Brain Fiction. Self-deception and the riddle of confabulation*. Cambridge, Massachusetts & London, England: A Bradford Book.

Hofstadter, Douglas (2007): *I Am A Strange Loop*. New York: Basic Books.

Horgan, John (1999): *The Undiscovered Mind*. New York: The Free Press.

Horgan, John (2003): *Rational Mysticism. Dispatches from the border between science and spirituality*. Boston & New York: Houghton Mifflin Company.

Humphrey, Caroline & Laidlaw, James (1994): *The Archetypal Actions of Ritual. A theory of ritual illustrated by the Jain rite of worship*. Oxford: Clarendon Press.

Huron, David (2006): *Sweet Anticipation. Music and the Psychology of Expectation*. Cambridge, Massachusetts & London, England: The MIT Press.

Isidore of Seville: *Etymologies*. See Barney et al., 2006.

Itti, Laurent; Rees, Geraint; Tsotsos, John K. (ed.)(2005): *Neurobiology of Attention*. Amsterdam etc.: Elsevier.

James, William (1890): *The Principles of Psychology*. 2 vols. Reprint: Dover Publications, New York, 1950.

James, William (1902): *The Varieties of Religious Experience*. Reprint: Fount Paperbacks, Glasgow, 1979.

Johansson, Sverker (2005): *Origins of Language: Constraints on hypotheses*. Amsterdam – Philadelphia: John Benjamins.

Jouvet, Michel (1999): *The Paradox of Sleep: The story of dreaming.* Cambridge, Mass.: The MIT Press.

Jucker, Jean-Luc (2007): "Des marqueurs rituels. Ethnographie d'une messe tridentine." *Ethnographiques.org* 13 (juin 2007). http://www.ethnographiques.org/2007/Jucker.html

Kahneman, Daniel (1973): *Attention and Effort.* Englewood Cliffs, New Jersey: Prentice-Hall.

Kahneman, Daniel (2011): *Thinking, Fast and Slow.* New York: Farrar, Straus and Giroux.

Kandel, Eric R. (2005): *Psychiatry, Psychoanalysis, and the New Biology of Mind.* Washington, DC & London, England: American Psychiatric Publishing.

Kandel, Eric R. (2006): *In Search of Memory. The emergence of a new science of mind.* New York – London: W. W. Norton.

Kane, Robert (ed.)(2002): *The Oxford Handbook of Free Will.* Oxford University Press.

Kaplan, Marcia (2004): "Psychoanalysis and psychopharmacology: art and science of combining paradigms." = Panksepp, 2004: 549-569.

Kaplan-Solms, Karen, & Solms, Mark (2002): *Clinical Studies in Neuro-Psychoanalysis. Introduction to a Depth Neuropsychology.* Second Edition. New York – London: Karnac.

Katz, Leonard D. (2006): "Pleasure." *The Stanford Encyclopedia of Philosophy* (Summer 2006 Edition). Ed. Edward N. Zalta. URL = http://plato.stanford.edu/archives/sum2006/entries/pleasure/

Kawai, Nobuyuki & Matsuzawa, Tetsuro (2000): "Numerical memory span in a chimpanzee." *Nature* 403, 39-40.

Kentridge, R. W.; Heywood, C. A. & Weiskrantz, L. (1999): "Attention without awareness in blindsight." *Proceedings of the Royal Society of London.* Series B, Biological Sciences 266, 1805-1811.

Kirk, G. S. (1974): *The Nature of Greek Myths.* Penguin Books.

Klein, Stefan (2002/2006): *The Science of Happiness. How our brains make us happy — and what we can do to get happier.* Translated by Stephen Lehmann. Da Capo Press.

Knight, Chris; Studdert-Kennedy, Michael & Hurford, James R. (ed.) (2000): The Evolutionary Emergence of Language. Social function and the origins of linguistic form. Cambridge University Press.

Koch, Christof & Tsuchiya, Naotusugu (2007): "Attention and consciousness: two distinct brain processes." *Trends in Cognitive Sciences* 11(1), 16-22.

Komisaruk, Barry R.; Beyer-Flores, Carlos; Whipple, Beverly (2006): *The Science of Orgasm*. Baltimore: The Johns Hopkins University Press.

Komisaruk, Barry R.; Beyer, Carlos; Whipple, Beverly (2008): "Orgasm." *The Psychologist* 21(2), February 2008, 100-103.

Kramer, S.N. (1969): "Sumerian myths and epic tales." = Pritchard, 1969: 37-59.

Kraus, Manfred (1987): *Name und Sache: Ein Problem im frühgriechischen Denken*. Amsterdam: B.R. Grüner. (Studien zur antiken Philosophie, 14.)

Kringelbach, Morten L. & Berridge, Kent C. (ed.)(2010): *Pleasures of the Brain*. Oxford University Press.

Kuhn, Thomas S. (1970): *The Structure of Scientific Revolutions*. Second edition, enlarged. Chicago and London: University of Chicago Press.

Lachaux, Jean-Philippe (2011): *Le cerveau attentif. Contrôle, maîtrise et lâcher-prise*. Paris: Odile Jacob.

Laski, Marghanita (1961): *Ecstasy. A study of some secular and religious experiences*. Indiana University Press. Reprint: Greenwood Press, New York, 1968.

Lawson, E. Thomas & McCauley, Robert N. (1990): *Rethinking Religion. Connecting cognition and culture*. Cambridge University Press.

Lear, Jonathan (2005): *Freud*. New York and London: Routledge.

LeDoux, Joseph (1996): *The Emotional Brain. The mysterious underpinnings of emotional life*. New York: Simon & Schuster.

LeDoux, Joseph (2002): *Synaptic Self. How our brains become who we are*. Harmondsworth: Viking Penguin.

Bibliography

Lee, Jonathan L. C., et al. (2005): "Disrupting reconsolidation of drug memories reduces cocaine-seeking behavior." *Neuron* 47(5), September 15, 2005, pp. 795-801.

Lehrer, Jonah (2007): *Proust Was a Neuroscientist*. Boston – New York: Houghton Mifflin Company.

Leoshko, Janice (2003): *Sacred Traces. British Explorations of Buddhism in South Asia*. Hants, England & Burlington, USA: Ashgate.

Lévi-Strauss, Claude (1971): *L'homme nu*. (Mythologiques, IV.) Paris: Plon.

Levitin, Daniel J. (2006): *This is Your Brain on Music. The science of a human obsession*. London: Penguin / Plume.

Lewis-Williams, David (2010): *Conceiving God. The cognitive origin and evolution of religion*. London: Thames & Hudson.

Lewis-Williams, David & Pearce, David (2005): *Inside the Neolithic Mind. Consciousness, cosmos and the realm of the gods*. London: Thames & Hudson.

Leyton, Marco (2010): "The neurobiology of desire: dopamine and the regulation of mood and motivational states in humans." = Kringelbach & Berridge, 2010: 222-243.

Libby, William L.; Lacey, Beatrice C. & Lacey, John I. (1973): "Pupillary and cardiac activity during visual attention." *Psychophysiology* 10(3), 270-294.

Lillard, Angeline (1998): "Ethnopsychologies: cultural variations in theories of mind." *Psychological Bulletin* 123, 3-32.

Linden, David J. (2011): *The Compass of Pleasure. How our brains make fatty foods, orgasm, exercise, marijuana, generosity, vodka, learning, and gambling feel so good*. New York etc.: Viking.

Llinás, R. R. & Paré, D. (1991): "Of dreaming and wakefulness." *Neuroscience* 44(3), 521-535.

Lloyd, G. E. R. (2007): *Cognitive Variations. Reflections on the Unity and Diversity of the Human Mind*. Oxford: Clarendon Press.

Looren de Jong, Huib (2002): "Levels of explanation in biological psychology." *Philosophical Psychology* 15(4), 441-462.

Looren de Jong, Huib (2006): "Explication pluralism: Where the mind to molecule pathway gets off the track — Reply to Bickle." *Synthese* 151, 435-443.

Looren de Jong, Huib & Schouten, Maurice K. D. (2005): "Ruthless reductionism: a review essay of John Bickle's *Philosophy and neuroscience: A ruthlessly reductive account.*" *Philosophical Psychology* 18(4), 473-486.

Lorenz, Maria (1961): "Problems posed by schizophrenic language." *Archives of General Psychiatry* 4, 603-10.

Lutz, Antoine; Dunne, John D. & Davidson, Richard J. (2007): "Meditation and the neuroscience of consciousness: an introduction." *The Cambridge Handbook of Consciousness.* Ed. Philip David Zelazo, Morris Moscovitch & Evan Thompson. Cambridge University Press. Pp. 499-551.

Magistretti, Pierre & Ansermet, François (ed.)(2010): *Neurosciences et psychanalyse. Une rencontre autour de la singularité.* Paris: Odile Jacob.

Maldonado, Jose R. & Spiegel, David (1998): "Trauma, dissociation, and hypnotizability." = Bremner & Marmar, 1998: 57-106.

Malinowski, Bronislaw (1935): *Coral Gardens and Their Magic. Volume I: Soil-Tilling and Agricultural Rites in the Trobriand Islands. Volume II: The Language of Magic and Gardening.* London: George Allen and Unwin. Second Edition 1966. Indiana University Press. (Indiana University Studies in the History and Theory of Linguistics.)

Mallick, Shahbaz Khan & McCandless, Boyd R. (1966): "A study of Catharsis of aggression." *Journal of Personality and Social Psychology* 4(6), 591-596.

Marshall, Jessica (2007): "Future recall." *New Scientist*, 24 March 2007, pp. 36-40.

Maslow, Abraham H. (1964): *Religions, Values, and Peak-Experiences.* Reprint: The Viking Press, New York, 1970.

Maslow, Abraham H. (1968): *Toward a Psychology of Being.* Second edition. New York, Cincinnati etc.: D. van Nostrand.

Maslow, Abraham H. (1971): *The Farther Reaches of Human Nature.* Harmondsworth etc.: Penguin Books.

Matson, Wallace (1987): *A New History of Philosophy.* Vol. I. New York: Harcourt, Brace, Jovanovich. (not seen)

Maunsell, John H. R. (2004): "Neuronal representations of cognitive state: reward or attention?" *Trends in Cognitive Sciences* 8(6), June 2004, pp. 261-265.

McCauley, Robert N. (2007): "Reduction: models of cross-scientific relations and their implications for the psychology-neuroscience interface." *Philosophy of Psychology and Cognitive Science.* Ed. Paul Thagard. Amsterdam etc.: Elsevier / North-Holland. Pp. 105-158.

McNab, Fiona & Klingberg, Torkel (2007): "Prefrontal cortex and basal ganglia control access to working memory." *Nature Neuroscience* 11, 103-107.

Medin, Douglas L. & Atran, Scott (2004): "The native mind: biological categorization and reasoning in development and across cultures." *Psychological Review* 111, 960-983.

Meyer, Catherine (ed.)(2005): *Le livre noir de la psychanalyse.* Paris: Les Arènes.

Michaels, Axel (2006): "Ritual and meaning." *Theorizing Rituals: Issues, Topics, Approaches, Concepts.* Ed. Jens Kreinath, Jan Snoek & Michael Stausberg. Leiden – Boston: Brill. (Numen Book Series, Studies in the History of Religions, 114-1.) Pp. 247-261.

Michaels, Axel (2007): "'How do you do?' Vorüberlegungen zu einer Grammatik der Rituale." *Der Mensch — ein "animal symbolicum"? Sprache – Dialog – Ritual.* Ed. Heinrich Schmidinger & Clemens Sedmak. Darmstadt: Wissenschaftliche Buchgesellschaft. Pp. 239-258.

Miller, Courtney A. & Marshall, John F. (2005): "Molecular substrates for retrieval and reconsolidation of cocaine-associated contextual memory." *Neuron* 47(5), September 15, 2005, pp. 873-884.

Mithen, Steven (2005): *The Singing Neanderthals. The origin of music, language, mind and body.* London: Phoenix. 2006.

Moors, Agnes & De Houwer, Jan (2007): "What is automaticity? An analysis of its component features and their interrelations." = Bargh, 2007: 11-50.

Morenz, Siegfried (1957): "Wortspiele in Ägypten." *Festschrift Johannes Jahn zum 22. November 1957*, Leipzig 1957, pp. 23-32. Reprint: Morenz, 1975: 328-342.

Morenz, Siegfried (1975): *Religion und Geschichte des alten Ägypten. Gesammelte Aufsätze*. Köln – Wien: Böhlau.

Morris, Desmond (1967): *The Naked Ape*. London: Cape.

Mulcahy, Nicholas J. & Call, Josep (2006): "Apes save tools for future use." *Science* 312, 1038-1040.

Naccache, Lionel (2006): *Le nouvel inconscient. Freud, Christophe Colomb des neurosciences*. Paris: Odile Jacob.

Nader, Karim (2003): "Memory traces unbound." *Trends in Neurosciences* 26(2), p. 65-72.

Nahmias, Eddy; Coates, D. Justin & Kvaran, Trevor (2007): "Free will, moral responsibility, and mechanism: experiments on folk intuitions." *Midwest Studies in Philosophy* 31, 214-242.

Nakamura, Hajime (2000-05): *Gotama Buddha. A biography based on the most reliable texts*. Two Volumes. Translated by Gaynor Sekimori. Tokyo: Kosei Publishing.

Naqshbandi, Mariam & Roberts, William A. (2006): "Anticipation of future events in squirrel monkeys (*saimiri sciureus*) and rats (*rattus norvegicus*): tests of the Bischof-Kohler hypothesis." *Journal of Comparative Psychology* 120(4), 345-357.

Nathan, Debbie (2011): *Sybil Exposed. The extraordinary story behind the famous multiple personality case*. New York: Free Press.

Nelson, Kevin (2011): *The God Impulse. Is religion hardwired into the brain?* London etc.: Simon & Schuster.

Nemiah, John C. (1998): "Early concepts of trauma, dissociation, and the unconscious: their history and current implications." = Bremner & Marmar, 1998: 1-26.

Newberg, Andrew & d'Aquili, Eugene (2001): *Why God Won't Go Away*. New York: Ballantine Books.

Newton, Michael (2002): *Savage Girls and Wild Boys. A history of feral children.* London: Faber and Faber.

Nisbett, Richard E. & Masuda, Takahiko (2003): "Culture and point of view." *Proceedings of the National Academy of Sciences of the United States of America* 100(19), 11163-11170.

Nisbett, Richard E. & Miyamoto, Yuri (2005): "The influence of culture: holistic versus analytic perception." *Trends in Cognitive Sciences* 9(10), 467-473.

Nisbett, Richard E.; Peng, Kaiping; Choi, Incheol & Norenzayan, Ara (2001): "Culture and systems of thought: holistic versus analytic cognition." *Psychological Review* 108, 291-310.

Oberlies, Thomas (1998): *Historische Grammatik des Hindi. Die Genese seines morphologischen Systems aus dem Mittel- und Altindischen.* Reinbek: Inge Wezler. (Indologische Lehrmaterialien, 3.)

Ofen, Noa; Kao, Yun-Ching; Sokol-Hessner, Peter; Kim, Heesoo; Whitfield-Gabrieli, Susan & Gabrieli, John D. E. (2007): "Development of the declarative memory system in the human brain." *Nature Neuroscience* 10(9), September 2007, 1198-1205.

Padoux, André (1989): "Mantras — what are they?" = Alper, 1989: 295-318.

Pagnoni, Giuseppe; Cekic, Milos & Guo, Ying (2008): "'Thinking about not-thinking': neural correlates of conceptual processing during Zen meditation." *PLoS ONE* 3(9), e3083.

Panhuysen, Geert (1998): "The relationship between somatic and psychic processes." *Annals of the New York Academy of Sciences* 843 (*Neuroscience of the Mind on the Centennial of Freud's Project for a Scientific Psychology*, ed. Robert M. Bilder and F. Frank LeFever), 20-42.

Panksepp, Jaak (1998): *Affective Neuroscience. The foundations of human and animal emotions.* New York - Oxford: Oxford University Press.

Panksepp, Jaak (ed.)(2004): *Textbook of Biological Psychiatry.* Hoboken, New Jersey: Wiley-Liss.

Paper, Jordan (2004): *The Mystic Experience. A descriptive and comparative analysis.* Albany: State University of New York Press.

Parrinder, Geoffrey (1976): *Mysticism in the World's Religions.* London: Sheldon Press.

Penrose, Roger (1994): *Shadows of the Mind. A search for the missing science of consciousness.* Reprint: Vintage Books, London, 2005.

Piaget, J. (1925): "Le réalisme nominal chez l'enfant." *Revue Philosophique de la France et de l'étranger* 99, 189-234.

Pinker, Steven (2002): *The Blank Slate. The modern denial of human nature.* London etc.: Allen Lane.

Pinker, Steven (2007): *The Stuff of Thought.* London etc.: Penguin.

Plato: *Cratylus.* With an English translation by H. N. Fowler. The Loeb Classical Library 167 (Plato IV). Cambridge, Massachusetts: Harvard University Press; London: William Heinemann. 1977.

Plotkin, Henry (2007): *Necessary Knowledge.* Oxford University Press.

Plotkin, Henry (2007a): "The power of culture." *Oxford Handbook of Evolutionary Psychology.* Ed. R. I. M. Dunbar & Louise Barrett. Oxford University Press. Pp. 11-19.

Pribram, Karl H. (1998): "A century of progress?" *Annals of the New York Academy of Sciences* 843 (*Neuroscience of the Mind on the Centennial of Freud's Project for a Scientific Psychology,* ed. Robert M. Bilder and F. Frank LeFever), 11-19.

Pribram, Karl H. & Gill, Merton M. (1976): *Freud's 'Project' Reassessed.* New York: Basic Books.

Pritchard, James B. (ed.) (1969): *Ancient Near Eastern Texts relating to the Old Testament.* Third Edition with Supplement. Princeton, New Jersey: Princeton University Press.

Proudfoot, Wayne (1985): *Religious Experience.* Berkeley etc.: University of California Press.

Proust, Marcel (1913/1981): *Remembrance of Things Past, Volume One: Swann's Way; Within a Budding Grove.* Translated by C. K. Scott Moncrieff and Terence Kilmartin. New York: Vintage Books.

Bibliography

Pyers, Jennie E. & Senghas, Ann (2009): "Language promotes false-belief understanding: evidence from learners of a new sign language." *Psychological Science* 20(7), 805-812.

Pyysiäinen, Ilkka (1993): *Beyond Language and Reason. Mysticism in Indian Buddhism.* Helsinki: Suomalainen Tiedeakatemia. (Annales Academiae Scientiarum Fennicae, Dissertationes Humanarum Litterarum, 66.)

Pyysiäinen, Ilkka (1996): *Belief and Beyond. Religious categorization of reality.* Åbo: Åbo Akademi. (Religionsvetenskapliga skrifter, 33.)

Pyysiäinen, Ilkka (2001): *How Religion Works. Towards a new cognitive science of religion.* Leiden etc.: Brill. (Cognition and Culture Book Series, 1.)

Raby, R. C.; Alexis, D. M.; Dickinson, A. & Clayton, N. S. (2007): "Planning for the future by western scrub-jays." *Nature* 445, 919-921.

Raichle, Marcus E.; MacLeod, Ann Mary; Snyder, Abraham Z.; Powers, William J.; Gusnard, Debra A. & Shulman, Gordon L. (2001): "A default mode of brain function." *Proceedings of the National Academy of Sciences* 98(2), 676-682.

Ramachandran, V. S. (1994): "Phantom limbs, neglect syndromes, repressed memories, and Freudian psychology." *International Review of Neurobiology* 37, 291-333.

Ramachandran, V. S. (2012): "Author response" to Brugger, 2012. *Cognitive Neuropsychiatry* 17(4), 359-366.

Ramachandran, V. S. & Blakeslee, Sandra (1998): *Phantoms in the Brain. Probing the mysteries of the human mind.* New York: William Morrow.

Rank, Louis Philippe (1951): *Etymologiseering en Verwante Verschijnselen bij Homerus.* Dissertation Utrecht.

Rappaport, Roy A. (1999): *Ritual and Religion in the Making of Humanity.* Cambridge: Cambridge University Press.

Rees, Geraint; Frith, Christopher D. & Lavie, Nilli (1997): "Modulating irrelevant motion perception by varying attentional load in an unrelated task." *Science* 278, 1616-1619.

Reich, Wilhelm (1967): *Reich Speaks of Freud*. Reprint: Pelican Books 1975.

Reinders, A. A. T. Simone; Willemsen, Antoon T. M.; Vos, Herry P. J.; den Boer, Johan A. & Nijenhuis, Ellert R. S. (2012): "Fact or factitious? A psychobiological study of authentic and simulated dissociative identity states." *PLoS One*, DOI: 10.1371/journal-pone.0039279.

Richards, Graham (2002): *Putting Psychology in its Place. A Critical Historical Overview*. Second edition. Routledge.

Rolls, Edmund T. (1999): *The Brain and Emotion*. Oxford University Press.

Rolls, Edmund T. (2005): *Emotion Explained*. Oxford University Press.

Rolls, Edmund T. (2008): *Memory, Attention, and Decision-Making. A unifying computational neuroscience approach*. Oxford University Press.

Rose, Steven (2003): *The Making of Memory. From molecules to mind*. Revised edition. London: Vintage.

Rose, Steven (2005): *The 21st-Century Brain. Explaining, Mending and Manipulating the Mind*. London: Vintage. 2006.

Rovee-Collier, Carolyn (1997): "Dissociations in infant memory: rethinking the development of implicit and explicit memory." *Psychological Review* 104(3), 467-498.

Rovee-Collier, Carolyn (1999): "The development of infant memory." *Current Directions in Psychological Science* 8(3), 80-85.

Sacks, Oliver (1995): *An Anthropologist on Mars. Seven paradoxical tales*. London: Picador.

Sacks, Oliver (2007): *Musicophilia. Tales of Music and the Brain*. London: Picador.

Sander-Hansen, C.E. (1946): "Die phonetischen Wortspiele des ältesten Ägyptischen." *Acta Orientalia* 20, 1-22.

Sauneron, Serge (1957): *Les prêtres de l'ancienne Égypte*. Éditions du Seuil.

Savage-Rumbaugh, Sue; Fields, William Mintz & Taglialatela, Jared (2000): "Ape consciousness – human consciousness: a perspective informed by language and culture." *American Zoologist* 40, 910-921.

Savage-Rumbaugh, E. Sue & Rumbaugh, Duane M. (1978): "Symbolization, language, and chimpanzees: A theoretical reevaluation based on initial language acquisition processes in four young Pan troglodytes." *Brain and Language* 6, 265-300.

Scherer, Klaus R. (2005): "What are emotions? And how can they be measured." *Social Science Information* 44(4), 695-729.

Schooler, Jonathan W. & Mauss, Iris B. (2010): "To be happy and to know it: the experience and meta-awareness of pleasure." = Kringelbach & Berridge, 2010: 244-254.

Schopen, Gregory (2006): "A well-sanitized shroud. Asceticism and institutional values in the middle period of Buddhist monasticism." *Between the Empires. Society in India 300 BCE to 400 CE.* Ed. Patrick Olivelle. Oxford University Press. Pp. 315-347.

Schouten, Maurice K. D. & Looren de Jong, Huib (2004): "Could the neural ABC explain the mind?" *Behavioral and Brain Sciences* 27(2), 311-312.

Schwartz, Jeffrey M. & Begley, Sharon (2002): *The Mind and the Brain. Neuroplasticity and the power of mental force.* New York: ReganBooks.

Searle, John R. (1995): *The Construction of Social Reality.* Penguin Books.

Searle, John R. (1999): *Mind, Language and Society. Doing philosophy in the real world.* London: Weidenfeld & Nicolson.

Searle, John R. (2004): *Mind. A brief introduction.* New York – Oxford: Oxford University Press.

Searle, John (2007): "Putting consciousness back in the brain." = Bennett et al., 2007: 97-124.

Searle, John R. (2010): *Making the Social World. The structure of human civilization.* Oxford University Press.

Seligman, Martin E. P. (2003): *Authentic Happiness.* London: Nicholas Brealey.

Siok, Wai Ting; Perfetti, Charles A.; Jin, Zhen & Tan, Li Hai (2004): "Biological abnormality of impaired reading is constrained by culture." *Nature* 431, 71-76.

Slater, Lauren (2004): *Opening Skinner's Box. Great psychological experiments of the 20th century.* London: Bloomsbury.

Solms, Mark (2004): "Freud returns." *Scientific American* 290(5), May 2004.

Solms, Mark (2006): "Putting the psyche into neuropsychology." *The Psychologist* 19(9), September 2006, 538-539.

Solms, Mark & Turnbull, Oliver (2002): *The Brain and the Inner World. An introduction to the neuroscience of subjective experience.* London – New York: Karnac.

Spiegel, Herbert & Spiegel, David (2004): *Trance and Treatment. Clinical uses of hypnosis.* Second edition. Washington, DC & London, England: American Psychiatric Publishing.

Spitzer, Carsten; Barnow, Sven; Freyberger, Harald J. & Grabe, Hans Joergen (2006): "Recent developments in the theory of dissociation." *World Psychiatry* 5(2), 82-86.

Staal, Frits (1984): "Ritual, mantras and the origin of language." *Amrtadhara. Professor R. N. Dandekar Felicitation Volume.* Delhi: Ajanta Publications. Pp. 403-425.

Staal, Frits (1985): "Mantras and bird songs." *Journal of the American Oriental Society* 105(3; Indological Studies Dedicated to Daniel H. H. Ingalls), 549-558.

Staal, Frits (1990): *Ritual and Mantras: Rules without meaning.* Reprint: Motilal Banarsidass, Delhi, 1996.

Staal, Frits (2006): "Artificial languages across sciences and civilizations." *Journal of Indian Philosophy* 34(1-2), 89-141.

Stace, W. T. (1960): *Mysticism and Philosophy.* London: MacMillan & Co.

Strivay, Lucienne (2006): *Enfants sauvages: Approches anthropologiques.* Gallimard.

Strobach, Anika (1997): *Plutarch und die Sprachen. Ein Beitrag zur Fremdsprachenproblematik in der Antike.* Stuttgart: Franz Steiner. (Palingenesia, 64.)

Tallerman, Maggie (2007): "Did our ancestors speak a holistic protolanguage?" *Lingua* 117(3), 579-604.

Tavris, Carol (1989): *Anger: The misunderstood emotion.* New York: Touchstone.

Taylor, John G. (2002): "Paying attention to consciousness." *Trends in Cognitive Sciences* 6(5), 206-210.

Taylor, John G. (2003a): "Recent advances in understanding attention." *Science & Consciousness Review.* (http://www.sci-con.org/)

Taylor, John G. (2003b): "An Attention-Based Control Model of Consciousness (CODAM)." *Science & Consciousness Review.* (http://www.sci-con.org/)

Tooby, John & Cosmides, Leda (1992): "The psychological foundations of culture." *The Adapted Mind. Evolutionary Psychology and the generation of culture.* Ed. Jerome H. Barkow, Leda Cosmides & John Tooby. New York, Oxford: Oxford University Press. Pp. 19-136.

Tooby, John & Cosmides, Leda (1995): "Foreword." = Baron-Cohen, 1995: xi-xviii.

Turnbull, Oliver & Solms, Mark (2003): "Memory, amnesia and intuition: a neuro-psychoanalytic perspective." *Emotional Development in Psychoanalysis, Attachment Theory and Neuroscience.* Ed. Viviane Green. Hove and New York: Brunner-Routledge. Pp. 55-85.

Turner, Mark (1996): *The Literary Mind. The origins of thought and language.* Oxford etc.: Oxford University Press.

Turner, Victor W. (1969): *The Ritual Process. Structure and anti-structure.* London: Routledge & Kegan Paul. (The Lewis Henry Morgan Lectures/1966.)

Underhill, Evelyn (1911): *Mysticism. A study in the nature and development of man's spiritual consciousness.* Reprint: Methuen & Co., London, 1949.

Van Driem, George (2001): *Languages of the Himalayas. An Ethnolinguistic Handbook of the Greater Himalayan Region.* Volume One. Leiden etc.: Brill. (Handbook of Oriental Studies, Section Two: India, vol. 10/1.)

Van Driem, George (2004): "Language as organism: a brief introduction to the Leiden theory of language evolution." *Studies on Sino-Tibetan Languages.* Papers in Honor of Professor Hwang-cheng Gong on his Seventieth Birthday. Ed. Ying-chin Lin, Fang-min Hsu, Chun-chih Lee, Jackson T.-S. Sun, Hsiu-fang Yang & Dah-ah Ho. Taipei: Institute of Linguistics, Academia Sinica. (Language and Linguistics Monograph Series W-4.) Pp. 1-9.

Van Eck, Dingmar; Looren de Jong, Huib & Schouten, Maurice K. D. (2006): "Evaluating New Wave Reductionism: The case of vision." *British Journal for the Philosophy of Science* 57, 167-196.

Van Laerhoven, Eddy (2010): "Re-introducing philosophical soteriology: Bronkhorst on absorption (*samādhi*)." *Acta Comparanda* 21, 157-170.

Vergote, A. (1997): *Religion, Belief and Unbelief: A Psychological Study.* Amsterdam: Leuven University Press.

Voegeli, François; Eltschinger, Vincent; Feller, Danielle; Candotti, Maria Piera; Diaconescu, Bogdan & Kulkarni, Malhar (ed.)(2012): *Devadattīyam. Johannes Bronkhorst Felicitation Volume.* Bern etc.: Peter Lang. (Worlds of South and Inner Asia, Vol. 5.)

Wall, Patrick (1999): *Pain: The Science of Suffering.* London: Phoenix.

Wallace, B. Alan (2006): *The Attention Revolution. Unlocking the power of the focused mind.* Boston: Wisdom Publications.

Wallace, B. Alan (2012): *Meditations of a Buddhist Skeptic. A manifesto for the mind sciences and contemplative practice.* New York: Columbia University Press.

Warren, Jeff (2007): *The Head Trip. Adventures on the Wheel of Consciousness.* Oxford: OneWorld Publications.

Warren, Richard M. (1999): *Auditory Perception. A new analysis and synthesis.* Cambridge University Press.

Watson, Peter (2000): *A Terrible Beauty. The People and ideas that Shaped the Modern Mind.* London: Phoenix.

Watt, Douglas F. & Pincus, David I. (2004): "Neural substrates of consciousness: implications for clinical psychiatry." = Panksepp, 2004: 75-110.

Wegner, Daniel M. (2002): *The Illusion of Conscious Will.* Cambridge, Massachusetts – London, England: A Bradford Book, MIT Press.

Weissweiler, Eva (2008): *Die Freuds. Biographie einer Familie.* Frankfurt am Main: Fischer Taschenbuch.

Werner, Heinz & Kaplan, Bernard (1963): *Symbol Formation. An organismic-developmental approach to language and the expression of thought.* New York-London-Sydney: John Wiley & Sons.

Wilson, John A. (1969): "Egyptian myths, tales, and mortuary texts." = Pritchard, 1969: 3-36.

Wray, Alison (2000): "Holistic utterances in protolanguage: the link from primates to humans." = Knight, Studdert-Kennedy & Hurford, 2000: 285-302.

Wray, Alison (2002)(ed.): *The Transition to Language.* Oxford: Oxford University Press.

Wray, Alison (2002a): "Dual processing in protolanguage: performance without competence." = Wray, 2002: 113-137.

Wray, Alison (2002b): *Formulaic Language and the Lexicon.* Cambridge: Cambridge University Press.

Wray, Alison & Grace, George W. (2007): "The consequences of talking to strangers: evolutionary corollaries of socio-cultural influences on linguistic form." *Lingua* 117(3), 543-578.

Wulff, David M. (2000): "Mystical experience." = Cardeña et al., 2000: 397-440.

Wynne, Alexander (2004): "The oral transmission of early Buddhist literature." *Journal of the International Association of Buddhist Studies* 27(1), 97-127.

Yong, Ed (2009): "East meets West." *New Scientist* of 7 March 2009, 32-35.

Zaleski, Carol (1988): *Otherworld Journeys. Accounts of near-death experience in medieval and modern times.* Oxford University Press.

INDEX

A

Abraham, Carolyn 160
absorption 3-5, 29-31, 38, 46, 132, 133, 141-149, 154, 155, 157-159, 164-167, 169, 170, 180, 183, 185, 193, 201, 202, 204-207, 216
activated 95, 99, 101-104, 114, 118-120, 123, 130, 133, 141, 148, 153, 154, 164, 165, 187, 193
activation 99, 101, 102, 106, 115, 120, 134, 146, 164-166, 187
Addis, Donna Rose 123
Aeschylus 51
Al-Biruni 74
Alper, Harvey P. 33
Ananda 200
Ansermet, François 112, 113, 115
anticipating the future 30, 119, 126, 130, 197
Arbib, Michael A. 59, 61
Arendt, Hannah 74
asceticism 174
Asoka 77, 78
associations 4, 10, 11, 24, 25, 28-31, 45, 52, 62, 120, 140
Atran, Scott 45
attention 3, 11, 15, 19, 20, 29, 32, 35, 43, 44, 63, 74, 82, 86, 98, 100-104, 106-108, 113, 115, 116, 118, 119, 128, 129, 132, 133, 137, 140, 142-145, 148, 152-155, 158, 159, 165, 166, 168-170, 172, 182, 183, 193, 201, 202, 204-206, 214
Austin 9, 11-13, 15, 24, 28, 34, 48, 54, 132, 172
automaticity 128
automatic pilot 128
awareness 30, 37, 39, 41, 42, 120, 128, 129, 131, 147, 179, 182, 189, 204, 216

B

baby 98
Bareau, André 76, 158, 200
Bargh, John A. 128
Barney, Stephen A. 66
Bateson, M. C. 32
Beckman, Gary 74
Beethoven, Ludwig van 44
Begley, Sharon 129, 161
Benson, Ophelia 40
Bentall, Richard P. 9, 25
Bentham, Jeremy 211
Beyer-Flores, Carlos 82, 144, 151, 152
Bickerton, Derek 13, 41, 49, 55- 57, 59, 62, 64-67
Biello, David 82
Blakeslee, Sandra 25, 75, 152
Blake, William 205
Blanke, Olaf 132
blank slate, see also tabula rasa 150
Bloch, Maurice 32, 77
Bloom, Paul 97
Boden, Margaret A. 82, 87
Bodhi, Bhikku 176
Böhl, Felix 51
Borch-Jacobsen, Mikkel 92
Boroditsky, Lera 46
Boyd, Brian 18
Boyer, Pascal 36
Bradley, Margaret M. 169
Brahmanical ritual 32
brain 12, 15, 26, 29, 56, 81-84, 90, 91, 95, 106, 109, 110-115, 117, 136, 150-152, 160-162, 169, 171, 172, 197, 209, 210
brain plasticity 161
Bremner, J. Douglas 107
Breuer, Josef 118

Index

Brockman, John 4
Bronkhorst, Johannes 5, 48, 67, 76, 190
Brouwer, Bertus 16
Brunet, Alain 115
Bruya, Brian 132
Buddha 53, 71, 75- 79, 82, 93, 132, 158-161, 164, 176, 177,
    183, 187-190, 193-195, 197-201, 216
Buddha-to-be 183, 187, 194, 195, 216
Buddhism 32, 77-80, 187, 216
  Tantric 32
Buddhist 73-81, 84-86, 90, 91, 93, 125, 127, 130, 132, 133,
    135, 137, 140, 144-146, 148, 151, 158-160, 162, 164,
    167, 170, 176, 182, 187, 197, 199, 205, 207
Buddhist morality 182
Buddhist religion 77
Buller, David J. 150
Burton, David 80
Buser, Pierre 112

C

Cammann, Schuyler 53
Candland, Douglas Keith 11
Carter, Rita 100
Cashman, Tyrone 18, 25
cathexis 106, 108, 146
celibacy 83, 178
Chagnon, Napoleon A. 40
character 19, 23, 46, 83, 118, 124, 194
child 21, 43-45, 62, 67, 91, 156
children 11, 12, 15, 48, 50, 57, 66, 67, 138, 145
chimpanzee 9, 62
Christianity 76
Cioffi, Frank 87, 92, 140
Clark, David H. 75
Clayton, N.S. 30
Clayton, Philip 212
Coates, D. Justin 211

cognition 4, 20, 27, 37, 39, 42, 45, 89, 203
cognitive 37, 82, 87, 90, 91, 92, 96, 112, 150, 160, 213
cognitive neuroscience 91, 92
Cohen, Jon 62
Cole, M. 45
complete cure 125, 157, 158, 161
complete psychotherapeutic cure 125, 126, 130-132, 134, 135, 141, 157, 197, 199
concentration 29, 31, 38, 132, 133, 140-148, 169, 195, 197, 202-207
concept 13, 19, 53, 55, 93, 112, 136, 212
conditioning 14, 151
conscious 14, 18, 23, 29, 30, 80, 81, 91, 103, 106-108, 110, 121, 128, 129, 133, 156, 193, 209-211, 213
consciousness 14-16, 22-24, 27, 30, 31, 38, 39, 82, 83, 91, 103, 106, 107, 109-111, 116, 128, 129, 131, 143, 156, 202-206, 210
core consciousness 22, 23, 31
Correia, Sérgio P. C. 30
Cosmides, Leda 150
Coull, Jennifer T. 168
Cratylus 65
Crews, Frederick 92
Crick, Francis 83
Crow, Tim J. 9
Csikszentmihalyi, Mihaly 74, 204
culture 4, 9, 21, 27, 28, 35, 41, 43-46, 174

D

Damasio, Antonio 22, 23, 24, 31, 95, 113, 114, 130
D'Aquili, Eugene 151
Darwin, Charles 81
Darwinian 26, 60, 103, 137
Davidson, Richard J. 116
Davies, Paul 212
Dawkins, Richard 175
Deacon, Terrence W. 11, 12, 16, 18, 20, 25, 29, 37, 40, 41, 44, 49, 68, 69, 97, 103, 211, 212

Index

Deady, Denis K. 83
deconditioning 151
deep unconscious mental state 91
Dehaene, Stanislas 110
De Houwer, Jan 106
de Jong, Looren 83, 212
Dennett, Daniel C. 16, 18, 60, 97, 110, 208, 209
desire 78-81, 83-85, 88, 137, 158, 163, 164, 171, 181, 183, 184, 186, 192
determinism 208, 211
de Tommaso, Marina 201
Deutsch, Diana 34
Deutscher, Guy 46, 69
Diamond, Jared 9
Dieguez, Sebastian 132
discharge 105, 106, 125, 129, 136, 137, 138, 152, 163, 164, 168
dissociation 107, 159, 160
Doidge, Norman 122, 161
Donald, Merlin 11, 106
dopamine 171, 172
Dormashev, Yuri 132
Doyère, Valérie 115
drive, see also instinct 86, 92, 173
dual processing 20
Dufresne, Todd 92
Dunne, John D. 116
Duyvendak, J.J.L. 75
dynamic core 110-112, 161

E

Eckhart, Meister 116
ecstasy 202, 203, 205, 206, 207
ecstatic 203, 206, 207
Edelman, Gerald M. 14, 15, 23, 83, 101, 109, 111, 112, 161, 169
Ego 92, 106, 108, 113, 124, 135, 146
Einstein, Albert 160, 212

Eissler, Kurt 86
Eliade, Mircea 52
emergence 59, 89, 150, 212, 213
emergentism 213
Emerson, Ralph Waldo 113
emotion 113, 114, 139, 170, 182, 197
emotional charge 115, 121, 122, 124
empiricist 87
energy 86, 106, 108, 132, 146, 174, 194, 204
enlightenment bump 160
epiphenomena 212
epiphenomenal 82, 213
epiphenomenon 210
episodic 15, 95, 122, 123, 125, 127
episodic memory 15, 123
equilibrium 99, 100, 118, 123, 124, 131, 150, 166
Etkin, Amit 161
etymologizing 36, 49, 50, 51, 65, 66, 67
etymology 32, 49
Evans, Jonathan St. B. T. 20, 207
Everett, Daniel 14, 46
evolution 12, 55, 59, 60, 62, 172, 211
evolutionary 9, 68, 81, 83, 150, 174, 211, 212
evolutionary psychology 81, 83
excitation 99, 101-105, 120, 130, 134, 136, 138-140, 142, 143, 164-166, 169, 187
excited 99, 103, 106, 118, 123, 124, 130, 133, 136, 165, 182
explanatory gap 82
extended consciousness 22, 23, 31
Eysenck, Michael W. 102

F

Falk, Harry 161
falsifiability 87
fantasy 121, 122, 130
Faxian 74
fear 40, 75, 76, 91, 96, 185, 194, 196, 197

Index

feeling 22, 25, 88, 114, 133, 181, 191, 208, 209
feral children 11
Fields, William Mintz 14
Flanagan, Owen 78, 82
flow 147, 204, 205
folk psychology 83, 90
Ford, Brian J. 96
Forman, Robert K.C. 116
formula 32, 33, 52
Four Noble Truths 78
Fox, Douglas 115
fractionation 60, 97
Franco, Eli 158
Franke, William 26
Freeman, Walter J. 96
free will 84, 208, 209, 211, 213
Freud 84-89, 92-94, 104, 106-109, 111, 112, 117-121, 124, 127, 135, 138-140, 146, 147, 151, 152, 168, 170, 186, 216
Freud, Ernst L. 138
Freudian 84-87, 92-94, 104, 108-113, 119, 128, 138, 169
Frosh, Stephen 87

G

Ganeri, Jonardon 213
Garner, Aleena 115
Gay, Peter 121
Gellman, Jerome 26
Georgiadis, Janniko R. 152
Gerschuny, Beth S. 107
Gill, Merton M. 186
Gleitman, Lila 46
global neuronal workspace 110
Gomez, Lavinia 88
Goodman, Felicitas D. 38, 207
Grace, George W. 46, 57, 58, 60, 61, 63
Grahek, Nikola 160
Greenfield, Patricia M. 45

H

Hacking, Ian 100
Halligan, Peter 150
Hawkes, Jacquetta 207
Hebb's law 186
Heisenberg, Werner 209
Heisterbach, Caesarius of 52
Helen Keller 11
Henderson, John B. 53
Heraclitus 51
hermeneutic 90
heterostasis 100, 105
higher-order consciousness 15, 23, 24
Hinduism 32
  Tantric 32
Hinüber, Oskar 77
hippocampus 15, 151, 152
Hirstein, William 19, 21
Hofstadter, Douglas 212
holistic 33-37, 39, 56, 58, 59, 61, 62, 64, 66-68
holophrastic 5, 32, 55, 56, 57, 59-64, 68, 69
Holstege, Gert 152
homeostasis 99, 100, 105
homeostatic 99, 168, 173
homeostatic equilibrium 99
Homer 51
homuncular 68
homunculi 96, 97, 98, 170
homunculus 97
Hooper, Rowan 43
Horgan, John 82, 109, 151, 203
Horowitz, Seth 82
human nature 5, 80
human science 5
Humphrey, Caroline 36
hunger 98, 99, 105, 133, 136, 137, 159, 166, 173, 187, 189
Huron, David 144

I

Id 108, 113, 146, 169
independent urge 187
ineffable 26, 206
instinct, see also drive 85, 86, 135, 138, 153, 173, 174, 175
integrate 97, 100, 110, 118, 157, 165, 166
integration 98, 99, 109, 115, 118, 120, 124, 125, 149, 165, 166
intentionality 16, 97
Isidore of Seville 66
Islam 38

J

James, William 26, 80, 81, 113, 170, 202, 208, 210
Jefferies, Richard 207
Johansson, Sverker 67
Jouvet, Michel 21
joy 156, 181, 202,-206
Jucker, Jean-Luc 32

K

Kaas, John 150
Kahneman, Daniel 141, 169, 211
Kandel, Eric R. 82, 86, 88-92, 96
Kane, Robert 208
Kanzi 13, 14
Kaplan, Bernard 50, 111, 168
Katz, Leonard D. 172
Kawai, Nobuyuki 62
Keller, Helen 11
Kentridge, R.W. 106
Kirk, G.S. 51
Kirkland, Patricia 83
Klein, Stefan 113, 151, 170
Klingberg, Torkel 29, 152
Komisaruk, Barry R. 82, 144, 151, 152
Kortekaas, Rudie 152

Kramer, S. N. 50
Kraus, Manfred 51
Kuhn, Thomas S. 3
Kvaran, Trevor 211

L

Lachaux, Jean-Philippe 116
Laidlaw, James 36
Lange, Carl Georg 113
language 4, 9, 11-14, 16-18, 24-26, 29, 30, 32-35, 37, 41-49, 51, 53, 55, 56, 58-61, 63, 64, 66-69, 81, 90, 91, 128, 176
Laski, Marghanita 159, 206, 207
Latin mass 32
Lear, Jonathan 82, 113
LeDoux, Joseph 113, 115, 171, 172, 197
Lee, Jonathan L.C. 169
Lehrer, Jonah 113, 156
Leoshko, Janice 74
level of cognition 4, 27, 37, 39
Lévi-Strauss, Claude 36
Levitin, Daniel J. 154
Lewis-Williams, David 31
lexigram 10-13, 28, 34
Leyton, Marco 172
Libby, William L. 169
liberated 181, 192, 200
liberation 80, 176, 182, 183, 187, 189, 190, 198
Liénard, Pierre 36
Lillard, Angeline 45
Linden, David J. 157
linguistic 12, 13, 25, 27, 30, 32, 33, 35, 36, 38, 44, 48, 49, 66, 69
Llinás, R. R. 21
Lloyd, G.E.R. 45
Lorenz, Maria 50
Luria, Alexander Romanovich 111
Lutz, Antoine 116

M

Magistretti, Pierre 112, 113, 115
main unit 100, 102-105, 107, 108, 110, 117-128, 131, 134, 146, 149, 157, 166, 169, 170
Malalasekera, G.P. 216
Maldonado, Jose R. 29, 119, 145
Malinowski, Bronislaw 52
Mallick, Shahbaz Khan 170
mantra 31
Marmar, Charles R. 107
Marshall, Jessica 123, 169
Maslow, Abraham H. 203, 204
massive modularity thesis 150
Matson, Wallace 208
Matsuzawa, Tetsuro 62
Maunsell, John H.R. 169
Mauss, Iris B. 147
McCabe, Candy 150
McCandless, Boyd R. 170
McCauley, Robert N. 36, 212
McNab, Fiona 29, 152
Medin, Douglas L. 45
meditation 25, 132, 148, 160, 161, 169, 180, 181, 182, 188, 189, 202, 216
Megasthenes 74
memory 4, 15, 56, 62, 77, 89, 95-106, 113, 114, 115, 118-125, 127, 132-134, 136, 137, 141-143, 145-149, 151, 153-159, 164-167, 169, 170, 186-189, 193
memory trace 95, 98, 99, 102, 105, 106, 118, 119, 122, 124, 127, 134, 141, 149, 153, 154, 155
Meng, Heinrich 138
Merzenich, Mike 150
metapsychology 84, 92, 93
Meyer, Catherine 92
Michaels, Axel 36, 38
Midgley, Mary 212

Miller, Courtney A. 169
mindfulness 148, 160, 179, 180-182, 190, 191, 193, 216
Minsky, Marvin 44
Mitchell, T.N. 87
Mithen, Steven 34, 35, 59, 61
module 60, 150
Moggallana 197, 198
Molière (Jean-Baptiste Poquelin) 174
Moors, Agnes 106
Morenz, Siegfried 51
Morris, Desmond 9
Mulcahy, Nicholas J. 30
multiple personality 100
music 34, 35, 101, 143, 144, 145, 154, 155
mystic 27, 116, 202
mystical 4, 25-31, 33, 38, 151, 169, 202, 203
mysticism 4, 25, 38, 116, 202, 205, 206
mythology 4, 41

N

Naccache, Lionel 110, 112
Nader, Karim 115
Nagel, Thomas 88, 89, 90
Nahmias, Eddy 211
Nakamura, Hajime 76
Nanamoli, Bikkhu 176
Naqshbandi, Mariam 30
narrative 15, 16, 18, 19, 24
Nathan, Debbie 100
Nelson, Kevin 26
Nemiah, John C. 107
neurobiological 96, 109, 161
neurological 4, 22, 23, 26, 29, 68, 81, 103, 109, 133, 160
neurologist 22
neuroscience 4, 81, 82, 83, 91, 92, 109, 112, 117
neuroscientist 14, 75
Newberg, Andrew 151

Newton, Michael 11
Nibbana 184, 185, 190, 198, 199
Nicholls, Henry 30
Nirukta 67
Nisbett, Richard E. 45
noetic 26, 203
non-symbolic 4, 20, 21, 23, 27, 28, 30, 34, 37, 40

O

Oberlies, Thomas 49
Ofen, Noa 141
opiates 152, 171
opioid 152, 171
orgasm 152
orgasmic 144, 151, 152
origin of language 55
Ovid (Publius Ovidius Naso) 207

P

Padoux, André 33
Pagnoni, Giuseppe 115
pain 50, 52, 147, 150, 159, 160, 170, 181, 190, 201, 202, 211
painful 147, 187, 191, 211
Panhuysen, Geert 86
Panksepp, Jaak 100, 113, 136, 152, 168, 169, 171, 172, 197
Papafragou, Anna 46
Paper, Jordan 26
Paquette, Vincent 82
Paré, D. 21
Parrinder, Geoffrey 151
Pascual-Leone, Alvaro 150
patient 50, 120, 121, 125-131, 133, 134, 141, 143, 149, 157, 170, 182, 189
peak-experience 203
Pearce, David 31
Peirce, Charles Sanders 11, 17, 45

Penrose, Roger 84
Pfister, Oskar 138
Piaget, Jean 50
Pincus, David I. 109
Pinker, Steven 48, 150
Plato 65, 116
pleasurable 95, 97-99, 106, 116, 141-143, 147, 156, 157, 163, 165, 172
pleasure 4, 105, 114, 135, 136, 139, 141, 143-149, 152-155, 157, 160, 163, 164, 168-172, 180, 181, 183, 188, 194, 202, 203, 207, 211, 216
Plotkin, Henry 45, 150
Plutarch 51
positivist 87
prelanguage 60
Pribram, Karl H. 83, 186
primary consciousness 23
primary trace 98
primate 61
protolanguage 55-61, 63, 64, 66-68
Proudfoot, Wayne 26
Proust 155, 156, 157
psychoanalysis 84, 85, 89, 90-93, 118, 119
psychoanalytic theory 84, 86, 89, 92, 93, 108, 109, 126, 153
psychological 4, 33, 73, 77, 79, 80, 82, 84, 87-89, 95, 96, 107, 109, 111-113, 117, 136, 140, 155, 160, 162, 170, 171, 176, 182, 186, 193, 197, 200, 208, 216
psychological theory 4, 73, 80, 87, 88, 95, 112, 113, 117, 160, 186, 197, 208
psychology 71, 73, 74, 80-83, 90, 96, 108, 135, 140, 167, 168, 169, 186, 208, 210-213
psychotherapeutic 118, 122, 125, 126, 130-132, 134, 135, 141, 157, 161, 197, 199
psychotherapy 117, 118, 124, 125, 131, 134
pupil dilation 169
Pyers, Jennie E. 16
Pyysiäinen, Ilkka 25, 30, 36

Q

quantum physics 209

R

Raby, R. C. 30
Raichle, Marcus E. 115
Ramachandran, V. S. 25, 75, 108, 150, 152
Rank, Louis Philippe 51
Rappaport, Roy A. 17, 32, 35, 37, 38, 41, 42
rapture 116, 148, 170, 180, 181, 183, 188, 194, 202, 203, 205, 207, 216
reality assessment 97, 98, 100, 105, 107, 117, 123, 141, 146, 157, 165, 170
rebirth 78
recitation 25, 76
reductionism 90, 212
Rees, Geraint 29
Reich, Wilhelm 86
Reinders, A.A.T. Simone 100
religion 4, 9, 25, 35, 41, 46, 60, 77, 89, 203
religious 4, 31, 41, 42, 46, 75, 76, 144, 202
representation 9, 12-31, 34, 35, 37-44, 46, 54, 56, 96, 103, 140
repressed 106, 107, 113, 117-131, 146, 149, 157, 158, 161, 166, 167, 170, 182, 183, 193
repression 85, 104, 106, 107, 108, 111, 112, 119, 121, 123, 124, 125, 130, 132, 133, 134, 149, 166, 167
resistance 121, 125, 166
Richards, Graham 82
ritual 4, 5, 25, 31-41
Rolls, Edmund 113, 172, 173
Rose, Steven 30, 81, 90, 95, 96, 97, 173
Rosetta stone 81, 82
Rovee-Collier, Carolyn 122
Rumbaugh, Duane 9, 14

S

Sacks, Oliver 45, 62, 129, 143, 144
Sander-Hansen, C.E. 51
satisfaction 86, 99, 100, 104-106, 120, 135, 137-141, 145, 147, 149, 152-155, 157, 158, 165, 187
Sauneron, Serge 50
Savage-Rumbaugh, E. Sue 9, 14
Schacter, Daniel L. 123
Scherer, Klaus R. 114
Schooler, Jonathan W. 147
Schopen, Gregory 77
Schouten, Maurice K.D. 83, 212
Schuchardt, Hugo 58
Schwartz, Jeffrey M. 129, 161
scientific 5, 74, 75, 82, 87, 89, 90, 92, 114, 169, 186
Searle, John A. 18, 21, 60, 91, 133
seclusion 148, 170, 180, 182, 188, 189, 195, 201, 207
secondary trace 97
seeking system 113, 168, 169, 197
Seligman, Martin E.P. 205
semantic 15, 36, 48, 49, 50, 53, 54, 62, 64, 65, 66, 67, 91, 122
semantic etymologizing 36, 49, 50, 66, 67
semantic etymology 49
Senghas, Ann 16
sexual instinct 85, 86, 138, 153, 173, 174, 175
sexuality 85, 92, 135, 137-139, 141, 147, 149, 151, 158, 173, 174
Shamdasani, Sonu 92
Sherman 9, 11, 12, 13, 15, 24, 28, 34, 48, 54
sign 43, 45, 104, 105, 145, 167
signless 144, 145, 146, 201, 216
signless absorption 146
signless-absorption-of-mind 144, 145, 201, 216
Siok, Wai Ting 45
Skinner, Burrhus Frederic 96
Slater, Lauren 80
slip 128, 129, 182

Index

social reality 18
Socrates 65, 66, 67
Solms, Mark 106, 108, 109, 111, 113, 122, 186, 197
speech 4, 31, 32, 34, 49, 53, 54, 60, 61, 128, 178
Spiegel, David 29, 102, 119, 145, 159, 160
Spitzer, Carsten 107
Staal, Frits 25, 32, 36, 38
Stace, W. T. 27
stage-of-meditation 148, 160, 180, 181, 188, 189, 216
Stangroom, Jeremy 40
Stephenson, F. Richard 75
Stitch, Steven 83
Strachey, James 216
Strivay, Lucienne 11
Strobach, Anika 51
Strong, John 79
sublimated 154, 158
sublimation 86, 87, 149, 153, 174
suffering 78, 79, 80, 81, 83, 135, 159, 181, 200, 201
Sumitani, M. 150
symbol 10, 17, 36, 56, 57, 68
symbolic 4, 5, 9-31, 34, 35, 37-44, 46, 48, 53, 55, 68, 69, 103
symbolic reference 11, 15, 16, 25, 27, 28, 29, 34, 35, 38, 39, 41, 42, 48, 53, 55, 68, 69
symbolic threshold 10, 12, 14, 21, 28, 30, 34, 42, 68, 69
syntactical 10
syntax 30, 43, 49, 60, 61, 68, 81
system of the unconscious 113, 169

T

tabula rasa, see also blank slate 108
Taglialatela, Jared 14
Tallerman, Maggie 57, 61, 62, 65, 66, 67
Tantric 32
Tavris, Carol 170
Taylor, John G. 115, 116

tension 99, 100, 103, 104, 106, 107, 117, 119, 120, 122-128,
    132, 134, 142-149, 151, 153, 154, 155, 158, 160, 163-
    168, 170, 171, 182, 186, 197, 207
Thayer, Julian F. 107
therapist 93, 119, 121, 122, 126, 127, 130, 131, 189
therapy 93, 118, 119, 121, 122, 126, 135, 160
thirst 79, 137, 159, 187, 216
Tononi, Giulio 109, 111, 112, 161, 169
Tooby, John 150
trace 69, 95, 97-107, 111, 113, 117, 118, 119, 121-124, 127,
    131, 134, 141, 149, 153-155, 161, 164-166, 169, 170
trace unit 97-100, 124, 134, 165, 166, 170
transference 93, 121, 126
Turnbull, Oliver 106, 113, 122, 186, 197
Turner, Mark 18, 36, 74

U

unconscious 29, 88, 89, 91, 92, 93, 108, 110-113, 121, 122, 161,
    169, 206, 210
Underhill, Evelyn 205, 206
unpleasurable 99, 106, 142, 145
urge 87, 99, 101, 102, 104-107, 117-120, 123, 127, 134, 136,
    137, 138, 141, 149, 171, 187

V

Van Bloss, Nick 129
Van Driem, George 16, 58, 68
Van Eck, Dingmar 83
Van Eeden, Frederik 16
Van Laerhoven, Eddy 5
Vergote, A. 87

W

Wallace, B. Alan 205
Wall, Pat 150

Walshe, Maurice 200
Warren, Richard M. 21, 49
Watson, Peter 81
Watt, Douglas F. 109
web 14, 24-29, 38, 44, 45, 46
Wegner, Daniel L. 129, 209, 210, 211
Weissweiler, Eva 119
Werner, Heinz 50
Whipple, Beverly 82, 144, 151, 152
Whitman, Walt 113
Wilson, John A. 50
Wilson, Sir David 53
Wong, Alana T. 123
working hypothesis 73, 74, 75, 76, 79, 84, 159, 175, 208
Wray, Alison 33, 56-64, 67
Wulff, David M. 26
Wynne, Alexander 78

X

Xuanzang 74

Y

Yanomamö 40
Yaska 67
Yong, Ed 45

Z

Zaleski, Carol 52
Zen 115

www.ingramcontent.com/pod-product-compliance
Lightning Source LLC
Chambersburg PA
CBHW021343230426
43666CB00006B/386